# So They Call You Pisher!

# So They Call You Pisher!

*A Memoir*

Michael Rosen

VERSO
London • New York

First published by Verso 2017
© Michael Rosen 2017

Thanks to Brian Rosen for permission to use
most of the photos in the plate section

1 3 5 7 9 10 8 6 4 2

**Verso**
UK: 6 Meard Street, London W1F 0EG
US: 20 Jay Street, Suite 1010, Brooklyn, NY 11201
versobooks.com

Verso is the imprint of New Left Books

ISBN-13: 978-1-78663-396-5
ISBN-13: 978-1-78663-398-9 (US EBK)
ISBN-13: 978-1-78663-397-2 (UK EBK)

**British Library Cataloguing in Publication Data**
A catalogue record for this book is available from the British Library

**Library of Congress Cataloging-in-Publication Data**

Names: Rosen, Michael Wayne, 1946– author.
Title: So they call you pisher! : a memoir / Michael Rosen.
Description: Brooklyn, NY : Verso Books, 2017. | Includes bibliographical
   references and index.
Identifiers: LCCN 2017010491 | ISBN 9781786633965 (alk. paper)
Subjects: LCSH: Rosen, Michael. | Jewish men – United States – Biography.
Classification: LCC E184.37.R65 A3 2017 | DDC 305.38/8924 – dc23
LC record available at https://lccn.loc.gov/2017010491

Typeset in Sabon by MJ & N Gavan, Truro, Cornwall
Printed and bound by CPI Group (UK) Ltd, Croydon, CR0 4YY

Remembering Harold and Connie, and for Brian.
For Emma and our children, Elsie and Emile.
For Joe, Eddie, Isaac, Naomi and Laura.

# Contents

1. The Missing     1

2. No Thank You God     27

3. The Opposite of Wax     39

4. My Other Lives     61

5. Stalinallee     81

6. The Underdone Sausage     99

7. Great Expectations     125

8. Eng. Lit.     147

9. In the Colonie     169

10. The Politics of Culture     191

11. International Connections     219

12. Not Doing Medicine     239

13. Rehearsing the Uprising     254

*Postscript: To Harold, Who Died in 2008*     293

# 1

## The Missing

About a year before I was born, my brother died; he was not yet two. I don't know the exact dates of his birth or the death. They were never marked or mentioned in our house or anywhere else. There was no memorial for him. There were no framed photos of him in our house. He was invisible. My arrival into the world must have been a mixture of delight and dread. Delight that I had come along to fill up the gap left by the one before. Dread that I could go too.

It's possible that I would never have found out about it, if it was not for the moment when I was ten, and my brother Brian and I were sitting on the floor of our front room, going through boxes of old photographs. I picked up one of my mother with a baby on her knee. I held it up.

'Is that me or Brian?' I said.

Our father, who we always called Harold rather than Dad, took it off me, looked at it closely and said, 'That isn't either of you. That's Alan. He died. He coughed to death in your mother's arms. It was during the war. They didn't have the medicines. He was a lovely boy.'

Brian and I sat right where we were, not knowing what to say. Mum looked so happy in the photo. For a moment I felt ashamed I had made this discovery. Maybe it would have been better if I hadn't found it.

I must have been the replacement child. Perhaps I was also a cough waiting to happen. Every snuffle, every slight rasp of a breath must have given them reason to worry. I'll never know if either or both of them voiced such thoughts because, as I say, my father only ever once told the story of the brother who died. My mother never told it, never mentioned it, never said the boy's name, never let on that she knew that our father had talked about it to us.

The first sounds I heard in the world were in a nursing home called 'The Firs' in Harrow, halfway between Harrow-on-the-Hill station and Harrow School. The road, Roxborough Park, ran up a hill to the school, disappearing into a dark, green alleyway of old trees. The houses on both sides spoke of double-fronted, Edwardian wealth, some showing their middle-class past through their stuck-on black beams. 'Mock-Tudor' was something my father would spit out on walks down the roads of Pinner, three miles away, where we lived. He had another phrase that topped mock-Tudor: 'phony barony'. He would look over the hedges along roads around Pinner and say with venom in his voice, 'Look at that – phony barony.'

Brian, four years old by then, can remember coming to see me at 'The Firs'. Mum held me up in the window while he and Harold waved from down below. I can imagine them walking in and Harold saying to her, 'Blimey, Con, I didn't ever think we'd bring a kid into the world in a phony barony place like this.'

Quite why 'phony barony' was such a problem has only seeped into me slowly as an adult, from when I got to know more about where my parents, Harold and Connie, grew up. The places of their childhood and mine are as different as the middle of Paris and the Lake District. There had been no mock-Tudor where they were brought up, though the streets where they grew up aren't any more 'real' or authentic than the ones in Pinner. I think it was something he needed to say in order to show us that he wasn't attached to Pinner and Harrow: in his mind it wasn't only 'phony barony', it was full of phony barons.

Harold and Connie came from a place of myth: 'the East End'. In reality, their East End was one small part of the eastern end of London, stretching from the River Thames in the south up to Bethnal Green in the north, with an eastern boundary at Bow and a western boundary at the City.

They talked of this area, or gestured towards it again and again and again. And yet, I was never taken on a trip to the streets of their childhoods. It never became a real place. By that time, Mum's parents, who we visited, had moved northwards, a mile up the road in Hackney. In contrast, Harold's mother had moved eastwards by a few miles to live with her daughter Sylvia's family in Barkingside. This put them near to where Sylvia's husband Joe worked, at Ford's.

While I was growing up, Harold and Mum decided not to bother with the scores of relatives that they each had. Aunts and uncles and cousins were mentioned – particularly on Harold's side – people called Lally and Milly and Rae and Leslie Sunshine and Hilda and Bernie and Murray and Sam and dozens more – but we never saw them. Harold even did an imitation of his grandmother calling out all their names as she tried to remember which one she really wanted to come and help her: 'Rosie, Addy, Milly, Lally, Rae ...!' But it was as if they had been lost or locked away, living in places that would take days or weeks to reach.

It was only as an adult that I looked at the streets they lived in, the old brick terraces and tenements of inner London. Yet as I grew up my father peopled the little house where he grew up in our imaginations. He told us of the eleven others living there, of sharing his bedroom with his Uncle Sam, who he didn't talk to. He refused to talk to Sam because, he said, he, Harold, had come home with a hat from 'the Lane' – Petticoat Lane Market – and Sam had turned it inside out and back again, and spoilt it. In the language that they spoke before I was born, Yiddish, he and Sam were *broygus* – not talking. Broygus but sharing a bedroom.

It was into this house in Nelson Street, behind the London Hospital in Whitechapel, that Harold arrived on a boat from America in 1922, aged three. He came with his older sister Sylvia, his younger brother Wallace and their mother, Rose. This was half a family. The other half stayed in the States. Harold's father Morris, a factory boot and shoe worker, stayed behind with my father's elder brothers Sidney and

Laurence. My father only ever saw Laurie again – the others never – though the story always was that one day Morris would come. He never did.

Harold's mother, Rose, the woman he called 'Ma', was an extraordinary, perhaps outrageous, person. The family story says that on the day she left America, these two oldest sons were working in the fields near to the 'row house' where the family lived in Plymouth Street, Brockton, Massachusetts. Rose gathered together my father aged three, the baby Wallace and my father's sister Sylvia aged five, and headed off without even saying goodbye to the boys in the field.

The little party headed for the train station to take them to a boat leaving Boston Harbor for Liverpool: it was the *SS President Harding*. But they needed help to get to the train station, so it was Max, Morris's brother, who stepped in, along with Max's son Ted, then aged twelve.

Over seventy years later, I went to see Ted and his wife Gladys in Manchester, Connecticut. I saw them several times in the 1990s. He told me what happened. I scribbled a few words down but I got muddled about what happened when, or what was left where or whose fault it was. It had to be someone's fault. I went again to see him – we all did, my own family, wife and two little ones, aged four and eight in 2009. Ted was 101 years old and afterwards he sent me a letter. I read it to myself in his slow, deep American voice:

Dear Michael,
Last night I read part of Harold's book. 'Stories and Meanings'. He describes his mother's pride in her 'black trunk'. I remember it very well. When your family moved to Rochester from Brockton, I pulled that trunk on our cart all the way to the railroad station.

Aunt Rose walked in front carrying Wallace. Sylvia walked with me, holding my left hand. My right hand held the handle attached to the cart. Harold varied his walk. Sometimes walking beside his mother and sometimes slowing down to walk with Sylvia.

When we reached the railroad station, there was about 20 steps to go up to the station. I left the cart and the trunk at the bottom and helped the children up those steps. The train had just pulled into the station.

I left them there and went down to get the trunk. I had to go around to a road that led up to the station. The road was a little rough for the cart and trunk but I finally got up to the station level. The train was leaving just as I reached the station. I watched it leave, and pulled the cart and the trunk all the way back to our store.

My father called American Express to pick up the trunk and send it to Rochester. They charged $4.95. I told my father that I thought it was a lot of money. He did not think so. It was a heavy trunk. After reading about the trunk, I agree. It was not a lot of money.

With fondest memories,

Ted

(That trunk. Yes, my father did write about it, and often talked about it. As he and Sylvia grew up, this trunk, he said, was full of stories; all they had to do was open it, and Ma would take out photos and bits of paper and talk for hours about who this person was, what happened to that person. For example, how Ma's grandmother Miriam had come from Odessa and settled first in Oystershell Row, in Newcastle. It was a mistake. She thought she was going to London.)

In Whitechapel, Rose, Harold, Sylvia and Wallace moved in with Rose's parents Bessie and Joseph, a sweatshop worker, and three of mother's sisters, and Uncle Sam. Were there really six of them already? That made ten of them in all. Almost immediately, Harold's baby brother Wallace died. The story was that this death was the reason why Morris, Sidney and Laurie never came: the moment Morris heard that Wallace had died, he sent angry letters to Rose, accusing her of neglecting the boy. Before that, Morris had been sending dollar coins to my father's sister, Sylvia. Not anymore.

In time they heard that Sidney ran away from Morris to join the Army. In turn, Laurie ran all the way back to England, working his way on a merchant ship, and joined the Hussars. By the time I was born, Laurie had died. When I was a kid, I had it in my head that he died from swallowing a mothball. I don't suppose Hussars die from eating mothballs. Sidney, we were told, lived somewhere impossible like Texas or Colorado with a wife called Bess, which meant that we would never see them.

Where did all these people come from? Our parents' grandparents all came from places we never saw, never visited. These were mostly called Poland, though sometimes exactly the same places could be called Russia. 'Poland was kind of in Russia then,' they would say, not that that explained anything. But Mum's mother came from a place she couldn't remember but sounded, she said, like 'Bill, come in.' Mum said it was Romania. One time Harold called it Austria. I've combed old maps. I think it may have been Bukovina. Bill come in? Bukovina? Maybe. All I know is that we didn't ever go to a place that sounded anything like 'Bill come in,' any more than we went to Poland, Russia, or even Whitechapel and Bethnal Green.

All these people were Jews, the oldest amongst them speaking Yiddish, which by the time I came along didn't exist as a flow of talk. It came interwoven into English, as words and expressions, remnants of one language alive and well in another. It was good for swearing, describing anyone as foolish, crazy or nonsensical; anything to do with eating, gobbling, slurping and things tasting good; anything to do with saying that people were bad because they were thieves, bastards, know-alls, blabbermouths, spongers, tramps or slobs.

It was good for distinguishing a useless person from a big shot. There was a raft of phrases and sayings to say the unsayable. There were three ways of saying you were in trouble. Not so bad trouble, you were in *tsures*; bigger trouble: 'You're in *shtuch*.' Serious trouble? 'You're in *dr'erd*.'

Do me a favour! (meaning, do me a favour by not saying what you're saying): *Tut mir ein toyver*.

Be good and help me out here: *Sei a mensh*.

And for any time you needed to say, 'kiss my ass', there was *kish mir mein tukkhes*.

If you didn't know whether to risk saying something, what's the worst that could happen? 'So they call you *pisher*!'

There were even words my parents said that they didn't

really know what they meant but they said them all the same: a plate of nice food in front of us, and my father would say, '*Shnobbrergants*'. It didn't mean the food was nice. It meant something like, if I was a shnobbrergants I'd gobble this stuff up – but he didn't know what a shnobbrergants was. And a mess, for my mother, was a *misherdamonk*.

My father used more Yiddish than Mum did. I'm guessing that when he saw me, he named parts of me: there was my *pipik*, my *tukkhes*, my *punim* (belly button, bum, face). Most likely he used Yiddish to describe this baby's bodily processes. 'Con,' he'd say (it wouldn't have been his job), 'he's *kvetsht* up his milk', 'he's *grepst*', 'he's *fotzt*' (he's puked up his milk, burped and farted). When I winced, 'Con, it's something in his *kishkes*' (guts); 'Ach, there's *shmalts* all down his bib,' and when I was washed and dressed, he'd say, 'Look at the little *lobbes*! He's as sharp as a matzo ball and twice as greasy' (the little yob). If he thought I was small he would have called me a *shnip*, if he thought I was the kind of new-born baby who bosses his mother about, he'd have called me a *gubba*. And for as long as I ever knew he told me I had a 'triangular tukkhes'. I know what Bubbe would have called me when she came: *tattele* – little chap. It's what she called me every time I ever saw her.

And because my parents were Jews, at the very moment of my arrival into the world in 1946 they were carrying with them the discovery that their uncles, aunts and cousins had disappeared. In our family, accounts of these disappearances came from France, Poland and Russia. There were also other unexpected stories. Just about the time I was born, a man in his twenties arrived on my father's sister's doorstep, scarcely able to speak English. 'Lady Sylvia?' he asked. He was their cousin, Michael Rechnik. His mother, Stella Rosen, was Harold's and Sylvia's aunt, the sister of Morris.

In Poland, Michael Rechnik's parents had put him on a train going east just as the German army was arriving from the west. The Russians were invading Poland from the east and demanded that the Poles take Soviet citizenship. He refused, so they sent him to a camp in Siberia, but when the Soviet Union was itself invaded by the Nazis, the Russians let Michael out so he could fight the Germans. He joined the Polish Free Army that fought on the same side as Britain and Russia, even though he hated the Russians and the Russians hated him. He fought all the way round the perimeter of Europe, up the middle of Italy and on to the battle of Monte Cassino.

Just as I came into the world he got himself out of a camp where the Americans and British had put him for fighting for them, and came to England. He carried the addresses of the French, British and American uncles and aunts, and was heading for the relatives in the US via London. Sylvia gave him a bed, so he stayed in London. He learned to drive a taxi and never left. He never saw his parents again. How, where and when they disappeared wasn't known to anyone in the family. I'm not even sure that they dared think about it. Certainly, they didn't ever talk about it.

The rest of the Rosens weren't in Pinner, weren't in London, weren't in England. They were in America or they were nowhere. On the other hand, Harold's mother's family were in England. They were the Brookstones. Rumour had it that one part of this side of the family had started up the Essoldo cinema chain, named after family members, Esther, Solly and Dolly. Was that a joke or was it true? Harold gave the impression that the house in Whitechapel was full of rumours like that. Someone had made serious *muzzume*, money, in South Africa. Or not. Uncle Leslie Sunshine was going to set him up in the law, Harold had to give him a call after he got his 'Matric' and Leslie Sunshine would see him right. Harold got his Matric and rang but Uncle Leslie Sunshine made out he hardly knew him. But wasn't it Leslie Sunshine who took him to Highbury to see Arsenal play in 1926?

'No, that was my *Zeyde*' (Grandad).

'Who was it that was going to make you a bar mitzvah suit but when your mother said you weren't going to have a bar mitzvah, he didn't make you the suit?'

'No, you got that muddled. My cousin Bernie was getting a suit because he was getting bar mitzvahed but because I wasn't, my Zeyde felt sorry for me and said he would make one for me all the same, but the jacket he found too difficult.'

'And it wasn't Leslie Sunshine?'

'No, that was the thing about being a lawyer.'

'And who was the great lady that you were taken to see?'

'I wasn't taken to see her, I went on my own. My mother used to collect people. I don't know how she did it but they would turn up in our house in Nelson Street. One of them was this grande dame type, called Beatrice Hastings. After a few of her visits, my mother said that I had been invited to see her in Belsize Park. So after what seemed like a journey that took all day on buses and trams, I walked down a street the like of which I had never seen before in my life: huge white buildings with big, big windows.

'I went in and this Beatrice Hastings lived in thick-carpeted rooms, with pictures hanging on every wall, and little bits and pieces from Paris. She asked me questions I didn't know how to answer. I sat on a chair at one end of the room, while she talked at me from the other end. And then I left. I must have disappointed her in some way because I never heard from her again. Only later I found out that she had been Modigliani's mistress. Every time you see a selection of Modigliani's pictures you'll see some of her.'

While Harold was growing up in this house behind the London Hospital, our mother was living up the road in Bethnal Green, over a shop. My father spoke of the shop as being something pathetic, somewhere where Mum's mother tried to sell hats that I think she herself made.

Bethnal Green, he made out, was like some dangerous place where a kid like him wouldn't dare to go, yet that was where she was from. Standing behind her in a cloud of vagueness from before the First World War was Mum's grandfather who 'did dairy'. In the vagueness, he makes cream cheese, sour cream, yoghurt and *shmatana*. He must have taught it to the rest of the family: the only good thing Harold ever said about Mum's mother was that she could make wonderful shmatana.

My parents met in 1936 in a room where the Young Communist League held its meetings. It's not hard to figure out how Harold got there. His mother Rose was a Communist and her father, Joseph, living in the same house, was a socialist who had joined the forerunner to the Labour Party and the Communist Party, the Social Democratic Federation. Mum's parents, on the other hand, didn't seem to me to be part of this kind of thing, though Mum did once mutter very disapprovingly that her father used to go to meetings which she described as 'Trotskyist'. A Trotskyist? It sounded bad.

Were there any clues in what Mum said to us, in the stories she told us? She often described her first sighting of our father. He was playing table tennis at the YCL's meeting place, she said. 'It was his hair, his beautiful auburn hair.' 'I knew straightaway', she would add, 'that he was the one. He didn't have a say in it.'

No, that didn't sound very Communist.

Much clearer was Cable Street. In real life this was the occasion when hundreds of thousands of people stopped Oswald Mosley, the leader of the British Union of Fascists, from trying to march through the East End. In our house, with my mother telling us the story over the kitchen table, it was about how she and Harold – who she had only recently started seeing, they were just seventeen – ended up down a side street, off Cable Street, on the wrong side of the barricades, with mounted police charging up towards them.

'Luckily,' she said, 'just where we were standing, a door opened behind us and someone pulled us into their house.'

Harold refined this by telling us that the mounted police had been blooded in India and used the long sticks they had tried out there. Brian Pearce, who Brian was named after, and who came to stay with us when he split up with Fanny Greenspan, told him that.

I figured out that Mum and Harold had been really brave at Cable Street but I didn't think the bit about being on the wrong side of the barricades was as funny as they thought it was. I didn't get the joke.

'We were on the wrong side of the barricades!'

No, I didn't get it.

But who was this Mosley? He hated Jews and was trying to stir people up.

So why did he try to come into a place where there were Jews? To show he was in charge. He wanted to be Prime Minister.

But why did the police keep charging at you, if Mosley was bad? Ah! And the point is, he didn't get through. We stopped him.

Did he get to be Prime Minister? Oh, no.

Was Cable Street the reason why Mum was Communist? Harold said, 'With your mother, boys, it was those girls at Central Foundation. They were the ones who really got her interested.'

Many years later, I remember an occasion when the son of an old friend of our parents was telling them that they had 'betrayed the working class' and Mum stood up and said very loudly, 'Who else was going to defend us, eh?'

Given that this was decades after they had left the Party and Mum didn't often speak of those times with me, I figure that this thought ran deep. She felt that that organisation had done a good job of defending her. She had gone out with Communist Bertha Sokolov and leafleted for the big East End Rent strike. Mosley had said that everyone was being exploited by 'Jew landlords'. And yet here were Jews like Mum and the *knakke* girls (know-alls) taking action against landlords. So, if Mosley was really against landlords then he would have supported the rent strike, wouldn't he? But of course he wasn't against landlords for being lousy landlords. He was just against Jews.

Mum didn't often give us a picture of her home or what she did, but with Harold you could make the connections between the kind of life he had and how he ended up being 'in the Party'. He described how when he was a little boy he had to read the *Daily Worker* to his Zeyde because Zeyde couldn't read English very well. Zeyde took him to the public baths with all his *chaverim* (mates). And Harold said that when you lay in the bath, you could hear the *alte kackers* from Poland (literally old shitters, meaning old guys) in the other baths, calling out to the attendant to put more hot water in. The taps were on the outside of the cubicles. 'A leetle bit more hot vater in nummer tree, plizz ... AYEEE! Not so much, not so much …' then after a long pause a great sigh of satisfaction: 'Ahhhhhhhhh.'

Why did you go to the public baths? Because we didn't have a bath at home.

Why not? Because the landlord hadn't put one in. Or electricity. We didn't have electricity in the house.

'Oh you do go on, Harold,' Mum said.

Some of the gaps in my mother's early life were filled in by him. She started life in the Mother's Lying-in Hospital on the Commercial Road, then was taken back to rooms in a building in Hessel Street, next to the market. They sold live chickens on Hessel Street. Mum talked of being embarrassed by her mother haggling over the price for it in Yiddish, and round the corner on the Commercial Road, she talked of being scared in winter when the dray horses from the brewery skidded and slipped on the ice.

One story Harold told us about Mum was one she never told us herself:

'One time,' he said, 'when they were doing Harvest Festival at your mother's school, they told the kids to bring in flowers. These teachers coming in to Bethnal Green from places like Harrow …' (he said 'Harrow' with such an irritated tone that he seemed to forget that this Harrow was where we lived). 'How was your mother supposed to get flowers? We didn't do flowers. You never saw flowers apart from outside the London Hospital. She went home and didn't say anything to her parents. She worried and worried. If she didn't go in the next day with flowers, she knew there'd be trouble, *tsures*.

'On the way to school the next day, she's thinking what to do, and then she remembered the little gardens in front of the Bethnal Green Museum. She loved that museum. On Sundays when the *meshpuche* (relatives) came over to play gin rummy, she took herself off to the Bethnal Green Museum. So, instead of going direct to school up Globe Road she took a left, nipped into the gardens, and broke off a flower. Your mother a *ganuf* (thief)! She won't tell you that story. I'm the only one who knows.'

But she told us how she was the only girl in her school to win a scholarship to the grammar school and they wrote her name up on a wooden board with gold letters. She often talked about those gold letters. And she went to a special place called Central Foundation School, or as she always called it, 'CFS'.

There she met up with a group of girls with names I used to conjure with, like Dinah Kesselman, Alice Kissin, Rene Roder, Bertha Sokolov, Fanny Greenspan – names that were nothing like the names of girls I knew. And these girls, my father said, were all knakkes.

That was all I knew about her time at school until fairly recently a piece of writing about her time at CFS, that she must have done in the early 1960s, turned up. Mum was there from 1930 to 1936, when a third of the school were Jewish girls, she says.

We stepped from one world into another every day of our lives. Our grandparents spoke no English and the common language at home was Yiddish. Grandparents and even parents felt themselves to be foreigners. They didn't understand the country they had come to. They had fled from persecution, and collected together in the East End as tightly as they could to establish an island of security. They tended to regard the outside world with anxiety and suspicion. They mixed with it as little as possible. They remained a tightly knit group from their overcrowded tiny homes to their synagogue to the occasional day on the sands, shared cheek by jowl with their neighbours and relatives.

I would walk down the Whitechapel Road, teeming at all times of the day and night with the young parading and ogling, the old in groups gesticulating and arguing, past Vallance Road where the street corner meetings shouted and jostled, to the Public Library where a seat between a schoolboy and a seaman was a rare and miraculous acquisition, to call on a friend who lived, like so many of us, with a family of four in two rooms. Aldgate Pump was the customs barrier beyond which the streets were empty and silent.

On Saturday morning I went to the baths. No-one I knew had a bathroom at home. I sat in the baths clutching my towel, crowded between girls wearing scarves over hair curlers and waited two hours to reach hot water. After dinner there was the library or the Old Vic. Saturday evening I visited my friends. Pearl's father played the violin, Gertrude's father philosophised, Helen's mother asked awkward questions, Lily's mother was fat and worried about the shop, and Bertha's sisters were off to a dance.

We then proceeded to our Socialist Students' Club, held in Father Groser's hall and talked and talked and talked religion and politics and sex, and solved the problems of life, literature and the world. We poured out at twelve o'clock, argued our way down streets alight and alive with people, to go and sit in steamy cafes to talk some more.

Our parents were alternately alarmed at late nights, undesirable companions, fearful of participation in anything outside the Jewish community, and yet on the other hand remarkably lenient (or ignorant) of the ideas and influences flowing into us.

Perhaps we reflected the same contradiction, apparently sophisticated in the world of ideas, politics, religion, literature, and yet so ignorant of the world outside school and home. We talked sex and did not notice the young ladies in dressing gowns who propped up window sills at the corner of the street all day long. We lived in sordid, unhealthy, crowded homes where people lost tempers easily and streams of curses and invective were a common occurrence, but not one of us had ever heard or knew the meaning of common swear words. We stood between the reality of our homes and the reality of our school, and achieved a state of equilibrium in a world of hazy ideas unrelated to either world.

We adored the school. Perhaps unconsciously, we realised that it would give us all that we needed. We needed to be absorbed, we needed an introduction to the life that we were going to live, which was not the life of our parents. But did the school understand about us? The uniform was odd and something to be grumbled about and something terribly desirable, but every item that wore out was an agony to our parents to replace. What was the use of saying the grant covered clothes and books when we knew it had gone months ago to pay for a gas bill?

We lived in a confused, noisy, crowded, unmethodical community which talked and ate at any time of the day or night, but the school, successfully, imposed upon us life-long taboos against eating in the street or going out without gloves or stockings. We knew nothing of our teachers, where they lived, what chairs they sat on or what relatives they had. They were all over fifty and wore brown or green dresses and had smooth hands. We listened and learned and had some h.s. [history sense], pretended to talk French nonsense to each other, sat in the book-case that was the library, and it was always something rather removed, incomprehensible and unattainable.

At the time we accepted the separation unquestioningly. We didn't think about it. We didn't ask to be understood. We were too self-absorbed, group absorbed, bound by too many threads, one of which might even have been the protective thread of arrogance and conceit. We accepted the vast gulf of physical and moral environment that separated us from our teachers, without a moment's wonder or concern. We accepted the code of the school which had been fashioned for a different age and a different people, and conformed or didn't conform according to our thermometers of mutiny.

It left on all of us an indelible stamp. We passed out of the gates, the same gates which were shut every day to protect us from the Smithfield porters, carrying something which had become our own. We took with us the most precious thing of all, especially for us, an English culture, and it was Miss Roberts who gave it to us. How did it come about? It all seems somewhat strange now, as though education is carried on at all levels of the conscious and subconscious.

I remember her as someone quiet, almost subdued and never, ever given to enthusiastic gushing. She maintained a rare and enviable balance between involvement and reserve, sincerity and good sense and subjective response and objectivity. Yet somewhere the three forces fused, her own enthusiasm, our susceptibility, and the passion of great literature. In front of the classroom, we half acted, half read Orlando and Rosalind, Ferdinand and Miranda, and on Saturday afternoons for years, we hurried across the ever-temporary Waterloo Bridge, past the tattoo shop to watch them all over again from our

9d. gallery seats at the Old Vic. We listened to and read with an amused tolerance 'Sir Roger de Coverley' and the 'Man in Black', and strangely, when left to choose a play to act at the end of the year, we chose *She Stoops to Conquer*.

We had our Saturday evening play-reading sessions and read *Hedda Gabler*, *Strife*, and *The Monkey's Paw*, and the following year we chose to act *Quality Street* and arranged rehearsals. Alice produced it, and in that extraordinary enlightened fashion of the school and the English teaching, we were left to get on with it with the minimum of staff supervision. How did we so avoid squabbles that we were ready to go with Miss Jay to the long, dusty, dark Theatrical shop full of masks and trunks and uniforms to choose our own silks and satins and hats and wigs, and were ready to present the play to our parents?

I remember the holiday tasks from *Tom Brown's School Days* and *Robinson Crusoe* and *Jane Eyre* and *Henry Esmond*, and there we sat on the first day of each term writing an essay about them. Could it be done today? Does it indeed still continue? I can't say but I know I read them all, enjoyed them all, except *Henry Esmond* who was never finished and who ended his days in the mud one long wet holiday, and have indeed re-read them.

We arrived at the Fifth Form, overcame the embarrassment of Lady Macbeth, learnt speeches about ambition o'erleaping itself, became Devil worshippers under the influence of *Paradise Lost*, fell in love completely and forever with the Metaphysical Poets, and emerged from the examination with demands of our own. Could we please read *Hamlet* and do something modern, and Miss Roberts read us T. S. Eliot and Edith Sitwell, and by that time I was ready to see *The Ascent of F6* with a nice auburn-haired young man, and to make my way through literature and life.

I don't think we were ready to face the menial side of life. We wore blue stockings and so met disasters with saucepans and pastry. We had tried to travel in 7 years [she must mean five] an immeasurable gulf from Middle Europe to suburbia, and too often met disasters in relationships with office people and landladies. But Miss Roberts helped to bridge the gulf.

She gave us something so important, so much more important than the gloves and stockings, something that would always be a source of inspiration. She introduced us to the wisdom and poetry of the centuries and it was something we could understand, respond to, make our own, take away, and was ours for evermore.

When I in turn read to the nine-year-olds I teach, the *King of the Golden River*, or the *Princess and the Goblin*, or tell them about *A Midsummer Night's Dream*, and read them the Fairy Song, I remember the two worlds of my schooldays, and the bridge of English Literature that Miss Roberts provided, which enabled us to move from one world to another.

Reading what Mum has written, some forty years since she died, I find myself thinking that she talks of things here that she didn't ever give voice to in conversation. I don't think she ever mentioned Miss Roberts to me and, to my shame, I don't think I knew that she read those books. It was Harold who read that kind of book. There are dense knots of feeling about herself, culture and change that I don't remember her unravelling like this. Which means, I think, that she must have felt there wasn't the space in our home for her to say these things. It wasn't because such views and attitudes were forbidden. It was more that through subtle, unspoken ways she wasn't given (or she didn't take?) the space for that kind of reflection and thought; the airwaves were taken up by Harold, me and Brian.

This was the time, then, that she was referring to when once she told us about her panic and horror lying in bed at night thinking she would never get married. How would she find someone? In the end she did find that 'auburn-haired young man', but whether it was because he wasn't acceptable to her parents, or whether it was because Mum rejected them, she left home and went to live with Harold's mother, Rose. Somehow or other Mum patched it up with her parents – well enough for them to be around when I was born and throughout my childhood. But it was awkward.

I think now that this awkwardness arose from the shift my parents had made in how they wanted to live. And it left them with ambiguous, ambivalent attitudes to what that East End, east European Jewishness meant. Say, if my father muttered a Yiddish curse – strange antiquated phrases like 'may you get cholera' (*chaliera zolste nimmen*) or 'I've got you in my hole' (*ch' 'a' dich im loch*) – my mother would shout: 'Don't say such things!'

'What did he say? What did he say?' we'd call out. (It had suddenly got interesting.)

'Don't tell them,' she'd say.

'Why not?'

'It reminds me of my relatives.'

Relatives? What relatives? What were their names? What did they do? Where were they? She didn't ever tell us. All she'd say was, 'Every Sunday, they came over and sat in the back room playing gin rummy and cursing. I can't stand the sound of it.'

But why were they there? Why were they playing cards?

By the time I was born, our parents had not suddenly become wealthy or posh. In fact, someone at my primary school once explained to me that I was 'common'. This was probably true, but since his time of living in Whitechapel my father had studied at what one relative called 'psycollege'. He got himself a degree in English. And, during the Blitz of 1941, he'd started teaching in secondary schools in Leicester and Nottingham. They moved to North West London in 1944. Yet at the moment I was born my father was either still in the army or just demobbed. Not the British Army – the US Army.

For reasons we have never got to the bottom of, my father remained a US citizen. Born in Brockton, Massachusetts, at that time the centre of the shoe- and boot-making industry, he never chose to naturalise. 'Naturalise' was a word in our lives, repeated every time we all went through the worry of him applying for a renewal of his US passport, or every time we came through passport control separately on our ways into and out of France for our holidays.

Our parents often tried to explain to us how our father was

'the enemy'. Being a Communist meant it would have been difficult to get British citizenship and, in those days, he would have had to 'renounce' his US citizenship first before applying to be British. He could therefore end up with no passport or being 'stateless' – whatever that meant.

As a result, the US call-up reached him sometime around the end of 1944, and he went off to the British-based US Army University in Shrivenham in Berkshire. The gag here was that as he was 'away' from the US, he was on foreign pay supplement. Earning extra in England, we should all be foreign, they said. This moment in Harold's life touched me in my very first days and has marked me ever since. My parents named me after a great friend he made at Shrivenham: my middle name is Wayne, after someone who, through my childhood was an occasional visitor to London, legendary for his height, beard, bass voice, mid-West accent and kind fathering. He'd come from a background in the Mormons, which right from their time in Shrivenham, Harold always called the Normans. In fact, even as I lay in my cot, he probably stood over me, telling me that I was named after a Norman. Later in my life, much later, big, bass-voiced, bearded Wayne would become Wayne C. Booth, a much-admired literary theorist.

Harold was shipped off to Frankfurt, and on to Berlin. He was, he always told us, in the 'occupying army' and never saw action. He was billeted one time in the house of an SS officer, long since disappeared. He wandered round the rooms looking at this man's rise through the ranks. Along the shelves were books bearing the great names of German literature: Goethe, Schiller, Hölderlin. It worried Harold that reading that stuff hadn't stopped this man being in the SS. The army was one thing, but the SS, for Christ's sake?

His time in the US Army spanned from the end of the war in Europe, through the end of the war in Japan and onto the first months of the occupation of Germany. He did not see much of my mother, and instead he stood in line waiting for pancakes and maple syrup with his metal camp kitchen kit. Maple syrup. When he joined the army, my mother said, he was all skin and bone, and when he came out he had a 'pot', she said pointing out his belly.

As well as filling out he had moved from being an ordinary private into what he called the 'Education Corps', teaching America's soldiers first in Shrivenham, then in Berlin. There are photos on the web of lines of young, white, clean-cut men, all in uniform, with their twin-peak US Army hats. These teachers, my father amongst them, were issued with course books, which around my birth he started to bring home: anthologies of modern American poetry – Carl Sandburg, Robert Frost, Muriel Rukeyser, Hilda Doolittle, Langston Hughes; the 'New Criticism' of Cleanth Brooks, histories of the United States, collected writings of the Founding Fathers, most of them issued in uniform grey, each one stamped and numbered according to what was to be taught.

There's something very planned and ordered about this, but the books themselves were stunningly liberal, self-confident and American. A collection of over 400 of these books has been given to the Bodleian Library in Oxford. We had about fifty. I've still got five or six. But of all the surprises and jolts my father and mother were going through, this may well have been one of the most profound. In the Cold War battles to come, this pile of liberal, humane books from the US Army, of all places, would complicate things for them. For me as a child they were no more than odd, grey, dusty paper-backs, from a place and time I could never go.

At some point in 1945, my father was due to be sent to the Pacific. He liked to talk about his training; how he had to fix a bayonet to his rifle and run up a hill towards a scarecrow-like figure made to look like a Japanese soldier. They were under instructions to scream and yell and swear as they ran towards it, before 'killing' it with their fixed blade. My father said that he was less than keen and did his bit of yelling with a distinct lack of enthusiasm. He was spotted, hauled up and put on a charge. He came before the 'top sergeant' who noticed that my father had a degree. The man confessed he was having difficulty writing to a woman back home in the States, so could my father see a way to helping him? My father came to a deal: he would write the sergeant's love letters, so long as he didn't have to run about with a bayonet in his rifle screaming at scarecrows.

Then Hiroshima happened. No Pacific posting for him and it was all over. The post-war world had begun. But for my father, it did not yet mean demob. He stayed on in Germany and was in Berlin still teaching English to American soldiers at just the time I was born. He was also selected (he never knew why or how) to write a history of the US Army occupation of Berlin. Of all the things he might have imagined himself doing in the world as he grew up, this would never have occurred to him. Somewhere deep in the archives of OMGUS (Office of Military Government, United States) sits a report, written by someone who would come to be called in the following decades a 'card-carrying member' of the Communist Party.

'They suddenly realised that they had no records,' he would say, 'so they asked me to write up the history of the occupation. Me!' And so, in his words, he *krierched* (crept) about the base, asking questions. But they were all *mommzas* and *gonovim* (bastards and thieves), he would say. These colonels and generals were all fiddling something, making muzzume on the side, and so when this young English-sounding man arrived asking questions, they smelled a rat. They thought he was some kind of military policeman sent by the *gantse machers* (big shots). So they would try to buy him off. One colonel said to him, 'Do you like mushrooms?'

'I do and I don't,' said my father.

So the colonel took him down into the old Berlin bomb shelters, and there my father saw that he was running a mushroom farm, rows and rows of mushrooms leading far away into the distance down one of Hitler's bunkers.

'Don't tell anyone,' said the colonel, and offered my father an unlimited supply of mushrooms.

Another time, he found himself in an office that held the files of SS men and committed Nazis. He was 'staggered', he would say, that it was an open filing cabinet. People were coming and going, taking files out, putting files in. Anyone could have done anything to those files. He didn't know then and wouldn't ever know that one file, taken out of those cabinets and spirited away to safety, referred to the man who had just done for his relatives in France.

Later, he often talked of the hell of Berlin after the war, the ruin of it, the poverty. The smell and taste of bombed-out Berlin must have settled on him as I came into the world. And there was something else that made him uneasy: when he got on a bus in his uniform, people leapt up to give him a seat. If he stood anywhere, in a matter of moments people would come up and offer him anything that they thought was of value: books, jewellery, clothes. The irony of it was painful: someone like him, who only months before was 'the enemy' in three ways at once – American, Jewish and Communist – here he was, at the heart of the wrecked Nazi empire.

My father must have told my mother the story of the Berlin Natural History Museum. His old college friend, David, and David's mother, Nan, had asked him to make a trip through the rubble to the Museum to make contact with the professor there, someone who Nan had known before the war. So, despite the snow, my father got himself to the street, where all the houses were bombed out, just heaps of rubble, people living in cellars and holes in the ground.

When Harold got to the museum, it too was ruined and the great dinosaur skeletons, one of them identical to the massive diplodocus in London's Natural History Museum, were standing with backs broken from the bombing, exposed to the open air, in the Berlin snow. He did find the professor, who was in a cellar under the museum and Harold passed Nan's note to him, but the old man scarcely acknowledged it; he was beside himself with grief. He had heard that his son had been killed, 'on the eastern front'. My father said that at that moment he couldn't find any feelings of sympathy.

He knew it was the war that had taken away his sympathy. But it wasn't 'the Germans', it wasn't 'all Germans' who did all that bombing and killing, he'd insist. It was the Nazis. Only a few years earlier, he and his friend David and David's mother might have spent a happy day with the professor talking about dinosaurs. That dinosaur in the snow is special. My brother became a palaeontologist – a fossil expert – and worked most of his life at London's Natural History Museum. He found out that the skeleton in London, which millions of us had stared up at until recently, was identical to the one in Berlin, the one my father saw. They were both plaster replicas of the original in the United States. There had been a time in the past when American, British and German palaeontologists shared dinosaurs.

All our parents' hopes had been wrapped up in that place in the east where the 'eastern front' was: Russia, the Soviet Union, somewhere terribly, deeply, totally important to them, but again, not somewhere we'd ever seen.

Before the war, Connie and Harold believed that a utopia was being built there, a utopia that one day would spread across the world. Whereas the leaders of Britain and France had 'cosied up to the Nazis', ignoring the persecutions in Germany, pretending that they didn't know the Nazis were rearming, hinting that they wouldn't be too bothered if Hitler went into the Sudetenland, even letting on that a war with the Soviet Union would be no bad thing. Those leaders had ignored the bombing of Spain by German bombers and, as the Communists had predicted, it was the same bombers that later bombed London. They, my parents' people, had been horribly right, they believed, and it was the heroism and sacrifice of millions and millions of Russians that had saved them.

'We would have been carted off and killed in the camps,' my mother told us, 'if Hitler had won.'

Over there was the bombed-out Reichstag building – a building that had had mythic importance for my mother and father, the site of the 'Reichstag Fire'. That fire was how the Nazis had managed to turn their electoral superiority into total power. They told us over and over again how the Nazis had used the arson attack on the country's government building as an excuse to bring in emergency laws against people like Harold and Mum: Communists, socialists, trade unionists and then Jews. The way they told the story as we were growing up made it sound as if the Nazis taking power had been a personal attack on them.

But there was a hero in their story, too. Dimitrov, the Communist who the Nazis charged with having started the fire, sat in his cell preparing his defence and, even though the Nazis had all the means to frame him, his brilliance, they would say to us, proved his innocence. A lone, studious figure, using his intelligence, his education and his learning to defeat the Nazis. That was good.

Even more to my father's liking was the fact that he was once in a room in Berlin with American soldiers playing chess with Russian soldiers. He had the photo of it. He loved that, but would then temper it by saying, 'They wouldn't let that happen again, though, would they?' For him, it was like the fabled moment in the First World War, when German and British troops celebrated Christmas together. A moment never to be repeated.

Turning over the photos he took in Berlin, he would show us pictures of a demonstration marching through the streets, holding banners in German. This, he told us, was a peace march. The remnants of those movements that had been so strong before the Reichstag Fire, before the decree and the laws that followed it, had gathered together and marched for peace. Harold shook his head.

'The Americans and British banned them.'

But all through 1946, when he was on leave – 'furlough' in the US Army – he flew to and from Germany strapped onto the wooden struts of a Dakota, to tell my mother and brother about everything he had seen. The air around my cot, I guess, must have been full of it. In my growing up, his time in the army was expressed through photos and a set of khaki clothes he wore at weekends and on holidays.

Mum used to tell us about the period before the war in Europe was over and while my father was away, the V1s, then V2 rockets coming over the city. She often talked about 'doodlebugs' and told us that they were given instructions: if you're in the street and you hear a doodlebug coming and the droning sound stops, you have to lie down in the gutter and count to ten. She said that on her way to the White City flats where she was living with Harold's mother Rose, there were plenty of times, halfway between the underground station and the flats, when she lay down in the gutter and counted to ten.

By now she was working in the typing pool of the Communist newspaper, the *Daily Worker*. Harold had an explanation for why she and her friends didn't do more study:

'Every one of them knew so much, read so much. But, you see, Mick,' he said, 'not one of them went to university. They all passed their Matric like I did, but they left school at sixteen. Every one of their parents would have said, "What's the point of that? Going to college doesn't make you a *balaboust*"' (a good housewife and home-maker).

Some sixty-five years later, I met Sam Lesser, who had been a journalist on the paper writing under the name of Sam Russell. He had fought with the International Brigades in Spain, and at the time I was born he was investigating the collaboration between the authorities in Guernsey and the Nazi occupiers; his account would be published as a Communist Party booklet, *Spotlight on the Channel Islands* (1945).

We met at an event, September 2009, looking at how and why Picasso's *Guernica* had come to be exhibited in the heart of London's East End at the Whitechapel Art Gallery. Only a couple of months before Harold died, he and I talked about *Guernica* and I told him I wanted to make a radio programme about how this version of the painting had arrived at Whitechapel in January 1939. I was looking for people who had been there.

'I was,' Harold said. 'I was there. I remember walking down the stairs from the Library to see it …'

'You were there?' I said. 'You didn't ever say!'

He shrugged the shrug of someone trying to say that it had been impossible to tell me everything, no matter how hard he'd tried.

When I introduced myself to Sam Lesser, he looked at me and said, 'Your mother was beautiful. Very beautiful.' That word 'beautiful'. It was exactly what Solly Kaye had always said about her. Solly Kaye, carpenter, Communist councillor, teller of the longest Jewish jokes there have ever been. Beautiful? My mother? *Sheyne*? Like the song, '*Biss du sheyn*?' Is that what people thought of her, Connie Isakofsky? And were they a 'beautiful' couple? My mother seemed to think so, with that talk of her first sight of Harold.

On my arrival, as I was a baby boy, a conversation would have taken place about circumcision. In those days, you didn't have to be Jewish to be what we called, in the showers at secondary school, a 'roundhead'. I learned, from Mum, I think, that my circumcision was like the one these boys had, a non-Jewish circumcision, because in those days the doctors thought it was a good idea. What kind of a good idea? She didn't say.

But in one of those peculiar moments that happen around funerals, after the death of my father in 2008, his second wife Betty said that she understood that there had been a row in the family about doing (or not doing) what Bubbe and Zeyde had wanted. Mum's parents I knew as Bubbe and Zeyde, Yiddish for grandma and granddad. It was they who had wanted my brother and me to be circumcised, and it was only because of them that we were 'done'. So it wasn't a medical circumcision, it was a *bris* (the Jewish term for it), after all. Or was it? For it to be a bris, a *mohel* (circumcision specialist) would have to do it. Or did a doctor do it? And would that have been enough for Bubbe and Zeyde? I don't know.

This conjures up a picture of relatives standing about looking at the baby me, arguing over whether I was going to have a bris or not.

Of course he is, one says.

Why? says another.

How can you forget thousands of years of history? We know a mohel. He could do it.

No, the doctor will do it.

A doctor? Why would you let a doctor get at his *shmekel*?

Because doctors do it these days. All the goyim do it.

But if a doctor does it, is it a bris?

What do you mean, 'is it a bris'? Either you have the thing on the end, or you don't. What's the difference if a mohel does it or a doctor?

How can you say such a thing? You know it's different ...

# 2

## No Thank You God

My mother was mysterious. One time, during a typhoid outbreak in South America, the papers, radio and TV were full of warnings: 'Don't eat the corned beef. Don't eat the corned beef.' I didn't even know that corned beef came from South America. My mother went over to the cupboard and it was stacked high with tins of the stuff. We could never be without food; we could never be without corned beef. We never knew when people might come over. If there was corned beef in the house at least you could open a tin and have corned beef. This time, she went over to the cupboard, picked out a tin and said, 'Better not open that till the typhoid outbreak's over.'

When I was three years old, my first job was to help my mother become a teacher. In the mornings she took me on the bus from Pinner to Wealdstone, where she dropped me off at a house lived in by two terrorists. They were sisters, aged about seven and five. They made me play their games in their backyard – chasing, catching, grabbing – but the moment I caught one of them, she would hold up two crossed fingers and yell, 'Fainees!' Which meant that I hadn't caught her.

After several hours of this, the mother took me next door to a place called Tyneholme Nursery, run by 'Hornby Teacher'. I figured out that my job was to be held in this nursery until Mum had done what she had to do to become a teacher. For some reason, this had to happen every morning. Forever.

I wasn't able to put all this into words at the time. What I said was, 'Gallicker's got a big gas stove.' This was in answer to the interrogation I received when I got home after the first day.

My father asked, 'How was it today, *boychik*?'

I said, 'Gallicker's got a big gas stove.'

Day two: 'How was it today, boychik?' 'Gallicker's got a big gas stove.'

Same for day three and day four. My parents behaved like the answer didn't have much to do with the question, but I stuck to my position: 'Gallicker's got a big gas stove.'

On day five, they let my mother in to the nursery to see how things were going. Hornby Teacher asked Mum how I was taking it. 'Fine,' she said, 'fine, but when we ask him anything about the place, he says, "Gallicker's got a big gas stove."'

Hornby Teacher – who my mother called Miss Hornby – took my mother off to the kitchens, where she met Mrs Gallagher and Mrs Gallagher introduced my mother to her large gas cooker. Like I said, 'Gallicker's got a big gas stove.' It wasn't the only time in my life that people just wouldn't get what I was on about.

Then, Hornby Teacher lowered her voice and said, 'Mrs Rosen, would you like Michael to ... er ... not take part in religious things?'

'No, no, that's fine,' said my mother, who, I suppose, had decided not to make any kind of political point about God. They would just run with it. No fuss.

'Are you absolutely sure that you're happy for Michael to join us in a little prayer we say? I know you're ... er ...'

My mother explained to me a couple of years later that 'I know you're ... er ...' is how people ask you if you're Jewish, and the way I should answer that is, 'Yes.'

'You see,' said Hornby Teacher, 'it's about grace. Before we sit down to eat, we say a little prayer: "Thank you God for what we are about to receive, may the Lord make us truly thankful." I ask the children to say this standing up. I say, "Put your hands together and shut your eyes" and then we say the grace ...'

'Yes,' Mum said.

Hornby Teacher went on, '... but you see Michael won't stand up. He stays sitting down and shouts, "No thank you God! No thank you God!"'

I can imagine that this posed problems for my mother. All I know is that the 'No thank you God' thing came to an end. I knuckled down. Well, not down, more like up. I knuckled up. I stood up, shut my eyes, joined my hands and said, 'Thank you God for what we are about to receive, may the Lord make us truly thankful.' I've never figured out how my mother convinced me that I should knuckle up, but getting people to do things you don't believe in must have been a skill my mother possessed.

But such carryings-on had their drawbacks. You can get people to do what you ask them but if, deep down, they don't want to do what you ask them, there might be consequences. Each afternoon, Hornby Teacher got out the beds. These were ex-army folding beds, made of wood and canvas. She then gave us each an ex-army blanket and told us we had to go to sleep. It was a routine, but I didn't go along with it. I lay down on the bed and covered myself with the blanket, but then I didn't do the sleep. No way. I wasn't going to give in to that sort of thing.

The other kids went out like a light the moment they hit the canvas. But I worked out a way of not giving in. I concentrated on the rough canvas of the bed, then on the hairy blanket. Again and again, I fingered the tiny bumps of the canvas and then turned my mind over to how the blanket chafed my neck with its hairy bits. Bumps – hairy bits; bumps – hairy bits. Again and again. All through the long, long hours they held us there.

Then Mum arrived, we got on the bus and went home. She told me where she had been. Somewhere on the other side of the universe at a place called Little Gaddesdon. 'I go to Little Gaddesdon,' she would say, as if that explained anything or justified the kind of treatment I had been subjected to or acknowledged my resistance. She said she was being 'Emergency Trained'.

What happened was that when it came to the end of the

war, the government discovered that they didn't have enough teachers. So they created 'Emergency Training'. At the end of the training course, Mum took me to see what it had been all about. Little Gaddesdon, it turned out, was a castle. We went up some steps into the castle hall and Mum had pinned up hundreds of bits of paper on the wall. There was her writing and her paintings, and in one corner she had stuck some brambles to a bit of card. I looked at her, and she was sparkling. When Mum was happy her eyes looked bright, she smiled across the whole of her face.

'I've done it, I've done it,' she said. 'I'm Emergency Trained.'

I grew to love Hornby Teacher. She was the second-best woman in the world. And once I got to love Hornby Teacher I started to love Tyneholme Nursery. I made friends with Jimmy, who wore a brown suit. Something special happened with Jimmy and his suit: as he put his hands in the pockets of his trousers, the jacket rucked up to make room for his arms. More than anything else in the world I wanted to be able to make my jacket ruck up like that. I wanted to be Jimmy. But I didn't have a suit.

Decades later, I received a letter from a Mrs Monica Forcer. A few lines into this first letter, she declared her real identity: Hornby Teacher. She remembered I had called her that. In my reply I told her how my hero was Jimmy. She wrote back to tell me that she remembered him, too. His parents were Irish, and she was very glad that all the children from that family came to Tyneholme. I wondered how many thousands of children she had seen in her time there. I told her it wasn't only the jacket that made Jimmy my hero. He could get to the top of the climbing frame, the chimney pot. I was too scared to go that high. 'Yes,' she said, 'you were quite a reserved child.'

On the way home from Tyneholme on the bus I tried to tell Mum about Jimmy's suit and the chimney pot. She said, 'You see there, over the road? That's Kodak. I used to work there. I was a secretary.'

That sounded much, much better than Emergency Training. Kodak was so famous that every morning at a twenty to eight they sounded a hooter. You could hear it all over Harrow.

You could hear it when you were in bed. Surely it would be much better to work in a place that had a hooter like that. What with the suit, the chimney pot and Kodak, I got the feeling that no one was listening to me.

At the end of that year I left Hornby Teacher and moved on to Mrs Perkins's class at Pinner Wood Nursery. It was fine, though I wasn't in love with Mrs Perkins and once she made me eat mutton. I said, 'If you make me eat that mutton, I'll be sick.'

'Eat the mutton,' she said.

'I'll be sick,' I said.

'Eat the mutton,' she said.

I ate the mutton.

I was sick.

I said, 'Get it? Next time, don't give me the mutton, OK?' I don't suppose I did say that last bit, but I hoped that she got the point.

Mum moved on from Emergency Training to Harvey Road, a school in a place far, far away called Croxley Green. Once there, she got to be very keen on italic writing, making lampshades and finding what she called 'bits'. She needed special pens for the italic writing, special sheets of crispy material bought from Dryad for the lampshades, and we collected the bits on our walks. Bits could be leaves, berries or brambles that we went out and found on Sunday mornings. We'd be walking along and see some berries, 'Ooh, bits!' she'd say, and pick them. It all went off to Harvey Road.

Every so often, I visited Harvey Road. One time there was a play and a girl was being the Herald. She told us what would happen next. Then she said, 'You must use your imagination in this play', and all the adults laughed. I liked the idea that you could say something like that and people laughed, even if I didn't know what they were laughing about.

Another time, when the half-term holidays of my school and hers didn't match up, I had to go with Mum to Harvey Road to be in her class. As we lined up in the playground at the end of break, I thought I would do something clever. I skipped round from the back of the line up to the front, round the front and back to the back.

'Go back to the classroom!' Mum said to me.

When I got there there was another boy who had been sent back to the classroom. We talked about getting into trouble. Then he told me a rhyme:

Inky pinky ponky
The farmer bought a donkey
The donkey died
The farmer cried
Inky pinky ponky.

On the way home, Mum said how upset she was that I had done that skipping round the line. She said that I had let her down in front of everyone. She tried to find out why I had done that. As I didn't know, I wasn't able to help her. But at least something good had come out of it, I thought, because now I knew 'Inky pinky ponky'.

Another important thing at Harvey Road was Mrs Warner. She had a husband called Wally. Wally Warner. Sometimes Mum and Harold invited the Warners over. After a bit, Wally would start talking about where he worked, Sun Engravers. He had found something out, something so big, so terrible, so awful that he could hardly bear to talk about it. He leaned forward. The whole place, he told us, was being run by a kind of dangerous, secret club. He had uncovered it. He had found out how it was a club that reached everywhere. It had taken over. He said he wasn't afraid: he was going to confront them all, and then tell the world about it.

I loved Wally coming over and talking like this. It sounded so spooky and sinister. And Wally was a lone, brave hero battling against these powers. And when it had all come out, Wally would be famous. To be honest I had no idea what it was about, but I decided that Wally was amazing.

'Is Wally a Communist?' I asked Mum.

She was furious. 'Of course he isn't,' she said.

I had no idea why it made her so angry.

The reason why I asked her was because on Tuesday nights my parents went to Communist Party Branch Meetings. They didn't have to go far, as the meetings took place in our front room. We lived in a flat over a shop in Pinner at the time, and I guess that 1950s Pinner was not the most encouraging place to start a branch of a political organisation aimed at world revolution. Anyway, every Tuesday evening our parents would say: 'Now, boys, off you go to bed, we've got a Party Branch Meeting.'

We didn't do anything of the sort. We sat halfway up the stairs, and the moment the doorbell went, we leaned over the banisters to see who was coming. This didn't go on for very long because not many people turned up for the event. There was a very tall couple who wore very long clothes. There was a man called Len, who my father said was terrific. He made aeroplanes, he said. And there was another man called Max who came on a bike and wore little leather shorts. But they didn't all come every Tuesday. I remember some Tuesdays, no one came. Even so, my parents still held their Branch Meeting. We sat on the stairs and they went into the front room and shut the door.

I've often wondered how those particular meetings went. Did they have a little preliminary discussion on how it would go?

'Right, Harold, who's chairing?'

'Why don't you do it, Con?'

'OK, you do the minutes, have you got the agenda there?'

'Here.'

'OK – agenda: one, the World Revolution. Two, sell more *Daily Worker*s. Three, bazaar in the church hall at Wealdstone.

'Moving swiftly on to point three ... haven't we got some of the boys' old books we could donate?'

My mother read to me every night. I don't suppose anyone had read to her every night. It was something she must have learned was a good idea. My father said that his mother used to take him to the Whitechapel Library, and the first book he ever borrowed when he was very small was about whales. Between them, they thought my brother and I should have books like that. For birthdays and Christmases we got Puffin picture books and Puffin story books. These were much influenced by the kinds of cheap, bright picture books that were coming out in the Soviet Union, France and the USA. We saw them too: the Russian ones came from Communist Party bazaars, the French ones came under the Père Castor imprint, a publishing house inspired by a theory called 'New Education', and the American ones were in the Little Golden Books series. This was an international movement to put cheap, attractive, colourful books into the hands of the youngest children, with ideas of freedom, enquiry and discovery at the heart of them. Lying behind those ideas was the feeling that now the Second World War was over, there was an opportunity to build a new world.

Somewhere in the conversations that my parents had with other people, there must have been some kind of discussion about books from all over the world. Unlike any other parents I knew, mine brought home books like the animal tales of Ernest Thompson Seton, a forest ranger from British Columbia, or *Miskito Boy*, the tale of a Miskito 'Indian' boy from Nicaragua. These sat alongside the books coming out of Moscow's Foreign Languages Publishing House, including *Naughty Schoolboys* by Nosov, or the nonfiction books by M. Ilin with titles like *What Time Is It?*, which began by asking readers to imagine a world without clocks.

I had favourites, and there was a pattern to these. I loved anything with a core of naughtiness. Beatrix Potter's *Squirrel Nutkin*, in which Nutkin taunts Brown Owl to the point where he is pinned to a tree stump with Owl's talons, was supplemented by the Père Castor *Mischief the Squirrel* who escapes out of a cage back into the wild, or the trickster stories of the German peasant folk hero, Till Eulenspiegel, or the brown bears in Thompson Seton who convince the grizzly that they're taller than he is by standing on logs. And there was Raff the Jungle Bird, who learns how to sing and whistle and talk to the point that he can deceive people he's a person, and Ukelele, a girl 'from the South Seas' who preferred her own home-made doll to the one that white sailors bring her.

In all it was a rich, diverse range of books, utterly ordinary to me at the time but now slightly mysterious: I wonder how it was that my parents found their way to them, or knew that it was a good idea to read them and give them to us. What networks of parents, teachers and librarians did they tap into in the 1940s that talked about such things – networks that led all the way into our flat and up the stairs into our bedroom where Mum sat on the end of the bed reading to us about Frou the Hare, who escaped from the hunters?

There was another escape. Something revolutionary and dangerous happened around the time of the Coronation. My parents had an idea that if they weren't around while the Coronation was on, they would be able to ignore it away. They met up with their friends the Aprahamians and planned their escape. 'Let's go camping,' they said. So, they hired punts at Pangbourne on the Thames, and paddled us up the river, camping overnight, till we got to Wallingford.

There were some adventures on the way. At one point, my mother was paddling and we started heading for a weir. Mum shouted for help, and several men in uniform came running up and saved us from drowning. While we were just avoiding death, my brother sat in the back of the boat moaning.

'I'm bored,' he said, 'this is so boring.'

Later on in the trip, Francis Aprahamian, the dad, who was a bald Armenian Communist with no neck, and our father decided to go into Wallingford for some beer. When they got back, they were furious. They said that they found a pub, and as they opened the door they could see that the room was packed with people huddled round a TV set. The moment the door opened, everyone turned round and went 'Shhhh!' Then as Francis and Harold looked in they realised they had opened the door at the very moment the Archbishop was putting the crown on the Queen's head. The whole purpose of the punting holiday was ruined.

Another way my parents were Communists at this time was their campaign for Equal Pay. 'We're fighting for Equal Pay,' they said.

I once found, tucked into a copy of The Marxist–Leninist

Library 20, *The Origin of the Family, Private Property and the State*, by Frederick Engels (signed inside: H. Rosen March '42), a piece of paper with Mum's writing on it:

**Equal Pay**
1. Why do communists believe in Equal Pay? (Struggle for Equality will educate women in class struggle)
2. Why do capitalists believe in unequal pay? (Exploitation keeping to minimum)
3. Why are many workers opposed to E.P.?
4. In what spheres and countries (USA) are there concessions on equal pay and why?
5. Would E.P. help Party in struggle for Socialism?
6. Soviet Union Social production

Mum later explained to us that though she and Harold were both teachers, doing the same kind of work, Harold earned more money than she did. I confess that I did secretly think that that was because Harold knew everything and maybe Mum didn't. I'm not proud of that fact. I didn't say it at the time, in case they thought I was part of a wicked outfit called the NAS. The NAS were against equal pay. But my parents were in the NUT, and they were for equal pay. After a bit they said they had won equal pay.

But it wasn't going to happen immediately. Mum wouldn't get her equal pay straightaway. It was going to take seven years. So each year she got an 'increment'. As a result there came a certain month in the year when she would get a letter. She'd open it up and shout, 'I've got my increment!' Then she would look closely at the piece of paper and say, 'That's the third one.' She held the paper up in front of us: 'See this, boys. I am three-sevenths of your father.'

At the time I thought being Communist meant that everything we did that was right or good was Communist. Like camping, or Marmite. Camping was definitely Communist, because we went with other Communists. Marmite was Communist because Mum said it was good for us. They liked going into old churches and saying, 'Just look at that font', and my father especially liked old walls. He knew a poem about an old wall and sometimes he recited it out loud. Old walls must have been pretty Communist too.

My parents thought the butcher we went to was very good. I once heard them recommend him to some Communist friends of theirs, so I assumed he was a Communist butcher, until one day I was playing football with the butcher's son and he said that his dad said that we should drop the bomb on Russia.

There were things we didn't have, and I did wonder if that 'not having things' was because we were Communists: no car, no television, no fridge. We had a larder. It was a cupboard at the side of the kitchen in our flat. Mum said that it kept things fresh. How did it keep things fresh?

It's colder in there, she said.

But it's not colder in there. It's just the same as the rest of the place.

It's colder, she said. So she put the milk in there.

Sometimes, when Brian and I came down for breakfast, it was sour. It had gone off. It smelled like sick. I went to put it down the sink.

'Stop that,' she said, 'don't go pouring it away.' Then she emptied it out into a bowl, with all the thick bits blurping out of the bottle and the rest of it dribbling after. Then she got a spoon and started eating it. 'Mmm, sour milk,' she said.

'Mum's eating sick,' Brian said.

One time she mulched up some beetroot and mixed it in. 'Borsht', she said, 'I love borsht.'

As well as these things she would sometimes go over to the window, gaze out, wave her arm in the air like a grand actress and say in a grand-actressy voice: 'Tread softly, because you tread on my dreams.' At the time I didn't know why she did that, or where it came from, or whether it had anything to do with anything else. It was just something she did.

She also said that on the night I was born the church next door burnt down. She said it so often I started to think that it was my fault. I burned the church down. You could see it next to the alleyway by our flat. Sometimes we climbed in there and found treasure: little lumps of coloured glass, melted from the stained-glass windows. I was glad that something good came from my crime.

Sometimes Mum came into our bedroom and said it was a misherdamonk.

'What's a misherdamonk?', I said.

'Your bedroom,' she said and walked out.

'I think she means it's a mess,' Brian said.

This was how I was beginning to get to understand our mother, but she was always a bit mysterious.

# 3

## The Opposite of Wax

When I was seven, three things happened to me at the same time: Harold's father died; I realised I had three parents; I went to the shiny new school on the other side of the park.

The death of Harold's father wasn't a big deal in our family, because Harold hadn't seen him for more than thirty years. Even when he was a boy, people used to ask Harold where his father was and he'd say he was dead. Then the *alte bubbes* (old grannies) would take pity on him and say, 'Ah, *nabbech*! What a shame! Please God you don't have to go to Norwood.'

Norwood was the Jewish orphanage in South London where all the children had to wear stiff brown suits. In fact, if his Ma died as well as his father, Auntie Millie and Uncle Bernie had already said they would take him in. They had a stall on Hoxton Market. When Harold was a boy, he used to spend Saturday with them and watch the man on the other side of the road chopping up live eels.

Harold seemed annoyed that his father had died. We wondered where or how he had died, and asked Harold, but he didn't know. Some stuff eventually arrived from America: papers, and a thick checked jacket like the one the dockers wear in *On the Waterfront*. He had been dead for a while, but no one had told Harold. Ten years later I discovered the jacket at the bottom of a wardrobe and I wore it to disguise myself as one of the guys in *A Man Is Ten Feet Tall* (which was, I thought, a Sidney Poitier, anti-racist version of *On the Waterfront*).

My third parent, it turned out, was my brother Brian, who decided to take me in hand. I assume he thought that Mum and Harold were leaving gaps in my parenting. Perhaps they were. As far back as I can remember, they often gave him the job of looking after me and at some point he clearly came to the decision that part of the job description was to educate me.

He worked to a principle: 'Anything I've been taught, I must teach Michael.' So, with him starting at secondary school at the same time as I was starting at the shiny new primary school, he got down to teaching me French ('*Où est Toto? Toto est dans le jardin*'), algebra, ox-bow lakes, the feudal field system, bunsen burners and stamens. It was tough going for a seven-year-old.

But he liked jokes. Especially doing take-offs, when he pretended to be his teachers. We shared a bedroom, and through his performances I met his teachers, their accents and their mistakes. I even learned to do the voices myself, though I'd never met them. His PE teacher was old and Swiss and believed in the hard knocks method, sending kids out into the snow up a steep hill on runs. He would drive alongside, sticking his megaphone out the window, yelling at them to run faster. He particularly disliked my brother's feet, but as he never knew anyone's name, he called him 'laddy' – or in his accent, 'leddy'.

'Pick up zose great flet feet, leddy,' my brother declaimed in the bedroom.

Brian was not only a teacher: he rehearsed my life. Anything I might be in for later, he experienced for me first. The biggest scope for this was in the matter of Harold.

I think that Harold was annoyed that Brian had a father. At some time pretty early on he decided that Brian had it too cushy. He wasn't grateful enough that he had a father (Harold), and he didn't do exactly what his father told him. At the same time, Brian liked cars, planes and trains. He collected car numbers and train numbers, underlined the numbers in books and spotted planes in the sky. He spent his pocket money on car, plane and train kits and sat in our room, sticking them together. Brian started to think that this

was more interesting than homework. It drove Harold nuts –
not that Harold expected homework always to be interesting,
either.

Harold did think that homework was necessary, because
if you didn't do it you would end up like the Michaelsons.
We never met or knew the Michaelsons. All we knew was
the myth, in which the Michaelsons were poorer than dirt
poor and lived in terrible conditions in a tenement. We didn't
know what a tenement was and had never seen one, but we
knew it was a place where you didn't want to live. With bed
bugs in it. There was an ever-present danger that Brian could
end up like the Michaelsons in a tenement. What Brian did
wasn't good enough. Though it didn't seem that way to me.
Brian was utterly brilliant, got brilliant marks at everything.
What was the problem? But Harold felt that Brian shouldn't
be spending all that time making cars and planes and trains.

Despite the disapproval, Brian went out and bought some
card train kits called Micromodels. These trains were only
about as thick as your finger, but the kit didn't say how you
stuck them together. With the first one he bought, Brian made
tiny little micro-hinges and micro-flaps from Sellotape and
stuck it together that way. It was only later he discovered
something called 'Balsa cement', that meant you could do it
by dabbing on tiny blobs and lines of glue.

During this exercise, Harold once came into the bedroom,
stared at what I thought was an incredible example of micro-
engineering, tutted and then made a strange guttural noise in
the back of his throat – like 'cherch', with the 'ch' sounding
like the the end of 'loch', and walked out. The moment he
was out the room, Brian tutted and said 'Cherch'. And then I
did the same. Tut-cherch.

From then on, 'tut-cherch' became a shorthand for us
whenever Brian started to do anything that wasn't homework. He might say, 'Hey Mick, I've got this great car kit and
…' but before he finished we would both say, 'Tut-cherch'.

The downside of Brian being my parent came whenever he
thought I needed to be brought into line. He said that I made
a noise when I was eating. We'd be having a meal and he'd
say, 'He's making a noise with his food.'

Harold replied, 'He's *fressing*' (gobbling like an animal).

'Well, tell him not to fress,' my brother demanded.

'Leave him alone; he's tired,' Mum said.

That's how it worked. Brian or Harold would see something wrong. They'd each have a go and then Mum would say, every time, 'Leave him alone, he's tired.'

Brian and Harold twigged this, so the conversation changed.

Mum would come into our bedroom and say to me, 'Pick your clothes up off the floor.'

'Yes,' Brian said, 'pick your clothes up off the floor.'

Harold walked in. 'Yes, Mick, you should pick your clothes up off the floor.'

I said, 'But he hasn't picked his clothes up.'

Harold said, 'But we're talking about your clothes.'

'Yes,' said Brian, 'we're not talking about my clothes, we're talking about your clothes' – and then he'd dive in quick and say, 'Leave him alone he's tired.'

My first day at the shiny school, West Lodge County Primary School, was a shock. The first thing I noticed was that some of the walls inside the building were like the walls outside. They were just bare brick walls. The ceilings were made of oblong chunks of painted straw. To keep the building up they had put metal girders where you could see them. We had never seen anything like it. It was obvious: they hadn't finished building it. Harold said that it was very exciting: 'Smashing modern architecture!' It proved that Communism was possible: brand-new, beautiful schools.

They had built us a new school because we were 'the Bulge'. It was explained to us that our fathers came home from the war and nine months later there were millions of babies. Mum said that at her school they had built huts. Brian said they had huts at his school too. I was the lucky one, because we had brick walls, straw ceilings and iron girders.

Our teacher told us we were lucky, too, and soon got us cracking on a project about what the Queen was up to. She was at that time on her boat, meeting the world. Our task was to bring in newspapers from home so that we could make a wall display of the Queen's trip around the world. When I told Mum about this, she explained that the *Daily Worker* didn't write about what the Queen was doing. I was worried that all the other kids would be bringing in loads of articles and photos about the Queen meeting people. What could I say? Mum said, 'Why don't you listen to the Home Service? They're talking all the time about where the Queen is.'

'You bloody bet they are,' said Harold.

'Then you can write down the Home Service things and take that in,' Mum said.

It was at times like this when I thought Mum was really not helpful at all.

Another time she really wasn't helpful was when I had to have new trousers (they were shorts, actually), and she gave me Brian's old ones to 'tide me over'.

I said, 'All the other kids have got new trousers.'

Harold said, 'They're fine. Not everyone gets to wear a new pair of *gatkes* every time they need some. I was supposed to get a new pair when I went to the Foundation School and my Bubbe said ...'

'Harold, why do you go on and on about that stuff?' Mum asked.

'Do I *have* to wear Brian's trousers?' I said.

'They're fine,' she said, 'don't worry about it. They're wearing them like that.'

'What do you mean, "They're wearing them like that"? They're not wearing them like that. The other kids have got light grey. These are dark grey.'

'Don't worry about it.'

It made me so cross. Then when I got home in the evening, she said, 'So, did they like your trousers?'

'What are you talking about, "Did they like the trousers?" Of course they didn't like the trousers. They said they were dark grey when they're supposed to be light grey. I told you.'

'We'll sort it out at the weekend. It won't hurt that you're wearing them in dark for a week.'

How could she be so wrong?

The Queen's trip abroad went on for a long time. I did look in the *Daily Worker* to see if there was anything on it. Instead I found a Children's Corner that I liked, containing stories, puzzles and articles about the Chartists. One time they said that they would have a competition to see who could write the best story and the winner would be printed. I thought I would go in for it. I thought about a book I'd read at school, about a cat called Solomon: Solomon gets thrown out and goes from house to house looking for somewhere to be put up. I could write a story like that, I said to myself. I called it 'Solomon the Cat' and I wrote how Solomon gets thrown out and goes from house to house asking for somewhere to be put up. I sent it in and won the competition. They printed it in the *Daily Worker*: '"Solomon the Cat", by Michael Rosen'. Then at Christmas they printed it in the *Daily Worker Christmas Annual*. Mum and Harold were very pleased.

Some time later, we got a letter from the paper saying that someone had written to them to say that they had just read a book about a cat called Solomon who gets thrown out and goes from house to house looking for somewhere to be put up.

'See this, Connie?' said Harold. 'Would you bloody believe it, the things people do! Some ganuf's stolen Michael's story and made a book out of it. I've a good mind to take this up with a lawyer and sue the pants off them.'

'No, no,' I said, 'I shouldn't bother.'

But there was nothing on the Queen, and as a result my contribution to the wall display was not impressive. If they had asked for stuff on the Rosenberg trial or British atrocities in Malaya and Kenya I could have brought in loads, but Miss Goodall didn't ask for any of that.

I loved this school and didn't regret leaving the old one, particularly as I had feared more than anything being taught by Mr Stonelake. He had beaten Brian with a plimsoll so hard that his legs became swollen and purple. Mum went up to the school and complained. I was glad I escaped that. Mind you, there were beatings at the new school as well.

The playground was divided into two – girls and boys, divided by a line. Miss Williams said that on no account was anyone to walk across the line, run across the line, or linger *along* the line. I ignored this last rule and was talking to a girl across the line about skipping. She handed me her rope and Miss Williams came up and stopped that straightaway. 'Frances, I'm really surprised you were passing something over the line,' she said. I thought, why is she 'surprised' about Frances doing something wrong but not me?

A few weeks later, an American boy came to the school and brought his American football. His name was Ritter but there was a cowboy on TV called Ritter – Tex Ritter, so I may have blurred the memory. Tex Ritter brought his ball to school, kicked it into the girls' playground and he went belting off after it. We all cheered and followed him. The whistle blew and everyone stood still.

Anyone coming into the playground at that moment could see that something awful had just happened. Most of the boys were in their playground. All the girls were in their playground, but there was a bunch of boys right in the middle of girl country. Miss Williams marched towards us. It took her a long time because, though she was absolutely furious, she was quite small. She marched up to Tex and said, 'Tex, I'm having that,' and tried to grab the ball off him. Tex thought, 'Hell man, she ain't havin' my ball,' and he hung on to it. Miss Williams now reached right round it and started to tug on it. Tex hugged it even tighter.

Smack in the middle of all this, I booed. I have no idea why I booed, or what I thought I was going to achieve by booing, but I booed. The moment I started booing, the other boys started booing.

Just then, the head, Mr Scotney, came bounding up the steps on the other side of the playground and now he was heading across the playground towards us. Everyone was standing absolutely still, not daring to blink. He moved over the ground much faster than Miss Williams. He had really loud, clicking shoes and looked very much like the conductor Sir Malcolm Sargent.

We stopped booing. The whole thing had got too big for booing. Then, in one of those quiet but steely voices, he picked out each one of us. 'You, you, you, you, you, you, you. To my study.'

And we headed off towards the main building. It took ages to cross the playground and everyone was staring at us, apart from the littlies who didn't dare look at us in case they caught some of our evil spirit. We lined up outside his study and several of the kids who had never done anything wrong before were crying. They were lost: 'I thought this was what happened to bad kids, why is it happening to me?'

Not long after, Mr Scotney came back from the battlefield, looking ashen. He walked along the line, muttering under his breath about which ones of us he wasn't surprised were there and which ones he was really shocked were there. I was among the not-surprised-about ones. He stood in front of us and started breathing loudly through his nose, and talking about the new school curtains. It was something to do with our parents saving up to pay for them. He talked about oak trees featuring on the school badge because when they built the school they had cut down some trees that had been there since Henry VIII had his hunting lodge, right here where the school is now. He said that when he became head teacher he knew that there would be a small group of boys who'd cause trouble, and here we were.

Some of the sobbing was getting quite loud now. These were kids who had strayed way, way into dangerous territory, trying to figure out how they had ended up on the wrong side of the law. They thought Mr Scotney was like the Queen. Or Sir Malcolm Sargent.

He announced that he was going to cane us. He really didn't like doing this, but it was the only way to get us to see sense. He warned us that he was going to write our names in the Punishment Book, where the event would be remembered forever. The cane was bamboo and he caned us across the palms of our hands.

I wasn't sure at the time whether he did write it down in the Punishment Book where it would be remembered forever, but the school has in recent years asked me to visit and they very kindly found the Punishment Book and showed me the page where it says that I received two strokes for 'Disobedience in the playground'. Even more kindly, they went to a cupboard and gave me the cane. I mean, they didn't 'give me the cane', they gave me the cane to keep.

I loved this school. I loved the school dinners. I loved the school caretaker Mr Tyrrell, who had a ginger moustache and the same name as the archer who killed the king. Mind you, I always made sure he wasn't carrying anything long and springy. I loved Mr Baggs. One day in May I came in with a May Day Badge on my school blazer. Mr Baggs looked at it very closely and said in a sneery way, 'Oh, we're Communists are we?'

As my parents said that they had met him in the NUT and said he was a 'good bloke' (which I thought meant that he was a Communist), I was puzzled about this. That night I told Mum that Mr Baggs had said, 'Oh, we're Communists are we?' and she looked into the distance for a moment, and then glanced down at my shoes. She gasped. 'Look at your shoes. You haven't polished your shoes. They're going to think that Communists are people who don't polish their shoes.'

For our last year at the school they announced that they were going to divide up the classes differently: one class wasn't better than another class, it was just that some people have hands and some people have heads. I went into the 'heads' class with Miss Williams and the 'hands' people went in with Mr Baggs. They were doing this, they said, because this was a very, very important year: the year of the Eleven Plus exam. If we passed that we would go to grammar school; if we failed we would go to the secondary modern school.

'At this school,' Miss Williams said, 'I want as many of you to pass as passed at my old school. Or more.'

I realised that this was as much a challenge for her as it was for us.

Every morning, and all morning, we did arithmetic. First we did it on paper, which was called Practical, and then we put our pencils down and did Mental Arithmetic. This was terrifying. The way Miss Williams taught Mental Arithmetic was to walk up and down the aisles between our desks pointing very violently at someone and shouting out sums. There were forty-eight of us in four rows of twelve, each of us at a desk for two.

'You! Fifty-nine take away eleven!'

If you didn't call out the answer straightaway she would

say things like, 'This is the sort of sum that you're going to get in the Eleven Plus.'

I wasn't good at Practical or Mental Arithmetic, and would spend a good deal of time during these sessions trying to vanish myself. I did furtive slippings-behind the kid in front so she wouldn't notice me. I could see that she often picked on kids who tried the looking-down-at-the-desk move; she was on to that in a flash, in the hope that they were dozing or thinking about Dan Dare and the Treens. Sometimes, I tried a counter-bluff technique by acting like a knakke: bright-eyed and staring at her, like I knew what nine sevens were. I never knew what nine sevens were. Ever. I was known as the kid who didn't know what nine sevens were.

In the afternoon it was spelling.

She wrote twelve words up on the blackboard and shouted, 'Learn them!'

We had to write them down in our homework book. Then we had a week to learn the twelve words. I used to practise on my way to school in the mornings. Then on Friday morning – the Test.

She used the same technique as she did with the Mental Arithmetic, up and down the aisles, pointing and shouting out the questions. 'You! "Eligibility"!'

The trouble was, she hadn't told us how to say the words. You might have learned how to spell 'eligibility', but you had no idea how to pronounce it. You thought it went 'edg-iballility' and here she was asking you some other word altogether. How could that be fair? And she didn't tell you what the words meant either, because this was about spelling. Once there was the word 'acquiesce'. I was sure you said it 'ack-weesky'.

'You! "Acquiesce"!'

'Which word is that, Miss Williams?'

'Rosen, it's the "acquiesce" one, you tomfool.' She called me Rosen rather than Michael because she called all the boys by their last names and all the girls by their first names.

Then, every Friday, Miss Williams gave us an Eleven Plus test: Practical Arithmetic, Mental Arithmetic, English and Intelligence. The English test always had 'opposites', and

Miss Williams was very keen on opposites. I remember thinking about opposites. Does everything have an opposite? I would sit wondering about things that might or might not have an opposite and in my mind, there was a little Miss Williams in there barking out a word and I was barking back its opposite: 'Hot!' 'Cold!' 'Table!' 'Chair!' 'Tree!' 'Tree? What's the opposite of a tree?'

Intelligence was about problems involving patterns, series and men digging ditches. I liked these but got a lot of them wrong. All this was important, because Miss Williams said that over the weekend she would mark the tests and 'average them out'. This meant that she could 'place' us in the class, so that each week we moved to our 'place' as worked out by averaging the marks. Because I was good at English (even though I said that the opposite of 'wax' was 'paraffin') but very 'poor' at arithmetic and only 'satisfactory' at Intelligence, I always ended up somewhere around the middle of the class. After we had all moved to our new places, Miss Williams stood in the centre of the room, opened her arms like a scarecrow and said, 'All children this side of the class will pass ...' (then she span round 180 degrees) '... and all children on this side of the class will fail.' I was often just on the edge of the abyss.

I worked out, using Mental Arithmetic, that this meant that they knew before we took the Eleven Plus that three-quarters of our school would go to the secondary modern. What we knew – or should I say, what we were taught without them teaching it to us – was exactly where each one of us was in a league table. We drank it in every day just by looking at where we were sitting: Sheena's five places better than me; Roger's ten places worse than me. And when Judgement Day came, we would know exactly who was in the 'good' quarter and who was in the 'bad' three-quarters.

My great aim with these weekly tests though, was to finish thirteenth. The person who sat at thirteenth would get, at eleven o'clock, 12.30, 2.45 and 4.00, a little nod from Miss Williams. Then they would get up, go over to the cupboard, pick up a brass bell with a wooden handle, go out of the room and shake it like hell for about ten seconds and then come back into the room. Only the child who sat at thirteenth got to do this. All year, I longed to be thirteenth so that I could have a go at the bell but I never did. I was often twenty-first and nineteenth; incredibly, one week I was fourteenth, but never thirteenth.

At home, I pretended that none of this was getting me down. Brian, I knew, was very, very clever. In fact, by now I knew he was so clever that at the grammar school they said to him, 'You are so clever, we are going to put you up a year,' meaning that he was going to miss out his second year altogether and go straight from first to third. Amazingly, he went on getting the same marks and still Harold said that whenever Brian got a chance he was 'loafing'.

Loafing was as bad as being a Tory. In particular, as bad as Stanley Baldwin who didn't give a damn about the unemployed. Harold said Stanley Baldwin used to appear in ads for St Bruno tobacco that were shown in the cinema, smoking a pipe and saying, 'My thoughts grow in the aroma of this tobacco.' Harold smoked a pipe, and nearly always would say as he lit it, 'My thoughts grow in the aroma of this tobacco.' He made Stanley Baldwin sound really rather a decent, folksy sort of a bloke, someone my father might have called a mensh. But even though Baldwin had provided my father with a line to say when he lit his pipe, he was not a mensh. I got that.

In bed at night, I would lie there thinking about what would happen if I failed the Eleven Plus. I thought of how Mum and Harold would be ashamed of me and when we went round to friends' houses they would say, 'Michael failed.' All the other Communist kids older than me were passing. Maybe there was something about being Communist that made it easier to pass the Eleven Plus, so why wasn't it working for me? Not that I did fall into the abyss below twenty-fourth, but on the day of the exam I could, couldn't I? I could go in there and not know the opposite of something?

I called out for Mum. 'Mum! I can't sleep.'

Mum came up.

'What's the matter, *muzhik*?'

'I can't sleep.'

'What are you thinking about?'

'Things.'

'What things?'

'What's the opposite of wax?'

Mum figured out what I was worried about, and said that as it was coming up to Parents' Evening she would find out how I was doing. 'Do you want some Bournevita?' And she brought me Bournevita.

'Did you put brown sugar in it?'

'You think I wouldn't put brown sugar in it?'

On the night of Parents' Evening, she came back and said, 'You've got nothing to worry about with your Eleven Plus.'

'Really?'

'I talked to Mr Scotney and he said you've got Head Teacher's Recommendation. That means even if you fail, you still go to grammar school. That's how it works. Promise me this: just don't tell anyone I told you.'

'Hah!' said Harold, 'you should have seen your mother giving him the old one-two. She got it out of him.'

'Don't tell anyone,' Mum said, looking fierce.

And I didn't.

But maybe it gave me just that little bit of a reason to be a knakke. One time in a lesson when we were supposed to be going through the arithmetic we had done the night before, I got bored. So I drew a picture in my homework book. I had invented a hero figure called Trev the Tramp, who had a huge beard and did something that at the time I thought was hysterically funny: he walked about looking for old cigarette ends and putting them in a great big sack. Various sad souls, even in Pinner, could be seen doing just this.

So, that day, while the other kids were going through their arithmetic, I was drawing Trev the Tramp. When I got to the end, I held it up to show Harrybo, who was sitting across the aisle from me at about twenty-eighth. Trev the Tramp was also one of Harrybo's favourites, alongside Douglas Bader, Gillingham Football Club, Brixham Harbour, Eamonn Andrews and Piglet.

The room was silent. I mouthed 'Trev the Tramp' and pointed at my picture. Harrybo ducked and did a tiny snort of a laugh. In less than a second, Miss Williams was leaping down the aisle towards me. I banged my book down onto the desk, flicking the pages forward from Trev the Tramp.

'I'll have that,' she shouted, and *chapped* (grabbed) the book off me. She started frantically flicking over the pages till she got to Trev: a full page of Trev with his beard and his sack of cigarette ends. (My parents called cigarette ends 'dimps', and in fact I called it his 'sack of dimps'.)

'In your homework book!' she said, in a voice that told me that I had spoiled something beautiful. 'Right, go downstairs and show this to Mr Scotney. Your parents are going to be hearing about this, Rosen. And you can say goodbye to being a House Captain.'

I showed my book to Mr Scotney, who sat looking at Trev for much longer than he needed to. He looked up and said, 'I'm going to write to your father. You can say goodbye to being a House Captain.'

I came back through the empty corridors thinking about something Brian had said: whenever you're somewhere empty and long, you get the 'lonely crappers': you start dying for a dump. I hung on. I wasn't going to cack my pants this time. I sat in the class feeling wretched. Maybe they would take that Headteacher's Recommendation away from me and I'd be on my way to the secondary modern.

In class, everyone looked at me like I was a Treen. At play-time they told me that I was going to 'get it' when I got home. You're going to get the whacks, they said.

At going home time, Mr Scotney came into the class and handed a large brown envelope to Miss Williams and nodded significantly towards me. She handed the envelope over to me and on it was written, in very large letters – gaw! there was no need to make them that big – 'Mr Rosen'. So it was even too serious to be addressed to Mum as well.

On the way home Harrybo tried to be nice about it, but reckoned all the same that I was going to be in big trouble. He told me how his dad had a belt that he kept in a special drawer, and whenever Harrybo did something bad, his dad would ask him to go and fetch the belt and then he'd whack him with it. Once we were playing in Harrybo's garden where his dad grew potatoes. Harrybo found a potato and chucked it. It hit Harrybo's dad in the middle of his back: boom! His dad told him to get the belt. That boom sound was great though. And what a shot.

After I said goodbye to Harrybo and walked up the stony alley round the back of the shops to our door, I thought: I can't face giving them this envelope, and seeing them open it and read it. The alley got longer and longer, I kicked the stones where we played football and cricket up against the garage doors, and where Jonny Calvert had jumped off the roof of the International Stores and broken his head. I walked through the yard where I used to play moon-trips in the coal bunker, and throw cherry stones off the old cherry tree in the corner into the back yard of the workmen's caff next door where the automatic potato-peeling machine went der-ummer, der-ummer, der-ummer every morning ... and as I walked I thought up a plan.

First I nipped upstairs and hid the big envelope in my bed. I had tea, we listened to the radio: 'Journey into Space'. Me and Brian used to cup our mouths with our hands and call out in spooky voices: 'Journey!!!! Intoooo!!!! Spa-a-a-a-a-a-ce!!!!' Or it was 'The Critics', talking about a play they didn't like. 'It's not one of Chekhov's *early* plays!' Harold would shout at them. He'd smack his forehead. How could anyone be so stupid as to think that this was one of his *early* plays?

I stared as I always stared at the paintings in our flat, Breugel's *Netherlandish Proverbs*. My friends loved that picture, with its great jumble of people living out compulsive hells in a barn-cum-house-cum-tavern, a man banging his head against the wall, someone stuck on a roof with pies, people dancing round a gibbet, a pig with a pair of shears stuck through its side, a man peeing on an inn sign of the moon, a huge queue of blokes with their trousers down backing into a little room ...

Bedtime, I went into the bathroom with the Ascot coughing and spluttering, past the cupboard in the passage where Harold made yoghurt. Every night he boiled milk, let it cool down, tested it with his fingertip until it was 'blood temperature' and then poured it into a green tureen, added the bald

Armenian Communist Francis's yoghurt 'plant', wrapped it up in old jumpers and put it on the shelf above where Simpkin had her kittens.

I hated the yoghurt. It had bits in.

'It's because I stir the skin in,' Harold said.

'So don't stir the skin in,' Mum said.

'I like the skin,' Harold said.

'And Michael doesn't,' Mum said.

'Leave him alone, he's tired,' Brian said.

And then upstairs to our bedroom, past another cupboard at the top of the stairs where there was a gas mask, a trunk that was stamped 'USA' that was so big it had hangers inside, and a wooden box Harold had made at the school he taught at, where he put all the letters he had sent to Mum from Germany. I only ever opened it once, and the first letter was instructions from him to her about what to do if Brian was coughing.

Then into our bedroom where by now Brian had covered the walls with wine labels. One of the shops on our corner was an off-licence, and out the back were hundreds of bottles. Brian used to steam the labels off and stick them on the wall. Then he made a catapult, lined the bottles up and we fired the alley stones at the bottles. A copper once caught us and told us that we were breaking the law and ought to clear off home. So we started walking towards our back yard which was about twenty feet away and he said, 'Hey, where do you think you're going?'

Brian said, 'Home.'

And the copper said, 'I've got your number, sonny.'

I reached down into the bed and the big envelope was still there. I pulled it out and went next door into our parents' bedroom, which was once Brian's bedroom, where he used to play trains on the floor with the Märklin train set that Harold brought back from Berlin and was nothing like anyone else's train set ever. Then I laid the envelope down on the bed, next to Harold's pillow.

I went back to my bed, got in, sucked on the corner of the sheet and went to sleep in a state of fear and misery.

In the morning, Harold came into the room. He didn't usually do that, because he had to be out the house early to

Greenford County School to teach English. Or maybe he had moved on to Kingsbury County by then, because the Head at Greenford had said that he couldn't be head of department because Communists can't be head of department.

'Oh dear,' he said, 'you poor old thing. You must have been so worried about that silly homework book. You couldn't face showing us, could you?'

I lay in bed saying nothing.

'Don't worry about it,' he said. 'I've written them a letter. You won't hear about this again.'

He looked at me. 'They shouldn't have done that House Captain thing to you. Mommzas.' And he was gone. I got up. Mum didn't say anything. They had a deal where if one of them talked to us about something big and bad, the other one kept quiet. Mum always stuck to the rule, but when it was Mum telling us off, out the corner of your eye you could always see Harold bobbing about, muttering 'Quite', 'Oh yes', 'Right'.

Then she went off to school. Brian went next. I met up with Harrybo and off we went.

'Did you get the whacks?' he asked.

'Nope.'

He thought I was lying.

When I got to school, the other kids crowded round. 'Did you get the whacks?'

'Nope.'

'What happened?'

'Nothing much.'

They were disappointed. It wasn't turning out to be much of a thing after all. I handed over the envelope to Miss Williams. She opened it in front of the whole class, took the letter out, and as she started to read it she moved her face into a smile and held it all the time she was reading. Then she put the letter back into the envelope, looked at me, and put it down on her table.

I didn't hear about the homework book and my picture of Trev the Tramp ever again. Neither Mum nor Harold ever told me what they wrote in the letter. I figured that it was some kind of secret teacher language, that meant that they knew what Miss Williams knew and she knew what they knew and – apart from the House Captain thing – it was sorted.

On Friday afternoons, having spent four and a half days on Eleven Plus training, Miss Williams let us do other things. One of the other things was a Nature Chart. We had to write up The Date, My Name and What I Have Observed.

If there was something you could bring in to prove you had observed it, so much the better. Maybe the effect of all the competitive training meant that even the Nature Chart became a competition. We desperately tried to prove that we each saw better things than someone else.

'I saw a robin.'

'I saw a duck.'

'I saw a robin *and* a duck.'

One night, while I was walking home through the Memorial Park, I was getting to thinking about what I could write up tomorrow on the Nature Chart. Wouldn't it be great to see something really good? Like a nest. I remembered how I had once seen a film of a bird that lays its eggs on the ground. Well … I could find a nest on the ground, couldn't I? Trouble was, there were no nests on the ground in the Memorial Park. But there was plenty of dead grass lying around. So, maybe I could pick up some of this dead grass and make 'something'.

I twisted the grass around, poked it about and made something that looked like a bird's nest. Then I worked out a plan that would prove it was a nest. When I got to school the next day, everyone would think I was brilliant at Nature.

I left my nest lying on the ground and walked home. Next morning, Harrybo called for me and we went off to school, through the Memorial Park. So I said to Harrybo, 'Hey, let's walk over this way, eh?'

'No,' he said.

'Go on,' I said, 'we might find something.'

'Oh, OK,' he said.

So I led off in the direction of the nest. I didn't want to lead him there and me find it. That would make him suspicious. I wanted us to see it together, maybe him a little bit first. The trouble was, I couldn't see it anywhere. I didn't know where to lead him. Maybe it had blown away.

'Come on,' Harrybo said, 'or we'll be late.'

'No, hang on,' I said.

'What are you doing?'

'Oh you know, just looking for Nature. Come on over here. You look.'

Then I spotted the nest, still there from the night before. He wasn't going to see it. My plan wasn't working. So I pretended to look surprised and said, 'Hey, Harrybo, I don't suppose this is anything, is it?'

He came over.

'Michael – that is a nest. That is a nest.'

'Is it?'

'Yep. Amazing. That's what it is, all right. We could take that into school and write it up on the Nature Chart. No one's ever found a nest before. Incredible.'

We picked up the nest and took it to school. We put it on Miss Williams's table. All the other kids crowded round: 'Where did you find it?' 'It's terrific.'

Harrybo put on his important voice and said, 'Look, er ... don't touch it, OK? It's a bird's nest. We were looking for Nature and we spotted it. I knew it was a nest straightaway.'

Miss Williams looked at us and looked at the nest. 'Looks to me', she said, 'like someone made it. Some little fingers or other made it.'

I looked at it sitting on her table. It didn't look much like a bird's nest at all. In fact, it looked just like what it was: a heap of dead grass that someone had twisted about a bit. But Harrybo was quite cross: 'Oh, no, Miss Williams. We found this when we were looking for Nature. It was there on the ground. Actually, Miss, if Michael hadn't said, "Let's go over the grassy bit", we'd've missed it. That was really lucky he said that.'

Miss Williams looked at me very hard. I said nothing.

'Can we write it up on the Nature Chart now?' Harrybo said.

'Not just now,' Miss Williams said.

We didn't get to write it up all that day, or the next. The

nest sat on her table getting looser and looser, until all it was was a heap of dead grass. I hated looking at it. Surely everyone could see it was a trick. Someone was bound to say that we made it. But no one said anything. And Harrybo kept going on about what a great find it was. I started to wish he would just keep quiet about it.

A week or two later, we got to school and the nest was gone. So was the Nature Chart.

Harrybo said, 'Miss Williams, why have you taken down the Nature Chart?'

'Oh,' she said, 'I thought it was time for a change. Anyway,' she said, looking at me, 'things were getting a bit silly, don't you think?'

'Were they?' I said.

'Yes,' she said, 'they were. But if you want your nest back, boys, I've put it under the sink.'

'That's OK,' I said. 'I haven't really got anywhere to put it.'

'I have,' Harrybo said, 'brilliant. I'll take it home and keep it in my room. When you come over to my place, Michael, you can look at it any time you like.'

'Thanks.'

That night he took it home and put it on his chest of drawers. Every time I went over to his place, he showed it to me. He never let me forget the great day we found a real bird's nest. He said that he just loved looking at it, thinking about the bird that made it.

In the middle of March we got our Eleven Plus results. I passed. This meant I was going to go to the same school as Brian and my first choice on the list of preferences that parents and children had to fill in before taking the exam; not my second choice Pinner County (in which case I would have got to know Reg Dwight, who later became Elton John), and not my third choice, Downer (in which case I would have got to know Long John Baldry), and not the one that was nearly everyone else's first choice but not mine, Harrow County (in which case I would have got to know Michael Portillo). My first choice was also the school where Harold had taught after he came out of the army.

On the morning I heard that I had passed the Eleven Plus I went out to wait for Harrybo and the moment I saw him, I said, 'Did you pass?' and he said in a cheery voice, 'Nope. I knew I wouldn't.'

I felt desperate. Why hadn't he passed? Harrybo was brilliant. He knew about so much stuff – radios, cars, books, gramophones, gardens, raw food, Winnie the Pooh. 'I'm going to Headstone Lane,' he said. 'I'll watch out for Sherbet Jacket, Mick,' he said, 'don't you worry.' (Sherbet Jacket was our name for Shane, known for miles around as the kid who got so angry he could rip you apart. He wore a jacket that had white flecks on it and we called him Sherbet Jacket to make him sound less dangerous.)

He did go to Headstone Lane, and almost immediately we stopped seeing each other. We bumped into each other in the street every so often and we were friendly enough. When I was seventeen we moved from Pinner, and for twenty years or so I didn't ever see him, but I wrote about him plenty of times. I wondered if one day I would bump into him and would show him all these things that I'd written about him.

Then, by chance, in the early 1980s, I was doing a reading at Pinner Wood, our first school – they didn't know I had been there – and a girl at the school said that her dad knew me. When her Mum came to fetch her, she asked whether I would come back with them to their flat.

Outside the school I met her Mum.

I said, 'Who's your husband?'

And she said, 'Jimmy.'

I racked back into my memory … Which one was Jimmy? A picture came to mind of a kid younger than us, standing with us when we were mucking about in the woods, and he was a bit giggly and had a little mannerism where he lifted his knee up and spun round.

Jimmy was waiting for us back at the flat and I was pleased that I did remember him. We talked our way through different people and then I said, 'Do you ever see Harrybo?'

'He died,' Jimmy said, 'he got a brain tumour when he was seventeen, and a few days after it was diagnosed, he was dead.'

Harrybo, my Harrybo, who was so alive in my head, in my poems, in my shows when I had acted out being him. I was so sure I would meet him again and talk about everything that had happened since we lost contact. But now I never would. And wasn't it terrible that we had moved so far apart that I didn't know about it at the time?

# 4

## My Other Lives

I had other lives.

On Sundays we went to see Bubbe and Zeyde, Mum's parents, or Harold's sister Sylvia. The trip to Bubbe and Zeyde's was on an old Edwardian brown electric train to Baker St that had separate compartments, and a brass handle on every door with 'Live in Metroland' engraved on it. I was proud that we lived in a country called Metroland, and I learned the names of the stations in the right order all the way to Baker Street.

Baker Street Station was a palace: notice boards that lit up electrically, a cartoon film theatre that ran cartoons non-stop all day, and a giant bomb left over from the war with a slot in the side where you were supposed to put money for wounded soldiers. And, best of all, a machine that made little metal signs. You put your money in, you chose a letter from a big dial, pulled down a lever, then the next, then the next, until you had written your sign. You pulled another lever and out came a metal strip with your message, with two little holes in it so you could pin it up. We promised each other that we'd come back one day and write 'bum'. How brilliant would that be? I had by this point made a long strip out of the white edges of the *Daily Worker* sellotaped together, and put all the rude words I knew on it.

Outside Baker Street Station, at the foot of tall apartment buildings where, I thought, it would be grand to live, we caught the 30 bus to Hackney. This was another country. The houses, factories and bridges were black from the coal smoke. Bubbe and Zeyde lived with their son Ronnie, Mum's brother, on Sandringham Road in Dalston, in a dark down-stairs flat. They had an outside loo that was damp and spidery and kept chickens in a run, up one side of the back yard. Zeyde was still working in the boys' cap factory. Bubbe was always worried and, according to Harold, always *kvetshing* (complaining). 'She kvetshes about the neighbours, about the weather, about Zeyde, about the chickens, about the land-lord, about the people upstairs. She's a kvetsher.' The only thing she never kvetshed about was Ronnie.

We sat in the back room on dark brown 'rexine' armchairs or round a dark brown table. On the wall hung a picture of our parents on their wedding day. A ship in a bottle, an ocean liner with four funnels and stuck to a blue painted sea sailed along the mantlepiece.

They had a TV. We didn't. It was dark brown apart from the screen, which was black and white. Well, black and white until they tied a thick plastic thing to the front of the screen, which turned the top third blue, the middle orange and the bottom part green. This was because Ronnie was working to develop colour television. He had studied physics at night school and when the result came through, it was a 2:1.

'So close,' Bubbe said, 'they couldn't have given him a first?'

Harold glanced at Mum. He was chalking up another kvetsh.

Then Ronnie went to work for Marconi, carrying on inventing colour television. 'He's getting on so well with it, please God,' Bubbe said, 'he went up to the Parliament place to see the House of Lords. Tell them, Ronnie.'

Ronnie said that he and the team at Marconi had indeed been to the House of Lords to demonstrate colour TV.

Zeyde was laughing. 'And the ashtray.'

Bubbe tutted. Ronnie laughed, and pulled out a big heavy cut-glass ashtray. On the bottom it said 'GR'.

Zeyde said, 'They're sitting there and these Lords go out the room and Ronnie here opens his bag and slides the ashtray into it.'

'You'll be beheaded for that,' Harold said.

'Please God, he won't,' Bubbe said.

Sometimes there were pauses and we stared at the walls. Then Zeyde would get out the *Reynolds News*, a left-wing Sunday newspaper that I once asked my parents why they didn't get. 'We like reading Kenneth Tynan and doing the Everyman Crossword,' Harold said. 'And reading Katherine Whitehorn,' Mum said.

'How's your Khrushchev doing?' Zeyde said, by way of starting another conversation.

'Mmm-mm,' Harold said by way of closing it.

Bubbe got out fresh beigels ('bei' said like 'bye'), chopped herring, chopped liver, shmatana, pickled cucumbers, and caraway seed rye bread.

I didn't know anyone else in the world who ate these things. It was the only moment in the time we spent there that our father looked even the faintest bit as though he was having a good time. '*Gehakteleber* – the best,' he said when he spread the chopped liver. '*Ess geht in alle gliede.*' (Literally, 'it goes through all your limbs', but means something like 'it goes down a treat'.)

Zeyde passed me a beigel. 'Save the hole for me,' he said.

'I'm going to make pickled cucumbers this year,' Mum said. 'How much salt do you put in?'

'To taste,' Bubbe said.

'What do you mean, "to taste"?' Mum said.

'You put in to taste. Till it tastes like it should taste.'

'But how much is that?'

'I said, "to taste",' Bubbe repeated.

'Pass the shmatana,' Harold said, 'this is the best shmatana I've ever eaten.'

He recalled an alte bubbe he knew who used to say, '*Kindele, kindele, ess, ess*, for here is food plenty.' (Children, children, eat, eat …) He always laughed at that, but no one else did.

Bubbe said to me, 'You're drinking too much water. You swell up if you drink so much.'

After we had eaten, Zeyde said he'd take me over 'Acknee Dans'. When I was older I understood that he meant Hackney Downs. When we got there he joined a group of men wearing suits and talking Yiddish. Among them was his brother,

Hymie, who lived in the next street. 'Is that your grandson, Frank?' one of them said.

Zeyde nodded.

'Nice-looking boy.' Then they went back to talking Yiddish.

On the way back, Zeyde said, 'What's to become of us, Mickie, eh?'

Indoors, Brian and Ronnie were talking science. Brian brought over his physics homework and Ronnie helped him with it. Zeyde got out the chessboard and draughts. First he beat me at draughts. Then he said, 'I'll show you how to play fox and geese.' Then he beat me at fox and geese. Then he got out the dominoes and beat me at dominoes.

'Don't get out the cards,' Mum said, 'I can't stand the cards.'

'I'll show them a trick,' said Ronnie.

'Alright,' Mum said, 'just one and then we're going.'

So Ronnie showed us a three-card trick and a 'I know what card you've chosen' trick, then Mum said, 'We're going.'

'Take some beigels,' Bubbe said.

Zeyde got out two half-crowns and slipped one into my hand and one into Brian's.

'You shouldn't do that,' Mum said to him.

As we walked off to the bus stop, Ronnie and Zeyde stood in the street waving to us.

No one at school knew about any of this.

In the holidays we went camping. No one in my school went camping. They stayed in boarding houses.

In the first years we went camping, we went with Communists. That was how I worked out that camping was Communist. Somewhere in one of those books by Karl Marx or V. I. Lenin on our shelves, I used to think, it must say, 'Communists go camping.'

Back in the myth, Mum and Harold already went camping, and once they went with their great friends, Moishe and Rene (also Jewish, also Communist, each going to the same schools in the same classes as our parents – they were so close you could almost swap them). Moishe and Rene got in a boat and rowed out to sea and the rescue people had to come and get them. Mum had kept the article that told the story.

'A man came down to the campsite,' she said, 'and he was nosing about for a story.'

'What sort of story?'

'We weren't married and we clammed up and wouldn't tell him anything, so he made stuff up.'

'Why did he make stuff up?'

'Because that's what they do.'

First, there was the 'getting ready' for the camp. This meant hours and hours of sewing. Everything, every year needed to be sewn: tents, bags, groundsheets, rucksacks, jackets, trousers. Harold was especially proud of a bodkin he bought.

'This bodkin is terrific, Con,' he said.

Then there was the big question of what to do about the table. Harold said that he could make a fold-up table using a music stand at school, with a bit of help from the metalwork teacher. He would spread sticky-back plastic over some plywood that the woodwork teacher had given him.

Mum said, 'What's the matter with you? We could buy one of those nice fold-up tables they sell in those camping shops.'

'What is it with your mother?' he'd say to us. 'I can make a perfectly good fold-up table, and she wants us to shell out on something that won't work and will break.'

'Why do you think everything you buy in a shop is *dreck*?' she said (crap).

He did buy a tiny wooden chair, though, and this sent him off into sniggering about which cheek of Mum's tukkhes would fit on it. One of his perpetually repeated gags came whenever she bent down on the other side of the room, and he would say to us, pointing at her backside: 'Interesting expression on your mother's face.'

Going camping was also a chance for Harold to get out all the US Army gear that he pretended he hated – the fold-up canteen he used when he'd got in line for pancakes and maple syrup, his 'field jacket', his 'entrenching tool', his army shirts and vests. Mum knitted us socks, jumpers and pom-pom hats.

There was a lot of talk about 'proofing' things. They bought some strong-smelling white liquid and soaked things in it; the air was full of words like 'flysheet', 'brailing', 'ridge pole', 'meths', 'primus stove', 'prickers', 'water-bags' and 'ordnance survey'.

Then, a few weeks before the summer, a vast British Road Service lorry inched up the pebble-alley out the back of our flat, and took the bags and trunks off to where we'd be going – Devon, Wales, even France. These camps lasted forever, the whole of the school summer holiday, nearly six weeks. When I was five we went to Les Rosaires in Brittany. At seven, it was Argelès, near Spain – both without a car.

I didn't know anyone who went to France. People talked about it as if it was posh or crazy, but it didn't seem posh to have to pump and fetch water at a campsite, or sit at Harold's rickety table eating chewy garlic sausage, or poo in a stinky open latrine, where you could see wasps and flies crawling over piles of it. Brian and I talked about how people pooed in different colours and wondered what it would be like falling into the pit and not being able to get out.

Brian and I had to help. We had to go to the pump with the water-bags, sweep out our tent, and do the washing-up. 'It's all for the collective,' Harold said.

Each of these holidays produced new family phrases or songs. In Les Rosaires, it was the fact that there was a nearby town called Paimpol, a name like the sound of the hooter that trains make in French: 'pimpon, pimpon'. This tickled Mum no end and for the whole holiday, every time she saw the train to Paimpol, she'd sing it out like it was 'pimpon'. 'Paimpol, Paimpol,' she'd sing.

Harold was a fanatical guardian of guy ropes. Once while watching a little boy hopping about near our tent's guy ropes, he warned us: 'Don't ever do that, boys. You'll either rip the tent or hurt yourself. He's in for a shock.' Next day they carried the kid off the campsite on a stretcher, and later he was back with his leg in plaster and spent the rest of the holiday lying in a chair. 'You see. What did I say?' Harold said.

The family in the next-door tent taught us a song about a servant-girl called Perrine who works for a priest. One day, her lover comes over to see her but when the priest comes back home, she jumps into a cupboard. Six weeks later the rats have eaten her. There's a bit in the song where everyone shouts, '*Les rats*' really loudly. I joined in.

The following year, our parents decided we should join the Muswell Hill Communist Party Camp in Ladram Bay, in Devon. This meant getting to know the ever-miserable Roy, an old friend of Harold's, but also – and much more eventful – getting to know Malcolm, the son of the Communist Armenian, Francis, and his wife Peggy (who was the sister of a suave-talking BBC actor, Malcolm Hayes). It started off badly, because Malcolm armed himself with a frying pan and I armed myself with Harold's US Army entrenching tool and we tried to kill each other. After that we became deep, deep friends.

One night a woman set fire to her tent. Mum blamed it on the fact that her husband hadn't come. That was Ivor, who said that in Buckingham Palace they've got taps with long levers on them so when your hands are dirty, you can turn them on with your elbows. 'Why haven't workers got taps like that?' he said.

A year later, they decided we'd go to the South of France. On the quayside, I liked watching the cranes hoisting cars in and out of the hold of the ferries, like they were picking up beetles. We travelled overnight in the train to Perpignan in an ordinary compartment, so I slept on the floor with my head on Mum's bum, Brian on one seat and Harold on the other. Every now and then Brian got up and peered out of the window into the dark, till there was a sudden light and a clang of a bell and he called out the stations: Limoges – Toulouse – Narbonne … We never forgot the names.

When we arrived in Argelès, the trunk with our tents in hadn't yet turned up. It was a disaster. We had nowhere to sleep. I could see my parents were worried. But then they bargained with the campsite owners for us to sleep in some army tents that belonged to them. I lay on an army cot like the one at Tyneholme and there was no groundsheet, so I played with the sand, running it through my fingers. It was the hottest day ever and I started to boil. 'You mustn't worry, lad,' Harold said, 'the trunk will be here in a day or two.'

A man in the skimpiest shorts in the world came round selling newspapers. 'He'll get into trouble,' Mum said, 'he's saying the paper's all lies.' My parents learned to shout: '*La Dépêche! Tas de mensonges!*'

There were more songs. A big boy with a little hat came into our tent in the middle of the storm and sang, '*Hé hop Pipo Pipo Pipo / Quand il était militaire*'. And everyone kept singing a song that had a chorus where everyone went '*Oui, oui, oui*' and then a moment later '*Non, non, non*'. I could join in with that.

Harold kept saying, 'I'm buggered if I can remember all the words to the one about the rabbi who gets drunk. I'd love to teach that to them ...' And he tailed off into singing, '*un*' *der tsimbel hat getsimbelt* ...'

'In France', Mum said, 'they eat aubergines.' She sent me to the camp shop to buy *deux yaourts et un kilo d'aubergines, s'il vous plaît.*

Brian said that at the end of 'yaourts' I had to make a little sound like it's going to be a 'g' but it never quite becomes one. I practised all the way there, got the yoghurts and the aubergines, and Mum fried the aubergines with onions in the pan without a handle. I said I loved those aubergines. I did love the aubergines. Au-ber-gines. 'You don't say the "s" on the end,' Brian said.

One day, Harold said we were going to climb a mountain. At the bottom of the mountain, there was a very old lady sitting on her terrace under a vine. She gave us some mira-belles that were sitting in a sieve, and said that when we came down from the mountain we had to call in again. She would be waiting for us.

We climbed for days and days, and I said, 'What's that?' and they said, 'That's a flying grasshopper.'

Harold had his metal US Army bottle which never ran out of cool water. Mum brought hard-boiled eggs. We never ran out of hard-boiled eggs. No matter how high we climbed we would never climb as high as Mount Canigou. Then we got to Château Valmy, where there were hundreds of bottles of red wine. 'Bloody good plonk,' Harold said. It went into the rucksack with the water bottle and the hard-boiled eggs.

Eventually, we came down off the mountain but we didn't visit the old lady under her vine.

'Are we going to see the old lady?' I said.

'No, not this time,' they said.

'But she said that we had to go back and see her.'

'Well we don't have to.'

'But she'll be waiting for us.'

'Oh, I don't think so.'

'She will.'

I thought of her sitting in the shade under her vine waiting to give us some more mirabelles, thinking, they never came back, they never came back.

Harold said that some people on the campsite were going to Spain and we could cadge a lift. We could buy some really cheap cigarettes. But Harold was the only one who would be able to actually go over the border into Spain, because he had an American passport. That was funny, apparently. Mum's British passport wouldn't let her and us in, so we would go to a border town called Le Perthus and he would nip over, get the fags and nip back.

At Le Perthus there was a barrier across the road, and Brian said we could watch people crossing in and out of Spain. We watched Harold going in and I wondered if we would ever see him again. Just then a white Morris Minor pulled up at the barrier. A tall man with dark floppy hair jumped out, leant on the door of his car and called out loudly, 'Is there anyone round here who can speak English?'

Brian started giggling.

'What?' I said.

'Did you hear him?' he said.

'Yes,' I said, 'why don't you tell him you can speak English?'

'He means is there anyone French who can speak English.'

'Does he?'

Harold came back with boxes of cigarettes. Brian kept saying, 'Is there anyone round here who can speak English?' in as loud and as posh a voice as he could.

We drove off and just outside Le Perthus there was a police check. We stopped, the policeman looked in.

'What does he want?' I asked.

'Just to see if we bought anything in Spain,' Mum said.

Harold was shaking his head. I heard him say, 'Non.'

I called out, 'Don't forget to tell him about the cigarettes!'

Mum looked at me and did her tight-mouth move and shook her head.

'The cigarettes,' I said, 'tell him about the cigarettes.'

The policeman was happy. We drove on. Harold was furious. 'What's the matter with you? All you had to do was keep quiet. Why are you such a *yachne*? I've never known such a yachne' (gossip, chatterbox).

Brian said, 'Is there anyone round here who can speak English?'

One time we were in Perpignan and there was a bullfight. We weren't going to go, but there was a hill next to the bull-ring and my parents were curious about what it was like. So we went and stood on the hill and from far, far away, we saw a bull being killed. It was like the corner of a photo, where the photo is full of people shielding their eyes from the sun, trees, sky and mountains, and far away in a corner there is a big drama of death.

After that we went to the market, where Mum spotted some mats. They were coiled straw with a red outermost ring. She bought them, along with three string bags. For years and years we used those mats, they became more and more stained, so she bleached them and then bit by bit they unfurled and fell apart. The string bags lasted forever.

The next year we went to Skenfrith.

The Easter beforehand, Harold's friend Nancy from 'the Institute' (who called him 'Johnny', after a bandleader called Johnny Rosen) offered to drive me and him round the Wales–England border to find somewhere good to camp. One time we were halfway up a hill and Harold looked out of the window, down to a valley where there was a river and a flat piece of land next to it. 'That's the one!' he shouted.

We all got out of the car in the rain to look at this dark green platform of grass, surrounded by woods and hills. 'That's the one!' Harold said. 'Bloody marvellous!'

It turned out to be Butler's Farm, run by a red-faced tenant farmer called Bert Fidler, his wife, Mrs Fidler, and their sons Desmond and Clive. They said we could camp on their field so long as we didn't mind sharing it with pigs, bullocks, hens and an old horse.

This time and many times after, we camped on the bank of the River Monnow with a bunch of our parents' Communist friends: the Flowers, the Spencers, the Kaufmans. At times there was a gang of children, Mart, Tony and Paul Flower, Chris and Dena Kaufman, the Spencer children whose names I've forgotten and sometimes friends of any of these, too – like Leebs, son of the Liebenthals who had escaped from Germany 'just in time' and ate a small meal of bread and cheese at about five o'clock off wooden plates. No one was sure if they got out of Germany because they were Jewish, Communist or both. If it was because they were Communist, the general reckoning was that they weren't Communist anymore. In fact, the general reckoning was that Leebs wasn't Jewish anymore, either. Most people reckoned that his parents were Jewish but he was giving Christianity a go now.

Skenfrith was a Communist Narnia.

The people we saw only at this place had a place in our family mythology throughout the year like characters from stories. Mr Foggo, who ran the village shop, 'Foggo's', became just Foggo, a confused provider of not quite enough. Desmond, a tractor-driving replica of a plaid-shirted, dungaree-wearing Midwestern American teen. Mrs Fidler's ancient brothers on the other side of the river, born in the 1870s, retaining ancient strengths that enabled them to pull apart jammed tent poles. Mrs Fidler herself, who could pluck a chicken so fast you couldn't see her fingers move. Alongside this, there were legendary beasts: the horse who liked to stand on your feet, the goat who ate hats, the pigs who ate washing powder; the badgers playing at night, and the buzzards mewing like cats above our heads.

There were legendary places, too: the Sugar Loaf, Skenfrith Castle, the Norman door at Kilpeck Church full of faces and beasts, and 'the wires'. This is what we called the way to get across the river where you had to walk sideways across two stretched hawsers, one four feet above the other.

Epic events also took place when we were there: the time a man called Gifford turned up, walked across the top wire like he was tightrope walking, caught a plateful of trout by flicking a fishing fly over the water and then disappeared. The occasion when the raft that we had made turned over and Mart got trapped underneath and couldn't breathe, until his older brother grabbed the whole raft, lifted it up and saved his life. The sheep dip high up in the woods, where we all helped to push 200 scared, eye-rolling sheep one by one under the disinfectant water. The otter hunt, when men and women with shouty posh voices turned up in leather gaiters and floppy hats, with long poles and a team of hounds looking for an otter that wasn't there. Milking time, when I was so proud that Bert Fidler showed me how to milk a cow by hand while a breathing, sighing, grunting cow twitched and flicked her tail. The Monmouthshire Fair, where you could sit a few inches away from huge Hereford bulls, and where Mrs Fidler presented her prize dressed chicken. Or, just as the sun was coming up, when Mrs Fidler told Bert that she needed a chicken and he took me to the coop, opened the door, caught one as it came through, knocked it out, put it under his arm, took it to the barn, strung it up, took out his penknife, slipped it into its mouth and did the rest.

The songs tumbled over each other. Many of them the adults knew from back in the myth: 'I'm the man, the very fat man who waters the workers' beer ...'; 'Five for the five years of the plan and three for the three years taken'; 'He sat down beside her and smoked his cigar, his cigar, his cigar ...'

And, to the tune of 'The Volga Boatmen': 'Russian pastry, Russian pastry, we don't want your Russian pastry. Beigels and platzels, beigels with holes in ... Russian pastry, Russian pastry ...'

A Burl Ives song: 'My father kept a boarding house, hulla-balloo ballay. Hullaballoo ballah ballay ...'

'If you get to heaven before I do, just dig a little hole and pull me through ...'

And then Harold's set piece: 'When this lousy camp is over, oh how happy we shall be ...', which they tried to explain was a song based on a First World War song that was based on a hymn. But anything with that much explaining got lost.

Then there was General Bate. One year, Mart wanted to catch fish but Bert Fidler said we needed a licence. He said General Bate owned the fishing rights, and we'd have to get a permit off him. He lived on the road to Ross-on-Wye. Mart got out the map and saw that we could take a short cut and we set out to ask General Bate for permission to fish.

We crossed on the wires and went into a field of bracken higher than us. Bit by bit the field turned into a slope, then into a hill, and we hacked our way upwards till we got to the top. The bracken stopped at a lawn in front of a mansion. 'This is it,' Mart said.

We walked across the lawn and rang the doorbell. We heard a sound from inside and a man shouted, 'Who is it?'

Mart said, 'We've come about the fishing.'

Someone pulled back some bolts on the door and it opened. There stood a man with one leg, leaning on crutches. He had white hair and a trimmed white moustache. He spoke in a way that I had never heard anyone speak before, and very loud: 'What d'ye want?' he shouted.

'We've come to get permission to fish in the River Monnow,' Mart said.

'Ye better come in,' he said, and manoeuvred himself around on his crutches. He took us into a front room where we looked about and saw tiger skins and the heads of animals sticking out of the walls and pictures of generals. 'How d'ye get here?' he shouted.

'Up the hill,' Mart said, 'and across the lawn.'

'What?!' he shouted again, 'no one comes up there. That's Tinkers Bath. How d'ye come up there?'

'We climbed,' I said.

He made a roaring noise and Mart explained that we were camping on Butler's Farm and wanted permission to fish in the river. He looked at us and said, 'I admire yer sporting spirit. I admire yer sporting spirit. Ye can fish as much as ye like without a licence.' He then gave us a glass of water each and we left.

Mart said as we walked along, 'Did you see his top lip? It

was quivering. When he said, "I admire your sporting spirit", his top lip quivered.'

Back at the camp, Mart told the story and Mart's dad and Harold walked about saying 'I admire yer sporting spirit' for days after. Harold said it was a bloody cheek that some old sod could decide who could or couldn't fish in the river.

That was the year Mart planned for us to walk up the Sugar Loaf and down the other side so that we would cross the border between England and Wales. He showed me on the Ordnance Survey map and as it was a long way, we left the campsite early and walked all day. At one point Mart said, 'We're at the border now, Mick. We've got to do something special to celebrate. Why don't we take our trousers down and walk into England with our trousers down?' So we did.

We walked along the path with our trousers and under-pants round our ankles. Which is not very easy. At one point we heard some people coming, so we quickly pulled up our trousers and pants, but when they'd gone by we carried on. After a bit Mart looked at the map and said, 'OK, I think we've crossed now,' and we pulled up our pants and trousers.

When we got back to the campsite, Fred and Harold asked us how it went and Mart explained the route and Harold said, 'You must have walked over fifteen miles. That's incredible.'

'Well done boys,' said Fred and as I was feeling really proud of what we'd done, I added, 'And we walked into England with our trousers down.'

Harold and Fred looked at each other. 'Explain that,' Harold said, so I told them the story. When it got to the end, Harold said, 'Con. Come and hear this. We've got a pair of bloody idiots here. First thing they do is do something really sensible: plan a long difficult walk and next thing – they walk round the bloody hills stark naked. Jesus Christ, what have we done?' I didn't see the problem. I thought we'd done something really brilliant.

Then the next year, they decided to go to France again but this time they had bought a car. It was a dark green Bradford 'utility' van that someone had cut windows into, and Harold put two chairs in the back for Brian and me. The number plate was KAR 49, so Mum only ever called it 'Kar 49', never 'the car' or 'the van'. Harold drove Kar 49 to the Jura Mountains in 1956, and we camped with the Flower family overlooking two lakes. There we discovered brown lavatory paper that Mum called 'wholemeal', and it rained every day.

One day we went to Ferney. My parents said that this was on the Swiss border and it was where Voltaire had lived. Voltaire seemed to be on their approved list. Voltaire. They kept saying his name: Voltaire. Every time Voltaire got into trouble with the authorities, they said, he nipped across the border where they couldn't get him. That was approved, too. And there were three potteries that sold wonderful dishes. They had been told to ignore the first one, ignore the second one, and only buy pots from the last one. They bought stacks of coloured bowls and brought them home and we ate out of them for years.

It went on raining and I started getting diarrhoea. It went on raining and then Mum got diarrhoea, and we both had a temperature. Harold said we had to give up camping, and he found us a room in a house. Me and Mum lay there till a doctor came and said that we had dysentery, and we had to put bullets up our bums: '*Les suppositoires*', he said, and made a gesture with his hand to signify round the back and up. Mum said it was the best way. 'The French have got this right.'

Brian went off with Mart's older brother Tony and some boys and girls on a camp hike, and when he came back he said the girls were amazing, and the *moniteur* killed a snake with his walking stick. Tony married one of the girls – not immediately; about ten years later.

All these holidays were like another school for me. They were the springboard for some different lives I could start having, staying over with the Kaufmans, the Flowers and the Aprahamians. Each of these worlds were sealed off from school and though these people knew each other, they were sealed from each other. I loved these separate ways of being.

Mum and Harold called the Kaufmans the 'Coughs', and sometimes Mum called Moishe 'Coughdrop'. The family lived in a council flat in Cricklewood, and when I went over there Chris and I went to see Spurs play at White Hart Lane. Chris kept football programmes under his bed. He knew the name of every player who had ever played for Spurs. I supported Arsenal but I didn't have hundreds of programmes. I had one: from the time Harold took me and Brian to see Arsenal play Manchester City, and Arsenal drew 1–1.

No one I knew at school went to see big club football matches, and I liked the way we travelled on our own on buses and trolleybuses, squeezed our way to the front of the stand, watched the game, came out, bought chips and talked about Ted Ditchburn and Smudger Smith like we knew them. One time an old man behind me pressed his willy against me and it spoiled that game. I didn't tell anyone about it. Ever.

On the way home we'd buy the pink evening paper that wrote up the game we had just seen. On Sundays we went out and played football-tennis in the playground in his flats. Some of the kids who came out and joined in were not like kids I'd ever met. They were, I thought, young versions of Zeyde, talking with a cockney accent, calling each other *shmok*, prick. Sometimes Chris's grandfather, Pops, came over. He always wore a suit with spats and sat out on the balcony talking with Moishe in Yiddish. I didn't understand what he said when he spoke to me, so Chris helped.

Moishe worked at a place called the National Rubber College, but he was more interested in plastic. He said that one day everything would be made out of plastic. We ate our meals off coloured plastic dishes. At breakfast Rene gave me a fried egg, and when I started to cut into it, my knife wouldn't go in. It was plastic. That was the Kaufmans' plastic joke.

One time Moishe said he was going to put on a science show in the communal laundry downstairs. He had a tank of liquid oxygen smoking away that was so cold, he could make a hammer out of mercury by sinking it in the liquid. Then he put a rubber ball in the liquid, took it out, threw it on the floor and it smashed into little bits. Everyone clapped. Then we all went inside and Rene sang a Russian song.

In the summer we had free tickets for county games at Lord's because Rene's brother, Alf, was a groundsman. We sat there all day watching Middlesex, and at the end Alf would come over to us, driving his big roller, and shout 'Hi Chris!' from down below. I once saw Dennis Compton come to the wicket, hurl his bat around for twenty minutes while his hair flailed in all directions, score loads of runs and then get himself out on the last ball of the day. 'Typical bloody Compton,' the man behind us said.

The Flowers lived in North Harrow, in a 1930s suburban semi with a garden out the back, where Fred grew potatoes and got a hernia digging them up. 'Bloody hell!' he shouted, 'I know what that is.' He was right, it was a hernia. After that, Mart made it into his way of typifying Fred. He used to walk around, then suddenly grab his middle and shout, 'Bloody hell! I know what that is.'

Fred and Lorna had three sons: Tony who was Brian's friend, Mart who was my friend, and their youngest, Paul. They built train sets, and their bedroom floor was hidden under a painted papier-mâché field and hill, with a tunnel and a cutting they'd built themselves. They could talk about trains for hours. I loved the way they made the field look like a real farm and when you got down at eye level the trains looked like they were speeding through the countryside on the way to Skenfrith. The Flowers were the only Communists I knew who had a smoked glass biscuit jar.

And then there were the Aprahamians and their son Malcolm. They lived in a flat in a red house on a steep slope in Muswell Hill, with trains at the end of their garden. We could sit on the fence and watch the trains go by. The Aprahamians lived upstairs while Roy, the most miserable Communist in the world, lived downstairs with Dorothea, who sometimes had to go to bed for months, and their two girls, Katy and Judy.

Muswell Hill was different from anywhere else in the world. All the houses and shops were red with white windows, many of them with little church-arch windows at the top. All the shops had one white arch over the display window. When Malc and I wandered round the streets, I thought it was like being in a foreign country.

Malcolm had a deep, gruff voice: it sounded as if it was hard for him to get his words out. 'We're going to Granny's,' he said. Granny was Armenian. Her house was quiet and smelled of herbs. She lived with her grown-up son, Malcolm's Uncle Felix, who had filled the house with gramophones and solitaire boards. The gramophones had His Master's Voice horns where the sound came out – if they were played, which they weren't – and the solitaire boards were full of coloured marbles. There was a grand piano, and shelves packed with music books. When I walked into the room, I thought the horns turned towards me, saying: 'We want you to listen to our music,' while the marbles on the solitaire boards rolled around laughing.

Granny talked to herself in Armenian, and Felix spoke like the critics on the radio. In fact, I think sometimes he was a critic on the radio. He had a black and silver goatee beard, like someone had stuck a little badger on his chin, and when he read he put on gold glasses.

Granny shouted at Malcolm and told him he was a bad boy, and Malcolm growled, 'I'm hungry, Granny.'

Felix said, waving his hand in the air, 'Oh, Malcolm my boy, you must tame your tongue.'

'I haff no food in the house,' Granny said.

'Nonsense, mother,' said Felix, 'you always have food.'

'Pilaff,' she said.

'I love pilaff,' Malcolm said.

We sat down to eat pilaff that was made with herbs and spices I never tasted anywhere else.

'I love pilaff,' I said.

'Me too,' Malcolm said.

'You must teach Malcolm to speak properly,' Felix said to me.

After the pilaff, Granny brought out dried apricots, dates and the biggest raisins you'd ever seen.

'I love raisins,' Malcolm said.

'I love raisins,' I said.

Felix drifted out of the room in his leather slippers, and the sound of him playing the piano filtered through the shelves and the smell of herbs.

We left. 'You coming back soon, Malcolm,' Granny said, hugging him while he wriggled to get out of her grip.

Back at Malcolm's, sometimes Francis wasn't there because he was on what he called a 'peace creep' in Czechoslovakia, or Hungary or Poland or Romania or Russia, with 'the Prof' (J. D. Bernal). When he came back from 'Czecho', he brought shoes and pink plastic plates. The shoes, he said, had been stuck together with fish glue, because under Communism nothing goes to waste.

If Francis wasn't on a peace creep he sang us 'Barnacle Bill the Sailor' before we went to bed:

> Who's that knocking at my door?
> Said the fair young maiden.
> Well, it's only me from over the sea,
> Said Barnacle Bill the Sailor.
> I'm all lit up like a Christmas tree,
> Said Barnacle Bill the Sailor,
> I'll sail the sea until I croak,
> Drink my whiskey, swear, and smoke.
> But I can't swim a bloody stroke,
> Said Barnacle Bill the Sailor.

'Right, now you two must get to sleep.'

'No, Dad,' said Malcolm, 'do "Archibald Arseolein".'

'Right, that's the very last one.' So he recited 'Archibald Arseolein', which got him saying really fast a whole rigmarole about 'A,r,c,h, there's your arch, i there's your i, there's your Arch-i...' till it got to him saying, 'A,r,s,e, there's your arse, there's your bald arse, there's your i-bald arse, there's your arch-i-bald-arse ...', at which point Malcolm lay in bed laughing his big deep husky laugh.

'Now I'm switching out the light, boys. You must get some sleep,' and he went out. Malcolm told me he hated Katy downstairs and went off on a long, long speech about how awful Katy was. As I lay there, I could smell his Communist shoes.

The next day, Francis took us to a gigantic brick building on the top of the hill looking out over the whole of London, Alexandra Palace. Far away down below a train raced along.

'That's the Tyne-Tees Express, boys,' Francis said. 'All the railways have been taken over by the government, you know. Look at all these houses and all the people in them. Think of what it could be like if everything we made belonged to everybody, like the railways. You've got to have hope,' he said.

Back in the flat, Malcolm was reading the same book as I was, called *Folk Tales of the Union of Soviet Socialist Republics*. We talked about one sad story where a man was being attacked, and he asked the cliff to bend down and protect him – and it did.

Then, on 4 November 1956, something happened that changed everything. We were in Trafalgar Square with thousands of other people to listen to Nye Bevan say 'No' to invading Suez. I could hear his far-off shouty voice coming through the speakers, just like I'd heard the far-off shouty voice of Harry Pollitt at St Pancras Town Hall when Harold was a delegate at the Communist Party Congress. In the middle of Nye Bevan's speech, Fred Flower's brother John arrived at our little group. His lips were tight.

He looked from Harold to Fred, to Connie to Lorna and said, 'The tanks have gone in.'

They all looked at each other with a hopeless, helpless look.

I wondered what was going on.

'They're in Budapest,' he said.

Budapest? Isn't that in Romania or Hungary or Poland? Why has Anthony Eden sent tanks there? Egypt is nowhere near. I listened to their conversation trying to catch the drift. Right, so it wasn't the British. It was the Russians. And Budapest was nothing to do with Egypt and Suez.

So was it good that the tanks had gone into Budapest, or bad?

# 5

## Stalinallee

Not long after we heard about the Eleven Plus, Mum and Harold started having meetings with someone called Dorothy Diamond, who was a friend of Nan's. It was Nan who had sent Harold off to find the dinosaur professor in Berlin. I was beginning to enjoy working out these connections.

Later that spring – 1957 – Mum and Harold said to me and Brian, 'This summer we're not going camping. We're going to East Germany. We're going to a place called Weimar with a group of teachers. It's been organised by Dorothy. While we're in Weimar there'll be trips to all sorts of places, so it's going to be terrific.'

Back in our bedroom, working through this news, Brian said that Harold had driven a jeep round Berlin during the war, and he'd know the way. Brian was doing German at school and had taught me to say, '*Ich bin, du bist, er ist, wir sind, Sie sind, sie sind*', so I was pretty sure that I was ready to face most situations.

Once summer came, we boarded a train heading east. Our group included some teachers from Kilburn, among them one called John Holly, who wore a bright blue suit and suede shoes and played the guitar. There was his friend Callaghan, whose beard completely covered his mouth, and Peter Wright, one of Mum and Harold's old friends who Mum said was amazingly clever – he could even speak Serbo-Croat. Peter put on Shakespeare plays with the boys at Kilburn and the boys also played the women's parts. We went every year, and when Falstaff lined up Mould and the rest in *Henry IV, Part 2*, I laughed and laughed till I was crying.

Mum said that the boy who was Shallow spoke the line, 'We have heard the chimes at Midnight, Master John' in the most moving way she had ever heard, and she had heard Lawrence Olivier speak it when she and Harold went to the Old Vic. Harold did his take-off of Olivier doing Mercutio: 'creep into any alderman's thumb-ring'.

'Lovely legs,' Mum said.

Also in the group was Len Goldman. He had a moustache that made him look like Terry Thomas, but when he spoke he sounded like Zeyde. He spent much time looking for puns. Whenever he heard a word that sounded like another word, he just said it. But he never laughed. Someone said they lived in Neasden: 'Ah, yes', he said, 'Paradise, the Garden of Neasden.'

I would sit next to him and say, 'Len, tell me a joke.'

'Give me an egg and I'll crack one,' he said.

I thought Len was a comedian. Harold said that all his jokes were old ones.

It was only once we got through West Germany that there was any problem with passports. People started standing up and sitting down. Men in uniforms with guns walked along the aisle and back again. There wasn't a problem with everyone's passports; it was only Harold's, again, with his American passport. Was he going to be left behind because he was American and on the wrong side?

'They're not going to stamp it,' Mum said.

Was this good or bad?

Once we arrived at Weimar, they let us stay in an old school. The first thing I noticed was that they kept dishing up fresh cucumber, sliced into a watery, vinegary liquid that I thought was fantastic. The second thing I noticed was that they dished up a dark brown slimy garlic sausage which I also thought was fantastic, though everyone else said it was giving them the squitters. If East Germany is this good, I thought, then Communism is as good as Francis said it was.

The first thing Mum noticed was that she could understand

what people were saying. We sat at a table on a cafe terrace, while a man played a tune by rubbing the tops of wine glasses. All around us people were speaking German. With a happy look on her face, Mum said: 'I can understand what they're saying!' This couldn't be right. It was Harold who spoke German. He was the one who sang German songs like '*Drum links, zwei, drei!*' But Mum said, 'For the first few years of my life, we only spoke Yiddish at home. I get what it is they're saying.'

I don't think anyone had ever told us exactly that Yiddish was rather like informal, spoken German. I don't think anyone had ever said exactly that Yiddish was Mum's first language. Maybe Mum was more surprised by Germany than we were. She became different at that moment, as if she had another person in her head, someone we had never heard of, a girl who could only speak Yiddish.

Once we had settled into the old school, our days quickly fell into a routine. In the morning Mum and Harold went off to 'sessions', while Brian and me had to entertain ourselves. After lunch it was 'visits', and then after the evening meal, if there wasn't another outing, different people stood up and started singing and performing. I understood that the 'sessions' were mostly about swapping ideas on how to teach. What I didn't understand was why anyone would want to spend their summer holidays doing that.

On our own, in our room, Brian practised his imitation skills. He did John Holly, the guitar teacher, by sticking his hands in his pockets, throwing his head back and jazz-walking up and down the room, talking loudly about politics and guitar chords. I loved it. He had spotted that Callaghan was a quiet tippler, who always made sure he got more wine. Brian sat very still, narrowed his eyes and leant towards an imaginary waitress with just a hint of lasciviousness, saying in what sounded to me like perfect German: '*Noch ein Glas Wein, bitte.*' I loved that one too.

Despite spending most of our time by ourselves, we were sometimes interrupted by the Idiom Pest. This was one of the German guys, who carried a notebook where he'd written down idioms he had heard, or thought he had. Then he came looking for us, to ask what the phrase meant and how to use it.

'Hello, please, young men. Please what is this "getting the dirty hands"?'

'Well,' Brian said, 'you might be mending a car or something and get dirty hands.'

'No, I am finding that people are saying, "He doesn't get the dirty hands".'

'Yes,' Brian said, 'that's someone who's got clean hands.'

'No, the people are saying, "he doesn't like getting the dirty hands".'

'Yes,' Brian said, 'no one really likes dirty hands.'

'Hah, this is true. No one really likes dirty hands.' He wrote it down. 'And I can say, "look at him – hah! – he doesn't like dirty hands!" and this means?'

We looked at each other. It wasn't easy. This was someone we really would have to avoid.

Later, when we met up with Mum and Dad we told them about the conversation, and they said that we had got it wrong: 'It's "he doesn't like getting his hands dirty".'

Brian got tetchy about that, because he likes to get things right and he said it wasn't him who got it wrong, it was the bloke because he said, "getting the dirty hands.'

From then on, even though we tried hard to dodge him, the Idiom Pest went on hunting for us. We'd be eating in the canteen, he would spot us, nip over and sit himself down at our table. 'Ah, boys, I haff one more question. You have the time to speak with me?'

In the mornings, we kicked a ball about in the schoolyard and played hours of table tennis. The afternoons were better, but there is a limit to the number of houses of famous people that an eleven-year-old can take.

Usually I loved castles, battlements, moats, portcullises, trebuchets, mottes, baileys and keeps. I was determined to make myself a castle expert. Once when we were going around an old English castle, Brian said that they had found talking-tubes in it. He explained that these were tubes that ran through the walls so that people could send messages via them. You spoke some words in at one end and then, a few days later, someone in another part of the castle might come to the end of the talking tube in his tower, pull the cork out and hear the first man's message from a few days back. What happened, he said, was that a few years ago, archaeologists were digging in the castle and they came across one of these talking-tubes that hadn't been opened for centuries. They opened it up – pulled out the cork – and out came talk from hundreds of years ago, all in olde Englyshe: 'Thou hast fain be loath to ...', that sort of thing, Brian said.

The houses we visited in Germany all belonged to the same three people I hadn't heard of: Goethe, Schiller, and Frederick the Great. They included their birthplaces, town houses, summer houses, winter houses and libraries. Soon one old house started to look like any other old house.

'This is Belvedere,' the guide said.

'Wasn't the other one called Belvedere?'

'No.'

'It's a bit like they're all Shakespeare,' Mum explained.

She started to talk about Goethe and Schiller as 'G and S': 'We're going on another G and S creep today.'

But when we got back to England she had to say, 'G and S – but not Gilbert and Sullivan.' She thought this was funny, in the Mum sort of a way where she would be the only one laughing.

As we moved around I noticed men with guns in the street.

'They're Russians,' Harold said.

There were some longer trips, like the one to Wartburg Castle. Here we climbed hundreds of steps till we got to the room where Martin Luther had sat for hours, translating the Bible into German. Dorothy Diamond translated the guide's words for us.

'In this room ... Martin Luther saw the devil, and threw ink at him. If you look at the wall, you can still see the ink stain.'

I looked. There was a dark patch on the wall, and some of the plaster was peeling off.

Brian was excited about Luther, because in the school choir he sang Luther's hymn that begins '*Ein Feste Burg*'. 'Which means, Mick, "a strong castle", remember? I taught it to you.

And here we are at a strong castle and it's where Martin Luther was. See? Do you get it?'

'Yes,' I said.

I had learned to say 'Yes' so that Brian would think I had got things even if I hadn't. I hadn't even got who Martin Luther was. I hadn't got why translating the Bible was such a big deal nor why the devil would think it was a bad idea. And I hadn't got why the hymn was about a strong castle, because I didn't get hymns. I sang them along with everyone else, but what did something like 'For All the Saints' actually mean? What, every saint? There were thousands of them, weren't there?

But I did like the idea that this Luther threw ink at the devil and the stain was still there, hundreds of years later.

On another occasion we went to Bach's house in Eisenach. I knew who Bach was, because Brian was also teaching me about classical music. He played me Beethoven and Mozart symphonies and concertos and got me to look out for the theme, the variations on the theme, and especially the modulations. With Bach, he said it was different. It was fugues.

Bach's house was full of musical instruments. Dorothy Diamond took me over to one and said, 'Michael, that is a cembalo. It's not a harpsichord and it's not a piano. It's a cembalo.' I've never seen nor heard of a cembalo since.

One night we went to the opera in Weimar to see *The Marriage of Figaro*. Before we went, Harold said that there was a bloody marvellous bit when Figaro marches this chap, who's had his balls chopped off, up and down telling him that he can't mess about with women anymore. He's got to go off to the army. And that it was a superb satire on militarism. Then Harold put on his opera voice and sang, 'One foot ...'

'Does that come when they're marching up and down?'

'No,' he said, 'that comes at the beginning when Figaro is measuring his wedding bed.'

Brian then explained that it was based on a French play.

'Will they be singing it in French?' I asked.

'No, Italian,' Harold said.

'German,' Brian said.

Then one day Mum said that there was going to be a trip but we couldn't come on it.

'Why not?' we asked.

'It's to a concentration camp.'

'Why can't we come?'

Mum said that they didn't know exactly what was there, but she expected it to be so awful and so shocking that we probably wouldn't be able to cope. They went to Buchenwald and when they came back, Mum looked dreadful.

She couldn't explain. 'Terrible things happened there,' she said. 'I've talked about it before, but this was awful.'

I tried to figure out how awful was this awful. I had been on a school trip to the Tower of London and went into the torture room and saw the thumbscrews, the rack and the iron maiden. Was it as awful as that?

'Worse', Mum said.

In the evenings everyone sang songs. Mum and Harold tried translating them for us. They said there was a really terrific German song about Columbus, and when he gets to America all the Indians shout, 'We are discovered!'

I sang along with the chorus: 'Viddy viddy vid, boom boom'.

Then there was one where we all had to pretend to be a steam train. A big smiley bloke called Horst taught us this one.

'It's in Swabian dialect,' Harold said, like that was something I needed to know.

I learned to sing the first line, '*Auf der schwäbsche Eisenbahne …*' and when the chorus came I joined in with everyone in the hall going 'chuff-chuff-chuff-chuff'.

There was one about a boat on a river that seemed to get faster until we all shouted 'HEY!', and another one about a man who shoots a cuckoo, with a chorus that was like a tongue twister that I really loved but couldn't quite get. '*Zimzala bim zala bim zala doozala day,*' I sang, but Brian shook his head.

'If only I could remember all the words to the one about the rabbi who gets drunk,' Harold said.

John Holly got out his guitar and sang American folk

songs, which started a big debate about whether he should have been singing English folk songs.

John Holly said, 'For Christ's sake!'

There was a man from Guinea who sang a song that went 'Everybody like Saturday night', which Harold said was very political because really they didn't like Saturday night. I found irony very difficult to understand indeed.

But then, after even more table tennis and quite a lot of clothes fights in our room, Mum and Harold sat us down and said that they had been talking to one of the German delegates and she had two cousins who lived on a farm, and they would be fine about having us to stay for a while. There would be two girls who were Brian's age and a boy and a girl who were about my age, and maybe it could be like Skenfrith: 'You could collect eggs. And you like cows, don't you?' Mum said.

'Yes,' I said, because I did like cows. Ever since Bert Fidler had taught me how to milk a cow and I had been to the Monmouthshire show, I'd been studying them. Just like Brian could tell the difference between the Flying Scotsman and the Royal Scot and the Master Cutler, I could tell the difference between an Ayrshire and a Dairy Shorthorn.

They put us on a tram-train out of Weimar heading to stay with people neither they nor we knew. We weren't even going to be put up in the same house. We were going to be a mile or so apart. And I couldn't speak German. Brian had been doing it for three years, and I had heard him talking to people in German. 'Don't worry,' he said, 'the older girls speak English.'

'By the way,' Brian added, 'I don't think we're supposed to be doing this. Children from other countries who come to East Germany are supposed to be on special summer camps, Communist Pioneer camps, not just going off to stay with people, so don't talk about it.'

When we got off the tram-train, Brian said it was the 'Thuringian Wald' and I was taken to a little farm where the couple smiled a lot. Meanwhile Brian went off somewhere else. This couple had a boy and a girl who were a bit younger than me and an older girl who was about Brian's age or older, and who I thought was unbelievably beautiful. I mean film-star beautiful. She had long blonde hair that swung around, and she tried very hard to speak English.

Her parents showed me my bed: it was in a cupboard in the wall. There weren't any blankets, just a big bag full of feathers. I had never seen a duvet. Duvets hadn't happened in England yet. I didn't know how to go to sleep in a cupboard under a bag of feathers.

The unbelievably beautiful girl came in and sat on the edge of my bed and said she was very happy that I had come. She sat there practising my name: 'Michael, Michael ...'

In the morning she went off, and I played with the younger children in the back garden. They kept saying, 'Kick me!' and running off and laughing.

I didn't get it.

It turned out that they didn't have any cows, but they did have chickens and I noticed a lot of potato plants.

They served the cucumber just like they had done at the old school in Weimar, so that was great. Then we met up with Brian and the girl from his family. She was unbelievably beautiful too, but in a suave sort of a way – short hair, blonde, glasses, and she spoke really good English. We all went for a walk, and both girls hooked arms with Brian. They walked on ahead, chatting and laughing away, talking in English and German. I ran about with the younger ones behind. We were following a sandy path in a forest somewhere. All I knew was that we were where Brian had said: the Thuringian Wald.

'Maybe they're saying "kiss me",' Brian said, and the unbelievably beautiful big girls laughed and laughed. Maybe Mum and Harold would go back home, Brian would stay with the unbelievably beautiful girls, I would stay with the kick-me children forever, and we'd become East Germans and go out and walk down long sandy paths in the forest again and again and again. We went up to the top of a mountain to a cafe that looked over a valley. 'Thuringian Wald,' Brian said.

We didn't stay there forever, though. After a few days, we got back on the tram-train to Weimar. Mum and Harold met us. Harold said that when they said goodbye to

us, he had turned to Con and said, 'What have we done?' but
Mum had said we would be OK.

Now it was time to go to Berlin. We were going to go first
to Jena and then overnight in a coach along the Autobahn,
which, Harold said, bloody Hitler built so that he could rush
troops to the border to invade the Soviet Union. I sat up the
front of the coach with the driver and watched the lights of
the cars and lorries streak past.

In Jena, we were taken to the world's first planetarium. We
sat on wooden chairs and looked up at the dome. Dorothy
Diamond explained that the stars we could see were in fact
tiny little indentations engraved on to lenses by the world's
greatest glass engravers. Brian was very excited by this and
told me a complicated story about the Zeiss camera works.
Once there was just Zeiss; then came the war, and Germany
was divided into East and West. Though Jena was in the East,
the people in the West wanted to have a Zeiss too and there
was lots of legal stuff that went on for years, so that now
there was Zeiss Ikon and Carl Zeiss.

'Which one are we at?'

'Carl Zeiss.'

'Are they the good Zeiss or the bad Zeiss?'

'I don't think it's like that,' Brian said.

In Berlin we stayed in a hotel. We had never stayed in a
hotel before. It was huge and had red carpets on the floor, and
a neon sign outside that said either 'Hotel Adler' or 'Hotel
Adlon'. Even after we got back from East Germany there
were arguments over which it was. Inside it had a lift with a
sliding metal grille door, like the ones in American movies. Or
like in the hotel that Emil and the Detectives keep an eye on
because Herr Müller is inside with Emil's money. Harold said
they hadn't changed the carpet from before the war. When we
looked out of our room, we could still see where one half of
the hotel had been bombed.

That night, Mum explained how the Russians came from
the east and when they got to Berlin they fought street by
street until they won. Harold said that when he got to Berlin
it was flattened and everyone was living in cellars. I imagined him in the army shirt he wore on our camping holidays,

walking around bombed-out streets while people peeped up at him from holes in the ground, calling for help: 'Hey, American! Help, we've been bombed.'

We went out in the coach one day and the driver took us to where Hitler's bunker was. You could see what looked like a giant piece of concrete cake sticking out of the ground. 'It was hit by a bomb,' Brian said, 'but the concrete was so strong, all it did was tip it up. That's what you can see there.'

'What happened to Hitler?'

'Shhh.'

One time we stood on the corner of somewhere that was so flattened from the war, it looked like it wasn't anywhere. We went with an older woman who was kind to Brian and me; she had been the link with Dorothy Diamond from the East German end. She said that where we were standing was called 'Unter den Linden'.

We stood there for a bit and then she said, 'Hitler loved linden trees.'

'Did he?' I said.

We walked on and I noticed that Mum and Harold were having a whopping great whisper-argument. I could see that Mum was angry and upset, while Harold was hissing something like, 'Not now.'

After a while the old lady went off to look after some of the rest of the party and I asked Mum and Harold what was the matter. Mum said, 'I don't bloody want to know whether Hitler bloody liked bloody linden trees or not. What does she think she's doing telling us that?'

Harold said, 'There's no need to say anything.'

Mum said, 'I want to say something.'

'What are you going to say? That you don't like it that she told us that Hitler liked linden trees?'

'Doesn't it matter to you?'

'Sure it matters.'

'It matters, so it matters.'

That night a big, big scandal blew up. John Holly and Len Goldman disappeared. Dorothy Diamond was furious. This wasn't allowed.

'Where have they gone?' I asked.

Mum said, 'The story is that they've gone off with women.'
'Which women?' Brian said.

'The Russian one,' Mum said, 'and I think she's got a sister.'

Dorothy Diamond called a meeting and they discussed John Holly, Len Goldman and the Russian women. The question was whether they would come back soon, later, tomorrow or never. The general view was that they would come back soon and it was no problem. The meeting broke up.

They didn't come back soon or later. They came back the next day, strolling into the hotel. Dorothy Diamond said she wanted to talk to them. As far as I could make out, they took no notice of anything she said. (I think Len Goldman married the woman he met and they lived together for nearly fifty years. I once bumped into them at the Tate Gallery, and I told him I'd read his letters in the *Guardian*.)

Then we went to Stalinallee. Stalinallee was something very special, they said. This big new street was where the very best things that the German Democratic Republic was producing could be bought. When we got there I thought the tallest buildings looked like the one near where Nancy and Jimmy worked – Senate House, the London University library. Or like the Shell-Mex building on the Thames that you could see from the South Bank.

On Stalinallee they bought six smoky wine glasses with the money Harold had earned by helping Professor Lamprecht write English textbooks for German children. We had been to his flat, and Harold had chosen some English stories and helped with the exercises and questions. On the way back to the hotel, Harold had said that Lamprecht gave him the creeps. He reckoned Lamprecht was trying to use him to get out of East Germany.

'Can't he just leave East Germany if he wants to?' I asked.
'No,' Mum said.

After the visit to Stalinallee it was finally time to go home. We got the train back to England, and on the way an enormous row broke out. John Holly blurted out that Stalinallee looked like a public toilet. If that was socialism, he didn't want it. People started shouting and poking their fingers at one another, and it all got nasty. There was a lot of exasperated sighing and shrugging and bloody this and bloody that. A kind woman called Rose Betts had a little cry about it.

When we all went our separate ways at Liverpool Street station, some people didn't even say goodbye to each other.

I loved the smoky glasses. Mum put me in charge of them. I thought they were beautiful and chic, like Juliette Gréco, the suave French cabaret singer. You could swan about holding a long cigarette holder with glasses like that. When people came over, I would give Mum a little 'Shall I get out the smoky glasses from Stalinallee?' look. As each one broke I became more upset. By the time I left home there was only one or two left. By the time my father came to move house, I looked in the cupboard and there were none.

That September I started at Brian's school. This was going to be a big thing.

Harold and Connie called me and Brian into the front room. 'We've got something very important to tell you,' Harold said.

We sat down.

'Connie and I have decided to leave the Communist Party.'

I looked at Brian. He looked like this was a big thing, too. Was it? If so, how big?

'Is it because you didn't like East Germany?' I said.

'No,' Harold said, 'it's got nothing to do with that. It has to do with internal democracy.'

It was one of those moments – and there were plenty of them – when my father sounded utterly convincing, even interesting, but made no sense at all to me. Worse, it looked as if for everyone else in the room he was making perfect sense. Internal democracy, eh? Fair enough. What was internal democracy?

I should say that there hadn't only been the arguments about whether Stalinallee looked like a public toilet. There was the Twentieth Party Congress explosion, and of course there had been Hungary. The way these had played out in our house and with people like the Kaufmans, the Flowers and the Aprahamians was like this:

When it leaked out that Khrushchev had said terrible things about Stalin at the recent Party Congress, Mum and Harold shook their heads and looked fed up. They were unhappy that they had read about it in the *Observer* rather than the *Daily Worker*. For years one of their Sunday pleasures was to read what Victor Zorza, the *Observer*'s Kremlinologist, wrote about the Soviet Union, and to dismiss what Zorza had written as *meshugas* (nonsense). But this time, clearly, Khrushchev's speech wasn't meshugas and they knew it. Still, as a party member you didn't want to find this out from the *Observer* because, as Harold pointed out to me many years later, 'We couldn't admit that things were going wrong. We didn't want to give an inch to the "buggers-are-we" [bourgeoisie].'

If there were arguments between them and their friends, I didn't hear them. I'm guessing there were, particularly between Harold and Peggy Aprahamian. She was always the most loyal, the most certain that it was all working out a treat in the Soviet Union and that Communism was just round the corner in Britain.

Then there was Hungary.

What started as a student revolt on 23 October 1956 turned into a nationwide revolution, until it was crushed by Russian tanks the following month. The Hungarian government collapsed and a network of workers' councils took over, promising free elections. At first it seemed the Soviet Union was going to stay out of it, but then a major Soviet force invaded. Over 2,500 Hungarians and 700 Soviet troops were killed, and over 200,000 Hungarians fled as refugees. A Soviet-friendly regime was installed and from the outside, by January, it was back to first base.

This historic moment was the nearest that Mum and Harold came to holding different political views. Harold thought that it was OK for the tanks to go in, because he bought the line that the Hungarian uprising was a CIA plot. I got the feeling that Mum didn't agree.

These events caused division between my parents and some of their friends. Harold's great friend and mentor, Brian Pearce, who had lived with us for two or three years between 1952 and 1955, left the Party as a result of events in Hungary. Harold never spoke to him again. This was 'Big Brian', as we called him, who had put all his books in the little scullery room next to the shop downstairs. He answered every question that I or little Brian ever asked him. And if he couldn't answer it, he got down one of his volumes of the *Encyclopædia Britannica* and had us look it up. One Christmas Big Brian gave me *The Merry Pranks of Till Eulenspiegel*, and as far as I was concerned it was one of the greatest books ever written.

But now, he was no longer welcome in our house. And the only reason we were given was that 'it was a matter of internal democracy'. Now, my parents were going to leave the Party too, and, as Brian and I sat there, I started to wonder what was going to happen to the Communist camping and all the Communist friends. Were we going to still see them?

We did. Most of them also left the Party. Some of them drifted off later, and some stayed for as long as there was a Party to stay in. We remained friends with all of them. Just about.

The twenty or so years our parents were 'in the Party' – from the age of sixteen or seventeen until their late thirties (that is, from 1936 to 1957), marked them for the rest of their lives. For years, I had hundreds of conversations with both of them about history, culture, politics – past and present, personal and global. Over time, their attitudes to the Soviet Union, the British Communist Party, individual Communists and Communist friends changed: one moment defensive, another moment regretful, then bewildered, sometimes grateful, often angry. In the end it would boil down to those moments, back in the myth, when their own skins depended on Communists defending them. Yet they were yearning for something bigger and more universal than freedom for Jews alone: it was the liberation of all humankind they were after. At that moment in their late teenage lives, as they heard about what the fascists were doing in Spain and Germany, and then when the bombs were dropping on London and the stories of the camps were coming out, the fate of everything started to depend incredibly but appropriately, in an awful way, on the great showdown at Stalingrad. And this is why they made their choice and stuck with it for so long.

So when they chose to leave, at that moment in 1957 it felt to them as if they were betraying the very reason why they were alive – even though they had come to the difficult conclusion that this was no longer the road to a better society.

But, as they told us, they hadn't left over whether there was bad stuff in the Soviet Union. They left over 'internal democracy'. And so, in all those hundreds of conversations, did I ever get to understand what that meant?

On one or two occasions, Harold said something about the branches within the party not being able to talk to other branches. Or was it that the District wasn't allowed to talk to the branches? It wasn't easy to follow exactly what he was saying. He clearly didn't like talking about it.

Another of the folks at the 'Institute' once offered a different theory. She said that by the time all those issues to do with the Communist Party came up, Harold and Connie were on a different route already: the freedoms they were talking about at work were coming more and more into conflict with what was being said in the Communist Party. They couldn't embrace both.

For years, this thing about internal democracy didn't really bother me (why would it? I didn't ever join, and they never re-joined); but a few years ago I started to wonder about this time in their lives, and in my and Brian's. Because it changed everything, didn't it? For one thing, what happened immediately was that an ever-widening group of people started to flow in and out of our home, all of whom came from outside the Party. The atmosphere changed.

So I started to nose around those years, 1956–57, hoping to find some mention of the defection of Harold and Connie Rosen in the records. I found that whatever was happening inside the Communist Party at that time was only partly a result of the Soviet invasion of Hungary. Hungary wasn't the whole story.

Rather, a group of people had started to wonder if the problem with the Communist Party in Britain wasn't just the immediate matter of its views on the Soviet Union, Hungary,

Czechoslovakia or even Stalin; it lay in how the Party itself was organised. They wondered how the Party could develop ideas and analyse what was going on in the world, while at the same time having freedom of discussion, the freedom of members to share what they thought. How could it be a place that encouraged discussion, while at the same time – and here's the trickiest part for any organisation, left, centre or right – deciding on policy and sticking to it in the face of opposition? This group believed that democracy could be guaranteed in the way policies ran upwards from branches to leaders. The members should be able to raise the question of how those leaders were chosen and – just as important – were changed. Small wonder Harold hadn't tried to explain this stuff to Brian and me. Most adults find such things unutterably boring to discuss, let alone a fifteen- and an eleven-year-old.

What happened in 1956 and '57 was that a group of people came up with some ideas about how a party calling itself 'Communist' could do things differently. They envisaged a new system that would do away with a leadership committee that never changed. It would put an end to the semi-secret, mysterious 'Political Committee' that seemed to decide things without telling anyone else. This new policy would allow people to have alternative 'positions' on things, and branches to talk to branches. The group pointed out that the organisation they had had so far (the Communist Party of Great Britain) had developed in a very different historical place and time: in pre-First World War Russia, rather than 1950s Britain. These members – including my parents – believed another kind of organisation was needed.

Who were the dissenters? At the heart of this group was none other than the historian who I read in the sixth form and at university in order to understand how Tudor society evolved into the great upheavals of the English Civil War (or Revolution): Christopher Hill.

As I looked closely at who said what to whom and how the Party went on to reject what the Christopher Hill group said, I made a note of how many of the people deciding these things were paid Party workers. It was their jobs that were under threat. The Communist Party paid them to act within a structure that the Hill group were attacking, and those same paid members sat on a committee that decided that what the Hill group said was wrong! Well, they weren't going to give the thumbs-up to a report that said their jobs shouldn't exist, were they? They weren't going to vote themselves out of the door.

I wonder if Harold and Mum were aware of all that. They might have been wrestling with these discussions as we were packing to go to East Germany, or as I was getting ready to go to secondary school, right up to the moment they called Brian and me into the front room for the chat. A few years later, Harold would regale me with stories of rigged committees for school exam boards, university academic boards or government curriculum bodies, where people who know how to run committees arrange it so that the committees produce the 'right' results. Surely he would have spotted that the Communist Party was doing just that?

But there's a farcical element, too, which I think they both would have noticed. Once Christopher Hill's little group had been seen off (and the Party had bled even more members than the thousands who quit over Hungary), the remaining leaders and committees congratulated themselves on the correctness of their position. They trumpeted the growing number of signs in that year – that month, even – showing socialism was just around the corner, and stressed the crucial importance of their own role in building it. Given that the organisation was by then tiny, I felt distinctly reminded of that moment when the King of Lilliput brags and boasts and threatens Gulliver, while sitting in his hand.

And yet these Lilliputians were strutting about in the shadow of what Khrushchev himself had announced from the podium of the Twentieth Party Congress: the terror of the Stalin era. It felt absurd and grotesque ... tiny little puppet clowns, sitting on podiums congratulating themselves for bringing us to the verge of socialism.

Did Mum and Harold see it that way?

# 6

---

# The Underdone Sausage

I was going to be an actor.

There were times when all either Brian or I had to say was that we liked something, and Mum and Harold jumped on the comment and made it into a project. It was like they turned a passing comment into a building.

Once, I said I liked insects; maybe it was the flying grasshopper in France that did it. Then I started noticing water-boatmen skating on the surface of the water in the pond on the way to school, the ends of their legs like tiny flat bubbles. And I liked watching beetles, the way they had their own territories in the worlds between grass stalks. Next thing, for Christmas I got a butterfly-catching kit: a net, a killing-jar, relaxing fluid, mounting strips, a book on 'Butterflies and Moths of the British Isles', a 'Butterflies of Britain' poster. Harold said that he knew someone who smoked cigars and he got me some cigar boxes, so that I could mount the butterflies I caught in the boxes. We went out and tried to catch butterflies.

But I didn't want to catch butterflies. I was happy looking at them. Maybe it was fun to 'spot' them and know their names, but that was it. I didn't ever catch a butterfly. I didn't ever kill or mount a butterfly.

'He never uses his butterfly kit, Con,' Harold said, 'I don't know why we get him these things. What is it? You don't like butterflies?'

This time, after I had said I liked plays, my parents just assumed that I wanted to join an acting group. That's not what I said, I told them I said I liked plays. Regardless, Harold found me an acting group in Ealing.

Mum said, 'Ealing? How's he going to get to Ealing?'

'I've worked it out,' Harold said. 'You get a bus to Rayners Lane, you get the Piccadilly Line to Ealing Common, and then you get a bus to Ealing Broadway, you walk from the bus stop down the road, then it's left behind the cinema, along Mattock Lane and there you are – at Questors Theatre.'

'And he's going to do this on a Tuesday night, and in winter, when it's dark and cold? How long is this journey you've worked out?'

'Under an hour, I bet.'

'He's twelve, Harold.'

The following Tuesday I got on a bus to Rayners Lane, took the Piccadilly Line to Ealing Common, another bus to Ealing Broadway, walked down the road from the stop, left behind the cinema, along Mattock Lane and there I was – at Questors. All because I said I liked plays.

My favourite up till then had been *The Big Rock Candy Mountain*. Alan Lomax, who we used to hear on the radio talking about American folk music, made up a show for Joan Littlewood at the Theatre Royal, Stratford. A hobo, played by Ramblin' Jack Elliott, travelled across America looking for the Big Rock Candy Mountain and singing lines like 'Take this hammer, *pow*! Carry it to the captain …'

At the time, I got the point that the kind of stuff at the Theatre Royal was 'ours'. It was written about in the *Daily Worker*, and it was the kind of thing people talked about when they came over to the house. Mum or Harold said that such stuff was 'bloody marvellous'. Little did I know, aged nine and ten, that behind the show lay years of theory about ballad operas, epic theatre, alienation effect, folk music – Piscator, Brecht, Maxim Gorky, Kurt Weill, Ewan MacColl and more.

The same went for the other shows that Joan Littlewood did for children. We went to her productions of *A Christmas Carol* and *Treasure Island*.

'Her actors can sing, dance, tell jokes – they can do everything,' Mum said, 'you watch that Howard Goorney fellow.'

Maybe they thought I was going to learn how to sing, dance and tell jokes by going to Questors.

When I got to the acting group at Questors, it didn't look at all like I thought it would. It was a corrugated-iron church under some trees. At the edge of the church was a house with a staircase up the side. On the stairs some people were standing laughing and drinking and wearing bow ties. On the other side was a new building that looked like a school gym: no windows at eye level, just a row of them high up, so you couldn't see in. There was a sign saying, 'Stanislavsky Room'. I went in. Harold had told me to look out for Miss Rice.

Inside the room were about fifteen teenage girls. They seemed to be Brian's age or older, and they all turned round and stared. I spotted Miss Rice. She was about Mum's age and walked as if she was giving instructions to her feet each time she moved them: 'Right foot, move up slowly, glide forward smoothly but crisply then down, noiselessly. Left foot, now you move up slowly, glide forward smoothly but crisply, then down, noiselessly …' She was wearing several shawls.

'I'm going to give you each a card,' she said, 'and when I point to you, I want you to get up and act out what it says on the card.'

She dished them out. I turned mine over. It said, 'Peel an apple'.

One by one the girls got up, became even older-looking, like they were women, and performed their action. The others called out what they thought it was, laughed, clapped, cheered. Then it came to me. I stood up and mimed peeling an apple. It all went very quiet. I looked round the room. Some of them were looking at the floor. One of them was doing another's hair.

'Very good,' Miss Rice said. 'Anyone?'

'Peeling a potato,' said one.

'You see, Michael,' Miss Rice said, 'not peeling an apple.'

I didn't see.

'I deliberately wrote "Peeling an apple", because peeling an apple is different from peeling a potato.'

I panicked. Was it?

Miss Rice looked at me.

'How is peeling a potato different from peeling an apple?'

I could feel the blood rushing up my neck into my cheeks. I tried to think how peeling an apple was different from peeling a potato. I hadn't ever done either. My job at home was doing the drying up, not peeling potatoes. And anyway, who peels apples? You just eat them.

Wrong! Of course we ate peeled apples. Was there ever a week when we did *not* have stewed apple in the house? Somewhere in Mum's Big Book of Life, it said: 'And you will have stewed apple'. There was always a pan of stewed apple on the stove. I wasn't mad keen on it. Brian adored it. Some days, I think it was all he ate. And he ate it all day. Mum struggled to keep pace with the amount of stewed apple he ate. More apples, more brown sugar, more cinnamon. But how did she peel them?

'How is peeling an apple different from peeling a potato?' Miss Rice asked again.

At least ten of the girls were smirking. Probably all of them.

I held up my imaginary peeler, I pretended to be Mum and made a round-the-apple movement.

Miss Rice looked pleased. 'Yes!' she said, and clapped her hands together in a bouncy sort of way. 'You showed us how the apple is round, and you showed us peeling round the apple.'

I glanced at the girls, hoping that some of them would notice that this time I'd done OK. No. Nothing.

'Now,' Miss Rice said, 'we walk.'

Everyone bounced to their feet. I started to think that a lot of things had to be bouncy in the Stanislavsky Room. And we walked round the room.

'Walk towards each other, don't look at each other, avoid each other ... faster ... put some bounce in your steps. Walk! Don't run! ... And when I say "Stop" I want you to go down on one knee, stretch one arm out, put your elbow on your knee and flick your hand forwards, towards someone in the room so you end up pointing straight at them ... Keep walking until I say "Stop" ... and stop!'

At high speed, every girl did exactly that, as though they'd been doing it for years. I waited till I could watch what they were doing – and then down I went, put my elbow on my knee and pointed at one of the girls. At the end of the class we started to break up. The girls were laughing and flicking their hair when Miss Rice said I had done very well, and asked, just loud enough for everyone to hear: 'And how old are you?'

The room went quiet.

'Twelve,' I said.

In the forecourt in front of the corrugated-iron church, I asked one of the girls if it was always in the Stanislavsky Room.

She said in a voice that sounded louder, stronger and haughtier than any voice I heard at school: 'It's never in the Stanislavsky Room, because the Stanislavsky Room hasn't been built. We do it in the Shaw Room.'

Then it was the bus to Ealing Common Station, the Tube to Rayners Lane, the bus to Pinner and walk home, up the stony alley and in.

They were desperate to know how it had gone. 'What did you do?' 'How was it?' 'Who else was in the group?' 'What's Miss Rice like?'

I was wondering if I wanted to do this again. I wasn't sure it had much in common with the fun and spirit of *The Big Rock Candy Mountain*.

'I peeled an apple,' I said.

'Why did you peel an apple?' Mum said.

'It wasn't a real apple. I mimed it.'

'That's nice,' Mum said.

'But why did you have to mime peeling an apple?' Harold said.

'Because it's not a potato,' I said.

'Ah,' he said, 'very good. Very good.' And he sat there miming peeling potatoes and apples, apples and potatoes.

Mum looked at him. 'Not that you ever do it. When was the last time you peeled a potato?'

'Anything else?' Harold asked.

I got up and walked across the room, suddenly stopped, went down on one knee, put my arm on my elbow and pointed at the picture of Netherlandish Proverbs.

Harold loved it. 'I like that one,' he said, 'that's terrific.'

'Don't you do it, Harold,' Mum said.

A few days later, he went along the shelves in the front room and pulled out *My Life* by Konstantin Stanislavsky. 'You might like that, Mick,' he said.

I read it, utterly fascinated. I loved the idea that actors study how people walk and then work out why they walk like that, and how that might be connected with what their parents were like. It seemed linked to Sherlock Holmes (which I was reading at the time), who could tell what kind of person a man was from how his shoes had worn. I was going to start studying people. And I was going to be an actor. Or a detective.

Even though I wasn't sure about that acting group, I went back. I went every week. The girls started to talk to me. Instead of getting the bus to Ealing Common on the way home, I walked most of the way with one of them. Her name was Estelle. Brian said that meant she fancied me. I protested that she was about sixteen. In truth, I didn't know how old any of them were.

'As you're walking along,' Brian said, 'just put your hand down and hold hers.'

'Are you crazy?' I said.

Around then a woman came from the council to check the class. She watched some of the improvs we were doing – the bus queue, the doctor's waiting room ... Miss Rice would call out a surprise event – 'The woman on the right has fainted!' – and we had to respond according to who we were. I often chose to be an old man: my family had all moved away and I was lonely.

The woman from the council said that she liked what we were doing, and asked me if I felt alright about being the only boy in the group. I shrugged. Did I want to go on and be an actor? I said, 'It's a bit early to tell, I'm only twelve.' There was a gasp. Not from her, from Miss Rice. And this was followed by more gasps from the girls. Some of them just put their hands over their mouths. What was the problem? They all knew I was twelve. We had done the whole 'You're twelve' thing.

The moment the woman from the council left, they all turned on me. 'You weren't supposed to say you were only twelve!' they shouted. 'The class is for fourteen and up.'

'We're not allowed to take anyone younger than fourteen,' Miss Rice said, 'We only get the money from the council because it's fourteen and up.'

I felt wretched. I had wrecked the class. It was going to close. Because of me. But then nobody told me that I shouldn't say how old I was. How was I supposed to know?

But the class did go on. Maybe the woman pretended she didn't hear me. Or Miss Rice told them I was lying. Or I was an idiot who didn't know what I was saying.

At the end of term, Miss Rice wrote us a show to put on for all the adults at Questors, all their friends, and we would do it in the corrugated-iron church. The script did little more than set the scene before going into the improvs we had been doing. So one went:

A: 'Michael, you can play the doctor.'
Michael: 'But I'm only twelve.'
[Laughter]
*Improv* (4 mins)

A: 'Why don't we do a scene from *The Cherry Orchard*?'
B: 'Yes, let's.'
C: 'Michael, you like playing old men, you can be Firs.'
Michael: 'But I'm only twelve.'
[Laughter]
*Cherry Orchard* (4 mins)

Afterwards I met Estelle's mum, who said, 'That's very kind of you to walk home with Estelle.' And her dad said, 'Much appreciated, old chap.'

I stayed at Questors for years. When some older boys joined, the girls were massively relieved. One of the boys wore a suit and suede shoes. The first night he came, he asked one of the girls out. Another had white-blond hair, wore a blazer and someone had told him it was comedic when he did a startled look. From then on, his thing was startled looks. He told me that one night he didn't get off the train and spent the night in the sidings – startled look.

At some point, Miss Rice got ill and I never saw her again. Larry took over.

Larry loved us. We made him laugh, and he got us to put on plays. We did *The Red Velvet Goat* for the Ealing Young Drama Festival, which was judged by Gordon Snell, the TV personality. I played a young Mexican man who was madly in love with a young Mexican girl – played by Jane, who was at least three years older. I had to dash across the stage towards her, grab her hand and say that her eyes were brighter than the stars, her mouth as tender as the night ... (I'm not sure exactly, but a great stream of stuff like that). It was agony.

I had never been madly in love with anyone. I had never grabbed a girl's hand. I had never held a girl's hand. I had never told a girl about why she was beautiful. There was another complication: I did think that Jane was beautiful. I mean, like you might be watching TV and someone came on and you thought, wow, she's beautiful; not like someone who was in your class at school, someone who theoretically – if the situation was right – you might go out with. So, each rehearsal I had to dash across the Shaw Room and grab beautiful Jane's hand and recite that stuff. It was unbearable.

And it wasn't as if she held my hand back. When I grabbed it, it just sat there like a flannel.

'C'mon, matey,' Larry said, 'give it more welly. You love her. Every night when you go to bed, you've been dreaming of this moment when you and she are alone and you can tell her. It all turns on this. Screw this up, matey, and you don't stand a chance with her. Get it right, and you're in there. C'mon. Once more. Go!'

Then came the show for the Ealing Young Drama Festival. Halfway through the play, we were supposed to sing 'La Cucaracha'. But for some reason we forgot. There was a silence. We all stood looking at each other. Then, from the wings, we heard Larry, in the croaky voice of a woman aged about ninety-six, start up with '*La cucaracha, la cucaracha* ...' and we joined in. I don't know why Larry did it in that voice.

After all the plays, it was time for Gordon Snell, the TV personality, to come out and tell us what he thought. He went through each play saying what he liked and what he thought didn't work. When he got to us, he said that he'd enjoyed it a lot but wasn't always convinced that he was in Mexico. He didn't feel the heat, he said. 'And there was a moment, wasn't there, when perhaps ... What was it? ... Someone was supposed to say something, and then one of you ... I couldn't see which ... tried to sing but couldn't, and then you all sang to cover it up ... I thought that was very good, very professional. We all have to think on our feet in theatre. And where's the boy who loved the girl?' He spotted me. 'You.'

Oh no, I thought, he's going to say how I was like some dithering, dull twit, and no more looked like I loved Jane than if I was a tree.

'You have a face,' he said. 'Believe me, my boy, you have a face. Remember I've told you that.'

We didn't win the Ealing Young Drama Festival, but at least it didn't seem as if it was my fault.

I told Mum and Harold about what Gordon Snell said about my face.

'Who's Gordon Snell?' Harold said.

'A TV personality,' I said.

'We've all got bloody personalities,' Harold said.

'That was nice, what he said about your face,' Mum said.

Harold looked at me, put his head on one side, made as if he was inspecting a car, and said, 'Don't see it, myself.'

At the same time I was also becoming passionate about theatre. I went to see Larry, our Young Questors' teacher, in *Waiting for Godot*, as well as taking trips to the Kilburn Grammar School to see Shakespeare put on by Peter Wright from the East Germany tour, and to the Theatre Royal, Stratford. I suddenly had an urge to see any and every play that came on in London. We went on a family outing to see Zeffirelli's *Romeo and Juliet*, and I loved seeing the stage filling up and emptying: fights, deaths, helpless love, disaster. 'That Juliet's quite broad in the beam,' Harold said.

'I thought she did really well,' Mum said.

It was Judi Dench.

I found out that if you were under sixteen and went to the Saturday matinee, you could get fantastically cheap tickets at the Old Vic or for the Royal Shakespeare Company who had a London home at the Aldwych. I started going to see plays like Brian had collected bus numbers. Mostly I went on my own. When I came back, I wrote the title down in my diary.

In the space of a couple of years or so, between me being fourteen and fifteen (1960–62), I went to *Sergeant Musgrave's Dance* (which I didn't understand), *Henry IV, Part I* (which I thought I did), *Twelfth Night* (which I loved), *The Visions of Simone Machard* (very unsure about that one), *The Rehearsal* (not sure about that one either), *Waiting for Godot* (loved it), *Luther* (with Albert Finney – loved it), *Dr Faustus* (loved it), *The Epitaph of George Dillon* (loved it), *Saint's Day* (odd), *The Shewing-Up of Blanco Posnet* and *Androcles and the Lion*, (double bill at the Mermaid Theatre, loved it), *Beyond the Fringe* (like an explosion in my head – unbearably clever and funny and everything I wished to do in life), *Tosca* (not sure I got what the fuss was about – I mean on stage, not the applause), *Macbeth* (at Harold's college, loved students creeping across the stage holding bushes), and *The Taming of the Shrew* (Vanessa Redgrave, so that was fine by me).

When the Royal Shakespeare Company did *The Caucasian Chalk Circle* I noticed in the programme that they were offering a weekend workshop for anyone interested in finding out more about Brecht. I went, and the director got us to do scenes from the play and explained 'alienation technique'. I liked the way he got us to do crowd scenes, moving round the room together and suddenly changing mood: doing collective horror, mockery, surprise, excitedly talking to the stranger next to us.

When I got back, Harold went to the shelves and said, 'You might like this.' It was the *Messingkauf Dialogues* – Brecht in conversation with Erwin Piscator about epic theatre. It's in the form of a dialogue, sketchily laying out what we call the 'Brechtian' theories of theatre. My first concern was whether this was a real dialogue, whether the people in the dialogue were real and whether this Piscator man may have invented

Brechtian theory rather than Brecht. Whoever he was, he seemed to be very certain that his way was the only way. I struggled with terms like 'epic theatre' and why exactly it was that when an actor was acting, we should know that he or she was an actor. Didn't Stanislavsky say the opposite? In which case, who was right?

Around that time, Joan Littlewood's *Taste of Honey* came out in the cinema. I didn't see it as a play, and though people said she was a 'Brechtian', it seemed to me much more to do with Stanislavsky – playing it for real. Rather than taking specific meaning from plays and films, I discovered it was their afterlife that mattered, in particular the way specific scenes and moments lasted in my mind: the rattiness on Robert Stephens's face when he's trying to get Dora Bryan out the house; the tenderness between Rita Tushingham and Murray Melvin when he says that he'll help her look after the baby; the sound coming out of the school of the children singing, 'The big ships sails on the illy-ally-o'. (I'm writing these things from memory, not having seen the film for fifty years.)

When people wrote or talked about the play in the media they obsessed over the fact that the author, Shelagh Delaney, had a life that resembled the Rita Tushingham character's experience, and that the young woman's mother was with someone other than her father, and she herself had a baby with a sailor who was black. In other words, for them it was all about what they called 'morals'. To me, even then, it was about whether these people – these kinds of people – could or could not love and care for each other. The scenes that lingered in my mind afterwards were those that caught the dilemmas or feelings most acutely. As for whether this was a unique or rare example of giving one kind of working-class life dignity and space in the mainstream, I don't think I cared about this directly at the time. That bit of cultural politics probably slipped past me. On reflection, though, perhaps some of it sank in without my noticing.

By the time I was fifteen, old enough to be in the Young Questors group legally, and had somehow caught up with the girls, I faced a dilemma. Our school planned to put on

*Much Ado About Nothing* and I got a part. But I couldn't do that play, as well as my exams, and go to Questors. So I left the group.

This school production of *Much Ado* was something of an event. In the years I was there, my grammar school had dropped the compulsory, one-big-production-a-year routine. The stage in the hall had been turned into a classroom, so a group of us started up a campaign to do a school play somewhere else on the premises but we weren't getting anywhere. I could look back across the previous five years and compare this with what Harold got up to. He had produced plays at the grammar school where being a Communist was a problem. At his next grammar school, he put on a play about a man who, though he didn't have a shirt, was happy. And now that he was a head of department at a comprehensive, he was producing plays all the time. I figured that 'Comprehensive' was replacing 'Communist': all the enthusiasm about the Soviet Union had turned into enthusiasm about Walworth Comprehensive. And they did plays there.

So, compared to when I started at the grammar school, putting on plays had become an optional extra or lost altogether. Then Barry Brown arrived. Harrow Weald Grammar School had never had a teacher like Barry Brown before. He wore suede shoes and had a Manchester accent and hair flopping over his forehead. Within five minutes of his arrival there were rumours that he fancied the geography teacher.

He soon put on a play called *Under the Sycamore Tree*, about ants. Everyone in the cast was an ant, and I got the part of a plenipotentiary ant. It was great, except that at one point I had to walk on and say that I was a plenipotentiary ant, but I couldn't say 'plenipotentiary'. Barry Brown tried every which way to help me and in the end, I got it. I was desperate for Mum and Harold to like it; I wanted to know whether they thought Barry Brown was as good as I thought he was.

Also in the play was another child of Jewish ex-Communists. Her father, known as 'Chick', was a doctor. A Jewish Communist doctor – even a Jewish ex-Communist doctor – was, in Mum and Harold's book, royalty. How they would all take the play started to matter a lot.

Mum said I was a very good ant. Harold said that the play was facetious. It was the first time I had ever heard the word. I pretended I knew what it meant, and later looked it up in our two-volume *Shorter Oxford*.

Barry Brown was so pleased with how I handled being a plenipotentiary ant, he said I might be interested in joining the Hatch End Players, a local adult amateur dramatics society. They were doing *The Merchant of Venice*, and the Prince of Morocco needed two servant boys. We were to come on with fronds, stand very still while the Prince of Morocco tried to open the casket, and then when he couldn't and flounced off, we were to turn and walk out after him, waving our fronds.

I didn't realise until the dress rehearsal that I had to do this in a loincloth, blacked up. I don't remember anyone saying that this was at all objectionable. It may have been 1960 (just), but the 60s hadn't happened yet. And so, every night, I sponged myself all over with brown liquid. On one of the nights, the moment I came on there were giggles in the audience. Throughout the Prince of Morocco's speech, 'All that glisters is not gold', people were whispering and laughing. At the interval, Barry came into the dressing-room and said, 'For Christ's sake, Michael, you didn't black up your belly. You look like an underdone sausage.'

He said that if I watched the man playing Shylock from the wings, I could learn a thing or two about acting. Barry Brown was Bassanio and the geography teacher was Portia. It seemed the rumours could be true, then, until I saw him snogging with Portia's maid, Nerissa, in the alleyway next to the church hall.

Mum said that the man playing Shylock was revolting, and she was sick and tired of the way people who played Shylock clawed the air and did all this lisping and funny 'r' sounds.

I thought I'd better not tell them that Barry Brown had said that I could learn a thing or two about acting from the man playing Shylock. I just went neutral on it – something I was getting good at – and asked them if maybe the things they didn't like about Shylock performances came out of the way Shakespeare wrote the character? I shouldn't have asked that. They had a conversation that went on for weeks. I picked up from this rolling debate that maybe Antonio was as bad as Shylock, and that was the point – the good guys were as bad as bad Shylock.

Mum went to bed and Harold and I went on talking. He said, 'You're looking at two ways of making money here. Shylock's lending. Antonio is speculating. Spokeshave is so on the ball, he's seen how the new way of making money is no better than the old way. On the surface the new-wealth ones look like the good'uns, but in the end, they are the persecutors.'

I hadn't seen any of this. As far as I was concerned, it was much simpler. Shylock was the bad'un, and Antonio, Bassanio and Portia got the better of him. Bam! Served him right. Was there some kind of code that Harold was reading? Was there Shakespeare – the plays you see and think you understand – and somewhere else a secret code-breaker that cracked Shakespeare open, showing you it's really about something else altogether?

At school, I told my classmates about Nerissa in the side-alley but they said Barry was still after the geography teacher. The girls said that meant he must be two-timing. Why else were they doing it in the side-alley? Good point. Maybe Nerissa and Barry in the side-alley of the church hall was the way the 60s began in Pinner, Hatch End and Harrow.

There was another kind of theatre: teachers.

Our French teacher was French. She told us that in France all pupils learn La Fontaine. 'He is our Shakespeare,' she said. 'You will learn "The Fox and the Crow", and "The Grasshopper and the Ant", but remember it's not a grasshopper.'

For days, probably weeks, we learnt '*Maître Corbeau sur un arbre perché ...*' and '*La Cigale, ayant chanté tout l'été ...*' They are perfectly balanced, she said. You must decide who behaves properly. We said it was obvious. The fox explains that the crow thinks he is better than he is; the ant explains that the grasshopper – she interrupted: 'It's a cicada' – shouldn't have been singing all summer if he wants to eat in the winter.

Very good, she said, but why should we believe what the fox or the ant say? The fox is a thief, he steals the crow's cheese; the ant could be kind and share what he has, but he doesn't. Are such people right? More code-breaking. Interesting. Very interesting.

Why had our French teacher come to live in England? Maybe she ran away when the Germans invaded France, we wondered. No one knew.

The Swiss PE teacher behaved as though we were in training for survival in Greenland. Bald, old, moustached, at times incomprehensible, he yelled in people's faces, particularly if they had asthma. He made us climb higher than we wanted to, run further than we wanted to, lined us up outside in our shorts on a February morning and left us there to see how many of us would die. The ones who were left alive, he yelled at for thinking we could stand on ze shtreet corner viss ze begging bowl. After several hours of yelling, he would break off, come over to me, and with his voice turned into Marlene Dietrich, shmoozed me saying: 'Mike, I sink you know my record. Spain, mm?'

He had been at the school for hundreds of years, he was there when Harold taught there. Harold told me that this PE teacher had joined the International Brigades and fought in Spain. No matter what kind of a person you were, if you had done that, as far as Harold was concerned, you were a saint. When my friends did take-offs of the PE teacher they turned him into an SS officer, torturing people with lit cigarettes. Mum heard me doing this and went bananas.

'It's just a joke,' I said.

'It's not funny,' she said, 'those things aren't funny.'

The PE teacher showed us the bullet stuck in his shin-bone. We imagined him running up a mountain with a machine gun in his hand, getting shot, rolling over and lying for days next to a rock.

We never actually saw him climb a rope, go up a wall bar, vault over a horse, or run anywhere. He smoked so many thick, yellow, rich-smelling cigarettes that the smell had soaked into the walls of the gym and changing rooms. Wherever you were in the school, you could smell if he had been there any time in the last week. Mart said that they were Turkish cigarettes. Tony said they were Balkan Sobranies. We reckoned he was about eighty, and had managed to avoid the retirement age. All of a sudden he married the domestic science teacher and she had a baby. Someone said that it was born with a bullet in its leg.

I enjoyed French, so Mum and Harold ruled that I should do German and Latin as well. The German teacher was a deeply pious Catholic woman, who was very serious one moment and the next collapsed into fits of self-induced giggling. She taught half in German, half in English, switching halfway through the sentence: 'Now then class, *alles zusammen*, open your *Heute Abend*, page *zwei und vierzig …*' (break for giggling) '*nun bitte …* no need for that noise, Michael …'

She had taught at the school when Harold taught there, and when I said she was a Catholic he said, 'She's Jewish.' I said, 'She's not Jewish, she's Catholic.' 'She's Jewish,' he said.

She liked to teach us German songs. She had a tiny, piping singing voice that she was rather proud of. One day it was Brahms's 'Wiegenlied', she started '*Guten Abend, gut' nacht / mit Rosen bedacht …*' then collapsed in a fit of giggles. Through the giggles, she said, 'It never occurred to me before … "Rosen"! "Rosen"! And we've got Rosen here!' She went on about it for quite some time, while the class waited patiently.

I thought there was something very strange about that. First she had taught with Harold, who was called Rosen. Then she had taught Brian, who was called Rosen. And now she was teaching me. It couldn't really have been the first time it had ever occurred to her that our name meant 'roses' and that it was in Brahms's 'Wiegenlied'. But why did we have a German name when Harold's father didn't come from Germany? No one knew.

A few weeks later, it was time for another little song. 'This one is Austrian,' she said, 'and it's in Austrian dialect. All over Germany people have different dialects.'

I put my hand up. 'When we were in East Germany, there was a …'

A look of complete horror came over her face. 'You were in

East Germany?' she said, and when she said 'East' she made it sound like something dirty.

'Yes, we were in Weimar. And I stayed in the Thuringian Wald.'

She shook her head as if to say I was lying.

I carried on. 'One of the German delegates taught us a song in Swabian dialect, "*Auf der schwäbsche Eisenbahne*" and you go "chuff, chuff, chuff …"'

I wasn't interesting her. '*Nun bitte*, in this little song, *von Österreich*, you'll hear that some of the words are contracted.'

Then she stood up straight, clasped her hands and began: '*Muss i'den, muss i'den* …'

Two girls at the back screamed. She stopped. 'Pat! Linda! What do you think you're doing. Stop that right away!'

It was odd. Pat and Linda wouldn't ever behave like that usually. We waited for it to calm down. Miss asked them to explain. Pat said how '*Muss i'den*' was an Elvis song. Miss frowned. That couldn't be true. Pat said Elvis was in the army in Germany, and he had a song out called 'Wooden Heart', and halfway through he sings '*Muss i'den, muss i'den*'.

Miss said that that was a great shame. She had been looking forward to teaching us a pretty little Austrian folksong, and she had no idea that Elvis Presley had decided to sing it. 'Well, we won't do "Muss i'den" this year,' she said.

Some of the teacher-characters in this great play called School had back stories. It was said that the Burmese physics teacher had the George Cross, or could have had the George Cross or should have had the George Cross. He had apparently led hundreds of children over a mountain to escape the Japanese. A history teacher had been engaged to a man who got killed in the First World War, and had never had a boyfriend since.

The religious instruction teacher (who doubled up on Careers and Life Classes) had been ordained as a Baptist Minister, but was now a secret atheist. In Life Classes, which were segregated, he told us that 'it's not only you boys who have orgasms, you know. Women have orgasms.' If the class-room door blew open in the wind, he would fall to the floor sobbing, grabbing his completely bald head, roaring, 'What do you want? Take me if you want to. I'm ready!' Then he would straighten up in a flash, as if he hadn't done anything out of the ordinary, and carry on with orgasms. We weren't 100 per cent sure if this thing with the door was an act or real.

And then there was the Latin teacher. A young man with limbs weakened or withered by polio, like many of his generation caught and held by an illness that had terrified people in the era just before I was old enough to know what had happened. This teacher was so good at chess that he could take on twenty of us at a time, going round from one board to another and winning every game. Then there was an announcement in assembly: he had been selected for the England chess team. What a hero.

Except that for some of us he was crazy, violent, dangerous and – the word we always used – Fascist. Every lesson was a war. He blurted out Latin verbs and nouns, then called us idiots and clowns. Every time he turned to the board, we created tank manoeuvres with our desks, lifting them with our knees and sliding them across the room. He retaliated with hand-to-hand combat, coming up to us one by one, grabbing us by the hair just above our ears, pulling our heads down to the desk and then smashing our skulls with the knuckles of his fist. We took up invisible humming, delivering volleys of quiet droning sounds, with our mouths just a tiny bit open and smiling so that it was impossible to spot who was droning. To this he would retaliate with detentions and lines. He got my number: 'If we'd had any sense, Rosen, we'd've been on the side of the Germans in the last war.'

On the other side of politics there was Merlyn Rees, expupil of the school, teaching history and trying to win Harrow East for the Labour Party. In the 1959 General Election, aged thirteen, I slogged round the suburban streets posting his leaflets through the kind of doors which seemed to say loudly to me, 'There's no one living here who would vote Labour in a million years.' He didn't get in. The day after the election he was back in school, teaching the same old Great Reform Act of 1832 to classes of kids, the parents of many of whom hadn't voted for him. Wise guys in the sixth form whispered that he didn't know the right people to get a safe Labour constituency to contest, so he would go on teaching history to us forevermore. Wrong: he got exactly that kind of constituency and ended up as Home Secretary.

And there was a chemistry teacher who was not just legendary; he was epic. His reputation went way beyond the school, beyond the borough even. His lessons started off as riots and got worse. He was a mix of the incompetent, impatient and oblivious. You could go past the lab and a whole class might be sitting outside, sent out for being impossible. Every teacher knew about it but no one did anything. Occasionally teachers would give us some kind of excuse: they would tell us that he was a world expert on organ music and organs, and that he had even made one. I'm not sure how this was supposed to pacify the mobs he faced every day.

I don't even know his real name anymore, because he was only ever known as 'Boris'. There are hundreds of people in their sixties, seventies and eighties – some who lingered in Harrow, some who spread out across the British Isles, some who went on the post-'60s grammar-school-pupil diaspora to work in Canada or Hong Kong and have happened to stay there – to whom you can say one word: 'Boris!' and they will instantly reply in a deep, enraged voice with a touch of West Country: 'Go out!'

Was it true that one teacher was having it off with a sixth-former in the school attic? Impossible. Of course not. Was it true that two teachers used to creep to the field next to the school field, and when they were caught doing it, nothing was done, even though the man of the couple had caught two fifth-formers at it a few months before and got them expelled? Impossible. Of course not. Was it true that the head was an alcoholic and people used to see him come out of school, down the hill, straight into the pub and not emerge till closing time? Impossible.

Because Brian had been taught by these people before me and was also the world expert in the Molesworth books, and because he could imitate every teacher and invent a voice for every Molesworth character, he turned them all into one long teachers' cabaret. Our teachers and the teachers in St Custard's started to blur and merge. When the English master in St Custard's says, 'o molesworth one you must learn the value of spiritual things', the phrase became ours, too. When there was the revolt of the prunes, or the exam paper: 'Are the Andes?', these were our school dinners, and our exams. And yet we didn't go to a little private school run on some kind of fiddle by a Headmaster Grimes. How come it seemed so similar? Because it was.

By now, at home, we had a fridge (bought), a washing machine (bought) and a TV (rented from Radio Rental). As a result, politics shifted from being a debate around the dining table to a dialogue that we had with the TV. Harold talked at the television as if the people could hear him. Mum would tell him that they couldn't. While I watched anything, anytime – game shows, kids' programmes, films, cowboy shows, discussions, sport, sport and sport – Harold and Mum spoke of it as a waste of time, apart from two programmes.

One was by a Marxist critic. John Berger had devised a show called *Drawn from Life* (thirteen episodes, 1961–62), where his guest was someone 'ordinary', not an expert or famous in any way. Berger chose two paintings and talked about them in relation to the artist's life and times, and then the pair of them talked about the ordinary person's life. It was Berger's task to guess which of the two pictures the guest preferred. I think some of Berger's 'ordinary people' were politically involved trade unionists and activists. Our parents thought all this was brilliant. They must have seen it as a new kind of Marxist criticism in action: instead of a Communist Party ideologue laying down the law about what was the true meaning of something, here you could see the personal and social response of 'ordinary' people, intermingled with the personal and social origins of a picture. I was interested but not gripped. After all, these were the days of black-and-white television and no matter how great an Old Master or a Fauvist masterpiece might be, when it's reduced to a small black-and-white screen it's no longer very great at all.

The other programme they liked was a panel discussion about politics, *Free Speech*, where the main two guests each week were Michael Foot and Bob (the future Lord) Boothby. This excited our parents even more than Berger. Though I didn't fully understand the arguments, I could see that Boothby wasn't the fastest hound in the pack. He often resorted to reminding the audience how he and 'Winston' had 'stood alone', while Foot countered his arguments with short, sharp thrusts.

Boothby's gruff, gravelly voice was in contrast to Foot's, which was crisp and snappy. I 'got' their voices, Boothby's in particular, and I improvised gruff, gravelly monologues about 'me and Winston'. Their demeanours were very different too: Boothby grand in his bow tie, with neatly brushed-back hair and plump face, Foot with hair flopping down on either side of a gaunt, bony face, staring at the table in front of him.

Apart from anything else, the sight of Foot cemented in my mind a category or type: the Left Labour politician, a socialist who wasn't a Communist and had never been one. Rather than just being a distant, shouty figure on the plinth at Trafalgar Square or Holborn Town Hall, Michael Foot was a person who I could now see on TV at work – and I liked him.

In spite of themselves, our parents were becoming 1960s consumers of TV and commodities. When these ex-working-class Jewish East Enders took themselves and us to Heal's in Tottenham Court Road, they spent hours debating whether to buy the armchairs with the rust-coloured upholstery or the blue tweed sofa. I guess that was the Arts and Crafts movement meeting consumerism.

To fight the draught in the front room, Harold spent months and months planning the great Courtier Stove adventure: how to block off the chimney; how to make a hole in the thing he blocked it off with (a piece of steel he got from the metalwork room at his school); how to paint the steel sheet; how to get the old fireplace out; how to get the stove in. And then once it was all done, it became a household god. In winter, every evening he tended the stove, talked to it, stroked it, dusted it, polished it, marvelled at it, recommended it. He told stories about how he got the metal plate and how he made the hole in it; he held forth on how one paint worked but another didn't; how you have to get to know a stove, because each has its own personality; how the British are insane about coal; how all over Germany they have stoves; how they burn a fraction of what we burn; how their houses are as warm as toast … And one day there'd be no coal left, he said, and at the very least when you have a nationalised coal industry you could plan for this sort of thing … But of course the bloody Labour government, first of all did the right thing by nationalising coal, and then they only went and handed the whole thing over to a bunch of sharks …

'You see the fire?' he said once. 'It behaves according to the dialectic: lots of little starts till the whole thing suddenly becomes one big fire, many small qualitative changes create one large quantitative change.'

More often, he said, 'Not a bad old fire there, lad.'

He said it so often we shortened it to NABOFTL. The coal would burst into flame and we'd turn to each other and say, 'NABOFTL.'

Halfway through 1958, there was a bus strike. The school was a half-hour bus ride from home, usually a time for arguing, fighting, flirting, doing homework, preparing for exams, eating and bag-losing. For months now, we'd had to find other ways of getting to school and back. The maths teacher went to school via our road, so he offered to take me in his black Morris Minor. It was grim. He didn't have very much to say to me. I didn't have very much to say to him. He was rather interested in the girls in the top three years of the school, and because that's where Brian was, he would quiz me about who was going out with who. I didn't know, or pretended I didn't, and didn't want him to know. I didn't like it that he wanted to know.

Mum said that I had to take money to the bus garage.

'Why?'

'For the strike fund.'

'How do you know there's a strike fund?'

'Of course there's a strike fund. That's what they're living off.' She gave me some money.

'How do I know where to take it?'

'There'll be a picket line outside the garage. You go up to the picket line and give them the money.'

That evening I told the maths teacher that I didn't need a lift, I would find another way home and I went down to the garage. There were two guys sitting in the entrance. I went up to them and said, 'I've got some money for the strike fund. My mum says that you've got somewhere for me to put it.'

They had a box and I dropped the money in. I felt them looking at me in my school uniform as I was doing it. No one else I knew gave money to the strike fund.

Dave, my best friend at the time, lived in Stanmore, and used to ask me over for 'Friday nights' – what my father called *shabbes benacht*, as if we observed the eve of the Jewish Sabbath. I had never seen or done these Friday nights. At Dave's house, there was Dave, his younger sister, his younger brother and his mum and dad. His mum was not a happy person, and could turn every conversation into a comment about why she wasn't appreciated. His dad was a jazz musician who had given it up to sell shoes in Wembley Market. 'It's not all about you selling shoes, Morris,' said Dave's mother, 'what do you think I do all day?'

When I arrived at the house he said, 'Lovely to see you, Michael, how's your aunty?'

I said, 'You don't know my aunty.'

'That's why I asked,' he said.

When we sat down he said if I didn't have a *kuppel* I could put my hand over my head, 'God won't mind.'

'Why do you say that, Morris? It makes it sound like I haven't got any spare. Just open the drawer and give the boy one.'

I put on a kuppel.

Morris said the prayer, poured the wine into a silver cup and drank it. 'Any of you men want some?'

'For goodness sake, Morris.'

'We were all Communists once,' Morris said, 'but I could see that it doesn't work. It's human nature.'

'You don't know what you're talking about, Morris.'

'Do you like jazz, Michael?'

'I don't know,' I said.

'Music is the most important thing in the world,' he said, 'I could spend all day playing jazz.'

'I know,' said Dave's mum, 'and you would, if it wasn't for me.'

'What size are you?' Morris said.

'Eight.'

'Eight already! What are you? A monster?'

He went out the room and came back with a box. It was a pair of corduroy slippers. 'Do you wear slippers?' he said.

'No,' I said.

'Then sell them. I know a very good place in Wembley Market. It's run by a good man called Morris. Reminds me: a very old friend of mine was dying. He called out for his sons to come to his bedside. "Harvey?" "Here, dad." "Monty?" "Here, dad." "Solly?" "Here, dad."

'And my friend said, "So, who's minding the shop?"'

Dave's mum said, 'Why do you do that, Morris? Michael doesn't know whether that's true or not. It wasn't his friend, Michael. It was a joke.'

I thought, it's a joke? What's the joke? The bloke wants to know who's minding the shop. If you had a shop, you'd want to know that someone was minding it, wouldn't you?

'Do you know, Michael, the other day a feller came into the shop and he said, "What is it with you, Morris, why are you always asking questions? Is that a Jewish thing?" and I said, "Why do you ask?"'

Dave and his brother and sister groaned.

Morris got out his guitar. It was a light brown, very shiny, semi-acoustic. He plugged it in.

'Turn that down, Morris, I can't hear a thing.'

He whispered to me: 'Why does she need to hear a thing? What is this thing she needs to hear? All my life she says, "Turn it down, Morris, I can't hear a thing …" and I've never found out what the thing is she can't hear.' He was vamping along as he talked, soft jazz chords … and Dave started playing the piano.

It all sounded so clever. I had never sat in a room with musicians like them. Morris and Dave just played and played without ever looking at a piece of music. It flowed out of them.

Then I went upstairs to Dave's room and he had a record-player. He said, 'This is the most amazing record that's ever been made.' He put it on. It was Miles Davis's *Kind of Blue*.

'The day after Charlie Parker died,' he said, 'all over New York, people wrote up on the walls, "Bird lives".'

Morris came in and asked me why I wasn't having a bar mitzvah. I said it was because we didn't believe in God.

Morris said, 'What's believing in God got to do with it? Your father had a bar mitzvah.'

'He didn't.'

'He didn't? What are you talking about? I was there.'

'Were you?'

'No, I was lying.'

'His Mum didn't agree with bar mitzvahs,' I said, 'He told me.'

'So how did he get his first suit?'

'He says his Zeyde made it.'

'That's clever. You're not fools in your family, are you? Do you know what a *schmendrik* is?'

'No.'

'It's a fool. Your father's no schmendrik.'

Dave had to learn speeches for the bar mitzvah. It involved reading pages of Hebrew. The books lay open in his bedroom.

'Do you think there'll ever be socialism?' Morris said.

'Yes,' I said.

'You're wrong,' he said, 'I see these people come into Wembley Market, they come in my shop, and I think, how can there be socialism when the world's full of *schmoks*?'

'That's awful,' I said, 'you can't think like that.'

'I try not to,' he said, 'believe me, I do. I'm just saying what I think. We have to say what we think, don't you agree, Michael?'

'Why do you talk such rubbish, Dad?' Dave said.

'Do you think I talk rubbish, Michael?'

I said, 'No.'

'Then you're the first person in the world to think that. Let me shake your hand.'

Dave's mum put her head round the door. 'Don't leave your teacup there, Morris. I spent hours tidying up the last mess you left.'

So by the time I got to fifteen, nearly sixteen, I was in the school production of *Much Ado About Nothing*, wearing purple tights, playing an insignificant servant called Conrad. Mart's friend Leebs and Brian's blues aficionado friend Jeff were in it too and it represented a victory for the campaign to put on a play. In fact, it involved what we thought at the time was radical staging: we put on the play at the 'wrong' end of the school hall, using the doors into the kitchen for school dinners as our entrances while the stage sat unused and dark at the other end of the hall. This was 'theatre'. But I had been through four and half years of teachers and homes (like Dave's), all of which I was just beginning to see formed another kind of theatre – if only I could remember enough of it to write down, before it flashed past.

# 7

## Great Expectations

In the summer of 1959 we went to Sandsend, near Whitby in North Yorkshire, with the also ex-Communist Flower family. There Harold promised to read us *Great Expectations*. And so every night he pumped up the Tilly lamp and settled himself on the little camp chair, and we all squeezed into the tent around him as he read.

He had voices for all the characters, Magwitch, Miss Havisham, Pumblechook, Trabb's boy, Jaggers, Herbert Pocket, Wemmick – all different voices. After each evening's reading, we would go off and repeat the voices, 'Give me wittles, boy!' 'What larks!' 'Beggar him, Estella!' 'Don't know yah!' 'How much? Five pounds? Twenty pounds?'

At the time it felt to me like a story with hopes, fears, snobbishness, self-deceit, unrequited love … I got all that. I got that Harold and Mum loved this story, Harold in particular. The way he read it with such passion showed that he loved it more than any of the other hundreds of stories on the shelves at home, more even than the plays at the theatres we went to.

Since then, I've come to see why Harold read it to us with such feeling. Like him, Pip doesn't have a birth father; Pip is attached to a kind and loving father substitute, like Harold to his Zeyde. Perhaps Uncle Pumblechook was like his uncle Leslie Sunshine, turning up at the house, talking big about what he was going to do for him out there in the world?

And who was Miss Havisham if she wasn't Beatrice Hastings, sitting in her carpeted Belsize Park flat surrounded with mementoes from her time as Modigliani's lover, who Ma had perhaps thought would see little Harold right in some way or another?

Even the Trabb's boy scene, when he walks down the street mocking Pip and doing the 'Don't know yah' line, with Pip feeling ashamed: wasn't that like a story Harold told us about someone called David Greenwood? He always recalled how ashamed he'd felt that when David Greenwood tried to get in touch, after Harold had gone from the East End Foundation School to the posher, Regent's Street Polytechnic, Harold had ignored his former classmate, who was so poor he had to shlep a wheelbarrow to earn a penny or two.

Was there a Magwitch in Harold's past? Maybe there were several Magwitches at the Whitechapel Library. Old migrants, sailors from all over the world, who sat in the library to keep warm, talked about 'the *heim*' and politics, and played dominoes. Sometimes one of them would ask the young Harold to help him read something and one or two asked him for a penny for a beigel. Every time I read *Great Expectations* or see it on TV or at the cinema, it merges so much with Harold and his family that I can't clearly sort out the differences between what I thought when Harold read it to us, what I've thought as his family history emerged, and what I think now. Perhaps all response to books is like this.

Before the end of that holiday, Brian had to head off to France, travelling via home in London, so we took him to Whitby station, waved him off and headed back to the car park. As we got into the car, Mum realised that he hadn't got his house key. It was in her bag.

Harold said, 'The train goes to Pickering. I'm sure we could get there before him.'

So we jumped into the car and drove over the moors to Pickering. Totally out of character. Harold transformed himself into a James Bond figure in a car chase. I remembered Miss Goodall had read us *The Thirty-Nine Steps* and it felt like that, too. Harold put his foot down and we belted along the switchback road over the moors. He asked me to look out for the train. By the time we got to Pickering, the train was in the station. Even more uncharacteristically, Harold jumped out the car and ran up the platform, shouting, 'Stop the train!' He found Brian's compartment and handed over the key.

'You must have been worried sick,' Harold said through the window.

'No,' said Brian, 'I was going to ask Mr Townsend to borrow his ladder and climb through the kitchen window.'

All the way back, Harold chuntered on about what was it with Brian? Why was he so bloody egocentric? Over the next few years, I watched and listened while the drive over the moors and 'Stop the train!' turned from something-lived into a story-told, and from a story-told into a family legend that visitors to our flat liked listening to. Without knowing it at the time, I was doing my apprenticeship for what I've been doing for the last forty years.

With Brian being four years older than me, he was by now on the threshold leading away from home. It felt like he was pulling me over the line with him. Back in London, my old friends Chris and Malcolm both said at different times, when I was over their places, that they had gone with their still-Communist parents on the Aldermaston Marches to ban the bomb for evermore. Now it was coming up to Easter again, and they asked me if this year I was going to march to ban the bomb for evermore too. Mum and Harold were going to the rally on the last day. I said I wanted to go on the whole march, and actually I was going anyway. On my own.

Mum said this was impossible, 'out of the question', and made her protest: 'Where will you stay? You'd have nothing to eat, you don't know anyone. What would you eat? You're not going. Harold, say something. He's too young. Look at him, he's packing. You can't go without a spare pair of trousers. How can he carry a bag like that for twenty miles a day? Stop him, Harold.'

As it got nearer to the moment of my leaving, Mum carried on in the same vein, while taking care that I had packed enough for the journey. 'He's thirteen, Harold. Go next year, wait till next year. They won't have banned the bomb by then, believe me.' Then she started handing me food. 'There's the chicken. Take the chicken. Harold, get the chicken. If you're taking a tin of beans, take two.' And on she swerved between complaint and advice:

'There'll be another march. Go on that one. You must keep eating fresh fruit. And you like dates. He's always liked dates, hasn't he? Just squeeze them in down the side of the bag. Couldn't he wait till the last day, when we'll all be there? We can all go to Trafalgar Square together ... Just because it's Easter doesn't mean it's warm. It can snow at Easter. Wear the string vest ... Who's organised the coaches? Do we know these people, Harold? ... One orange! Take five. And raisins ... He's thirteen. It's ridiculous. He can't go. Keep the chicken wrapped ... Phone us if you need more food ... Goodbye.'

Once I had joined the march, I found that it was highly organised. There was colour-coding of every demonstrator, so that we could be allotted sleeping quarters in schools and marquees. I was 'Magenta'. The first stretch of the march took us from the Aldermaston base, where they researched atomic fission, to the town of Reading. At the end of the day I found myself wandering on my own through the back streets in the rain, trying to find the Magenta designated school. By the time I arrived, I was late and I was shoved in an annex. I used my Magenta ticket to get some soup, and then looked at the food that Mum had made sure I took. I started on the whole chicken.

Just then two young women turned up at the hall, causing a sensation. They were like beanpoles, with long blonde hair and tight black jeans, smoking and repeatedly saying 'Fuck!' really loudly. I gathered soon enough that one of them was Anthony Greenwood's daughter. Anthony Greenwood was a Labour MP, one of the leaders of the march, identified by the national papers as a major figure in the evil conspiracy undermining Britain's defences.

At around ten, the Magenta stewards said that it was lights out so we had better start getting to bed. I got into my sleeping bag on the classroom floor. Then I realised that Greenwood's daughter and her friend were going to bed down close to me. They had one big bag they were going to get in together. They looked over to me.

'What are you looking at, boy?' one of them said, in a loud, Questors' voice.

'Nothing. No, I wasn't looking at anything.'

'Yes you were. That's because you've never seen a bra, have you, boy?' one of them said.

I mumbled something.

And then one of them said, 'We're going to take our clothes off now, boy, and I bet you're going to look now, aren't you?'

'No,' I said, 'really I'm not.'

'But you want to, don't you?'

'No,' I said.

Then they started laughing, got right down into their sleeping bag, giggled and shrieked, and re-emerged with men's shirts on.

'Where are you from, boy?' they said.

'Pinner.'

'Are you a socialist?'

'Yes.'

'What does your father do?'

'He's a teacher.'

'What does your mother do?'

'She's a teacher.'

This wasn't interesting enough, so now they just talked to each other. After a while they called out, 'Good night, boy.' They thought that that in itself was a really good joke, and went off into peals of laughter. And we all dozed off.

In the morning there were queues for the toilets, queues for breakfast, queues for washing. I saw Greenwood and her friend walking about in their very short men's shirts and, as I thought, not wearing anything else. They loved it that everyone was looking at them. But as we all trooped off, I noticed that they got into the back of the truck that was carrying our heavy kitbags on to the next Magenta centre in Slough, twenty miles or so up the road.

I found the march easy enough – a bit like the camping holidays, but with even more Communists, and more different kinds of socialist and left-wingers than I had ever seen in my life. I started collecting leaflets from people and reading about socialist and anarchist and pacifist and revolutionary groups and parties I'd never heard of. As I walked along I studied them, trying to figure out what they were disagreeing about, who betrayed who, and when. Some of the leaflets explained in great detail why they couldn't support the march: they were there, but against being there. Others explained why they supported it 'with no illusions': the first instance in decades to come of being begged to support something 'with no illusions'.

Suddenly out of the blue, amidst the banners and flags, there was Brian Pearce, the man who'd lived with us a few years earlier. We had lost touch with him since. He had changed a lot. He had swapped his old brown-rimmed glasses for little gold-rimmed ones, and he had grown a little grey goatee beard. His banner said, 'Nationalise the Arms Industry Now'.

'Hi Brian,' I said.

He nodded knowledgeably at me.

I looked at his banner. What did it mean? Why should we nationalise the arms industry? What did that have to do with banning the bomb? I looked back at him. And he went on nodding knowledgeably at me.

Later that day, I walked for a while with Malcolm Aprahamian and his father Francis, the bald Armenian (still Communist). I told Francis that I had met Brian Pearce. He frowned. 'So clever,' he said, 'a great loss.'

I thought he thought that I had said he died. 'No,' I said, 'I saw him.'

'I know,' Francis said.

What Francis knew (and I barely did) was that Brian Pearce not only left the Communist Party, he had researched the Party in depth, and written in great detail what was wrong with the Party and with the Soviet Union. I learned later that at this precise moment he was a Trotskyist, believing, as Trotsky had, that there was hope that the Soviet Union could be reformed back to the socialist path. Also at this precise moment, there were of course several Trotskyist and sort-of-Trotskyist groups each with their variations on the theme of a 'degenerated workers' state'. Brian Pearce at that very moment was moving through the Socialist Labour League (always referred to as 'the SLL') on his way to becoming a translator of such things as the transcription of the 1903 Second Congress of the Russian Social-Democratic Labour Party. This was when the Bolsheviks and the Mensheviks split in the upstairs room of the Crown and Woolpack pub at the Angel, Islington, London, which at the time of my writing these words is a hairdresser's called 'The Chapel'.

Every now and then on the Aldermaston March, the baggage trucks went slowly past us and they were half open at the back. In one of them I saw Anthony Greenwood's daughter and her friend leaning out over the tailgate and as soon as they saw me, they started screaming and waving, 'There's Boy! Hello Boy! Say hello, Boy!'

I waved back.

'He's waving!'

'Boy's waving.'

The people I was with said, 'How do you know them?'

I said that I didn't really, it's just that I was sleeping with them last night.

'What?'

'No, I mean they were in the Magenta school where I was last night.'

'That's Anthony Greenwood's daughter, you know.'

'Yeah, I know,' I said.

This happened several times. Either they were leaning out the back of the truck or, when we arrived at a speech rally on the route, they were hanging off some kind of rig, just where Chris Barber or Humphrey Lyttelton were filling the air with jazz. Somehow even in the middle of a big crowd they could see me, and screamed out, 'Boy! There's Boy!'

In Slough, Magenta section were given a giant marquee. Hundreds, if not thousands, of us slept in row upon row. At lights out, a few people were still talking, and there was a bit of shushing, until the great tent fell silent and we dozed off. Then, from nowhere, one lone and very loud voice started doing the monologues from *Beyond the Fringe*. First Jonathan Miller and the one about the trousers on the train. Then the Alan Bennett vicar one, with 'Is there a little bit of sardine left in the corner of your life?' This guy in the marquee, whoever he was, knew them by heart. Then he moved on to the sketches:

'Goodbye sir. Or is it au revoir?'

'No Perkins, it's goodbye.'

He did the intro to Dudley Moore's song: 'And the lover bemoans and bemoans and bemoans ...'

By the time he was getting into the songs, people were shouting at him to shut up, reminding him that we had a long walk tomorrow, that he was driving them mad. But he didn't stop; he just went through the whole show in the dark. It was like Jonathan Miller, Dudley Moore, Alan Bennett and Peter Cook were there with us in the tent. I thought how incredible it was that a group of performers could make up monologues and sketches, perform them, make a record and then people anywhere and everywhere could repeat them. The guy in the marquee in the dark may have been irritating the hell out of hundreds of people, but he also triggered off in me a yearning to do something like *Beyond the Fringe* in my own life.

On the March there was always a song, or a slogan being chanted. This, in turn, developed into an ongoing debate about folk songs and the blues.

In our family, this was the year the blues came to Pinner. Some people went over to Ealing to see it played in the Rhythm and Blues Club where Jagger, Jones and the rest were getting together. For me and Brian's friends it was on LPs, EPs, bootlegged reel-to-reel tapes, and occasional concerts at the Finsbury Park Astoria, the Dominion Tottenham Court Road, the Marquee, Charing Cross Road or the Hammersmith Odeon. We passed names around like secret passwords: Howlin' Wolf, Blind Lemon Jefferson, Muddy Waters, Lonnie Johnson, Leroy Carr, Gus Cannon's Jug Band, Son House, Elmore James, Memphis Minnie, Jimmy Yancey, and the mysterious and incredible Robert Johnson. Some of them dead, some of them disappeared, some of them rediscovered.

It was magical that many of this first generation of blues musicians who wailed out of our record players in our suburban bedrooms, whether from the Mississippi Delta or Chicago, were so out of reach. How had they created this incredible music? What did the words mean? Were they really men and women who were only one or two generations out of slavery?

On the road on the Aldermaston March, however, there was a rumble of debate about what was allowed and what was not. Could white people sing the blues? One row I overheard was about whether people should only sing songs from their own country. Another was about whether it was or was not OK to sing traditional English or Irish or Scots songs with a guitar. Some didn't give a damn and just sang political songs, Aldermaston songs, parodies of hymns, spirituals, campfire songs, with or without guitars, anything to get us further along the road.

'I belong to a family, the biggest on earth ...'

'I'm gonna lay down my sword and shield, down by the riverside ...'

'If I had a hammer, I'd hammer in the morning ...'

'One more river, and that's the river of Jordan ...'

'Och Jock, the monster's in the loch and we're gonna ban Polaris ...'

'It's a long way to Aldermaston, it's a long way to go ...'

'... just like a tree that's standing by the water, we shall not be moved ...'

A guy called George Clark, who had a megaphone, begged, pleaded, cajoled and roared at us to keep going. 'Tea round the corner,' he said. It was a lie. And the next time he turned up, we shouted back at him. 'Lies! It's all lies!'

More songs, more chants. The 'out-out-out' one was getting us down. Someone hollered the name of a politician, or a weapon, and we all responded 'OUT', again, 'OUT', and a last time followed by 'OUT, OUT, OUT'.

To make a change, I shouted 'Way!' and everyone shouted 'OUT!'

Again: 'Way!' Everyone: 'OUT!'

One more time: 'Way!' Everyone: 'OUT! OUT! OUT!'

I found myself walking along with two Indian guys, who took it on themselves to explain imperialism to me. They gave me a book list – word of mouth, not on paper. I remembered how Harold had described him and Brian Pearce sitting in the University College 'Refec' (cafeteria) in 1938, listening to Krishna Menon and Pandit Nehru tell them that independence wasn't far away. These guys warned me that I shouldn't have faith in the Labour Party, it was 'fatally compromised by imperialism' and always would be.

We arrived at Turnham Green and the group I was with now, mostly made up of my brother Brian's friends, said, 'Why don't we go to the Partisan?'

'Yeah, let's go to the Partisan.'

'What's the Partisan?' I said.

'A cafe in Soho.'

We queued for some time but got in, and someone said, 'Have the Spaghetti Bolognese.'

I had it. My first Spaghetti Bolognese.

That night I went home, and Mum and Harold said that Francis Aprahamian had thanked them very much for the chicken. He said that chicken had fed the whole of the Aldermaston march. Connie's chicken became North London Aldermaston folklore.

'Did you eat the beans?' she asked me.

I said that I did eat the beans, but there was food at all the stopping points.

'And the dried fruit?'

And the dried fruit, Mum.

They wanted to come with me to the march on the last day, but by now I was joining Brian on the threshold out and wasn't keen on them being there at all. Rather than walk with them, I preferred the image of myself reporting back to them about the people, leaflets and talk.

On that final day's walk into Central London, I got in with someone who objected to the Communists being there. 'Fatally compromised,' he said. This 'fatally compromised' thing seemed to be some kind of killer put-down, which demolished everything. 'They think the Russian bomb is OK, so how can they just object to the British bomb? The point is, no bomb is OK. If they object to the British bomb but don't object to the Russian bomb, the press can make out that we're here just to get Britain to be weaker in the face of what we think is the "good" Russian bomb, see? We're compromised by letting them come on the march.' He said there was going to be a split over this. I also got a leaflet that laid out a plan for Britain to become neutral. No need to be aligned with either Russia or America, it said.

And then I did bump into Mum and Harold after all. Mum said she'd noticed that the Quakers wore sensible shoes, very sensible shoes. Harold said that it was all bloody marvellous. The last time he had seen a march as big as this was the one for the Second Front (World War Two stuff I had heard about many times, so I didn't need to ask 'What Second Front?'). Maybe this march was bigger than the Second Front one. At Trafalgar Square we all sang along with Canon Collins, 'Don't you hear the H-bomb's thunder', to the tune of a hymn. It was like a huge Ban-the-Bomb school assembly.

When I got back to school after the Easter break, the kids in my class asked me about the march. I could see that for some of them, this was like I had done some majorly risky thing, that their parents would never have let them do. I was, after all, just a third-former, not quite fourteen. The only other people from school who went on the march were Brian and Brian's friends, but they were in the sixth form or had just left school on the way to university.

One girl wanted to argue with me about it: the bomb kept us safe, she said. In order to counter her I tried to remember what it said in the leaflets I had picked up along the route. I recalled one of them saying, why couldn't Britain be a neutral country? and tried this out on her. I had a feeling that it was the first time I'd looked to somewhere other than the *Daily Worker*, Mum or Harold for political ideas.

Ever since Harold had read us *Great Expectations*, in the back of my mind was the idea that one of the things we do when we grow up is 'make our way in the world'. On this Aldermaston March and subsequent ones, I had a sense that this was, in its own fashion, how I was 'making my way in the world'.

One morning it was announced out of the blue that Mum's brother Ronnie was getting married. It was 'out of the blue' because Mum hadn't ever said that something was cooking, or that Ronnie had met someone. The consensus was that he never would. Not so: he had got engaged to a chemistry teacher, and we were all going to meet her in Kingsbury. Kingsbury? That was over our way, in the suburbs, where Harold had taught and where I had learned how to swim.

Within seconds of meeting the chemistry teacher and her family, we gathered that from now on things with Ronnie were going to be *frum* (observant): a religious wedding at a synagogue, kosher catering – the whole thing. I had been in a synagogue before. When I was seven a boy had come up to me in the playground and said, 'You're Jewish. My Mum says you're Jewish and that you should come to Hebrew classes.' I went home and said, 'Peter Kellner says that I should go to Hebrew classes. His mum runs them in the old church in Marsh Lane.'

'Very well,' Mum said.

So I went to the old church and Mrs Kellner started to teach me Hebrew. I remember very clearly how she taught us the sound of two of the letters that looked a little bit like a seven. One has a dot above the seven, the other has a dot in the middle of the down stroke.

'How do you tell the difference?' I asked.

She said, 'When a football lands on your head, you say "Oh!", when a football lands in your tummy, you say, "Oooh!" That's the difference.'

I enjoyed the Hebrew lessons, and I liked Mrs Kellner very much. And for two or three Sundays I went with Peter Kellner to the synagogue.

When Bubbe and Zeyde came over, Zeyde couldn't believe it. He laughed and laughed. 'Michael's going to *cheder*!' (Hebrew classes, pronounced 'kayder'). I guess the bitter arguments about religion from before the war turned my cheder outings into a joke.

Once the Hebrew class went on an outing to Chessington Zoo. The mothers of the cheder kids said that we could all go off on our own, and meet up by the entrance at four o' clock. At least, that's how I heard it, so I did just that. I loved the zoo, but when I got back at four o'clock they came running towards me, shouting 'Where have you been? We've been looking for you for hours!'

I reminded them that they'd said we could go off on our own. So I had. And they started shouting all over again: 'You weren't supposed to wander off on your *own*! You were supposed to be in your *group*. Everyone else was in their *group*. You were the only one not in your *group*. Just think: you've ruined everyone's afternoon.'

I was furious. As far as I knew they hadn't said anything about groups. I never went back to Hebrew Classes.

Years later I asked Harold, 'Why did you let me go to cheder? You disagreed with that sort of thing.'

'You said you wanted to,' he said.

Back to 1960: Ronnie's wedding was going to be the *gantse magilla*, Harold said – the full thing. However, the day didn't go entirely smoothly.

At the service, Harold had one job: he had to stand one side of Ronnie, while the bride's brother stood the other side. He then had to pass the ring to Ronnie. The day was hot, and sweltering under the *khuppe*, the canopy where a Jewish wedding ceremony takes place. It was the big moment: Ronnie stepped forward, Harold started to give him the ring and Ronnie fainted. He gave way at the knees.

Bubbe – who saw the world as a series of crises – cried out from her wheelchair. Someone rushed over to console her. The rabbi seemed worried about how the service could carry on. Harold and Ronnie's brother-in-law improvised. They picked Ronnie up and propped him between them for the rest of the ceremony. As Harold put it, he was 'out of it' for the whole thing. Afterwards, Bubbe was inconsolable about Ronnie: 'It was a lovely wedding. A lovely wedding. Such a shame he missed it.'

Then we went to the poshest place I had ever been to. It was somewhere in the West End, in an underground banqueting hall. You couldn't tell from the front, though. It was just a door on the street. But inside there were mirrors and chandeliers and hundreds of guests, people from the bride's side I hadn't seen before, of course. The room also filled with people from Bubbe and Zeyde's side I had never seen before either. Great-uncles and great-aunts, cousins and second cousins: Isakofskys and Goldmans. The only ones I knew were Zeyde's brother, Hymie, and his wife, who lived in Hackney a few houses away from Bubbe and Zeyde.

One of these relations looked different to the others. She was related to Bubbe, but wasn't wearing the sort of clothes that everyone else was wearing. She had a red scarf on her head and large gold hoops in her ears. Mum told me who she was, but sadly I've forgotten. Afterwards Mum said, 'See, I always told you. There's gypsy in me.'

After the wedding, we visited Ronnie and his new wife in their new home in Kingsbury. The house was like all the houses my friends from school lived in. Harold said that the cheese cake was the best cheese cake he had ever tasted, real cheese cake, not that 'strange confection' you can buy in supermarkets these days. And then it stopped: we didn't see them anymore. Bubbe died, then Zeyde. Mum went to the funerals, saying that she preferred it if I didn't come.

Reading and rereading the leaflets I picked up at Aldermaston, I gathered there was an outfit called the Young Socialists who met upstairs in the Railway Tavern, Wealdstone. I decided to go. There, we sat on stacking chairs and I listened in silence as the others talked about Gaitskell and Greenwood. Gaitskell had lost the vote, then he won the vote. Greenwood had lost the vote but he was running again, and we had to support Greenwood.

I realised very quickly that people were talking in short-hand – which was fine, Mum and Harold did the same. Names of people stood for a set of beliefs or ideas, and if you weren't tuned in, you could get lost very quickly.

Greenwood I knew. Well, I didn't actually know him, but I had seen him at the head of the Aldermaston March, and of course I knew his daughter. Well, again, I didn't exactly know her, but there had been the whole 'Boy!' thing.

Some people in the room were for Greenwood, some for Gaitskell. Some Young Socialists were young. Some were old. I recognised one of them: Dave, who had been a school friend of Brian's. He was very intense in those days, walked fast down school corridors looking at the floor, with his hair bouncing on the top of his head in time with his walk. Now as he debated he grew more agitated.

I had seen him getting agitated before. When he was a prefect in the sixth form he had put me on detention. I had thought, how daft is this? You might be over our house later, and we'll be sitting round the table, Mum will have put a gigantic bit of cheese on the table, a loaf of bread and a jar of pickle and a fruit cake, and it'll be all 'Can you pass me the butter?' Brian liked him. Dave stood as the school Labour candidate in the school General Election of 1959, and Brian had been his 'agent'.

In the Railway Tavern meeting, the Greenwood vs Gaitskell argument went on for a while, until suddenly Dave stood up and said that the branch had been infiltrated by Trotskyists from the SLL. There was some hissing but Dave carried on, getting red in the face and his hair bouncing as it did when he walked down the school corridor and gave me a detention. He said there was no place for the SLL in the Labour Party, so the vote we were about to take was invalid.

Because at this stage I hadn't mapped Brian Pearce's road through Trotskyism, I whispered to the person next to me, 'Who are the SLL?'

'Socialist Labour League.'

It answered everything and nothing. Were they in the room? If so, which ones? And if they were in the room, should they have been in the room? If they shouldn't have been in the room, why were they in the room? I didn't know anyone to ask apart from Dave, but he was busy speaking and, anyway, he was pretending he didn't know me.

At this point, things got complicated because Dave said they had to vote on whether there should be a vote, because, he claimed, there were people present who shouldn't vote. People went over to the person chairing the meeting and whispered in his ear. The chairman then said that Dave could move an amendment. Dave said he didn't want to move an amendment, we needed to move to the vote. Someone said, 'Which vote?'

A guy stood up and said that we were all grown-ups – which wasn't strictly true, or if it was it shouldn't have been, because this was a meeting of the Young Socialists, not the Grown-Up Socialists. In the end there was a vote in favour of Greenwood, but I wasn't sure what that meant. I didn't know who was going to be told about the vote, nor whether any of these votes were going to go to Greenwood or not.

At the end, I got up to leave and two people came rushing towards me with a newspaper, which I bought, and they said they hadn't seen me at the branch before. Was I new to politics? I said I wasn't, and they said OK. I slipped away, and would have been interested in talking to Dave but he'd slipped away even quicker.

I decided not to go back to the Young Socialists. Dave went on to be famous, influential and much-loved, especially when talking about the environment. I suspect he didn't go to many more Young Socialist meetings either.

I did continue going on demos: anti-apartheid marches, and one at the US airbase in Ruislip, and then, when the Committee of 100 and Bertrand Russell announced that they were going to sit down in Whitehall in protest against a US submarine coming to Scotland, I went with Mart and we sat down. However, I got up when the police announced that they would start arresting us: I lost my nerve, and walked to the pavement. In the end, the police didn't arrest anyone that day, so afterwards I felt I had let people down by getting up.

By now Harold was teaching at a training college in West London. He had a whole new set of stories to tell: there was the time he was sitting eating lunch and the lecturer next to him was in full flow talking about someone he didn't like, and referred to this person as 'the nasty little Jew', and then he noticed that Harold was sitting there and the lecturer stopped talking.

When Harold got to the end of this story, I said to him, 'What did you say?'

'I asked him if there were any other kinds of little Jews,' he said.

The scope of our parents' friendships was widening. Students and teachers started coming over, and some would stay at our flat over a whole weekend. I loved this. I stayed up late at night with them talking and arguing. My favourite was Bertrand, the French 'assistant'. He wore thick dark-green glasses, had dark eyes, very tanned skin, a black chin-strap beard and a straight fringe. He loved to hear stories about my friends at school, and he told us stories about his parents and the village he came from in the Ardèche. He was desperate for me to teach him swear words, and we spent hours turning words from one language into literal but meaningless words in the other.

He had picked up that in the nineteenth century, street kids were 'urchins', so we started to talk about children as '*oursins*' even though it means sea-urchins and only sea-urchins in French. Soon our word for my friends and me was the *oursins*.

In the end Bertrand said that we should come out and camp at the *camping* in his village. He said there were loads of things to explore. 'You people like the walking and the hiking and there are the caves and the rivers where you can swim, it will be *formi* (great), and it will be full of *oursins* that you can play about with.'

So that summer Brian, Mum and Harold and I went to Laurac in the Ardèche and camped in the municipal campsite, in the middle of the village, next to a viaduct and a concrete swimming pool full of dark green water. Brian went off for two weeks camp-hiking with some friends, while Harold and I spent hours playing quoits. He complained that it was so hot he could only eat yoghurt. I practised underwater swimming in the pool that was growing darker and darker by the day. No one else swam in it. They said that seeing me slip beneath the surface, disappear completely, and re-emerge at the other end, was unnerving.

Harold started reading bits from the usual array of guidebooks he bought for our holidays, and told us that the region was famous for chestnuts and silk worms. The chestnuts are turned into purée and the silk was woven by the silk weavers of Lyon, who were, he said, revolutionaries. He suddenly remembered the song from his Yves Montand record of French traditional songs about *les pauvres canuts* (the poor silk-weavers), and walked about being Yves Montand, singing '*Qu'est-ce qui passe ici si tard? Compagnons de la Marjolaine ...*'

One night Bertrand said that they were going to show a Brigitte Bardot film in the village. When we arrived at the place, it turned out to be in an open courtyard, with washing lines loaded with shirts, pants and trousers running to and fro between the houses. Someone had set up a projector at one end and was showing the film on an old whitewashed wall at the other end. People of all ages gathered, ancient grannies dressed in black, children playing in the dust, couples, old guys drinking.

The film was *Les Bijoutiers du clair de lune* (The Night Heaven Fell), and people carried on talking and messing about even after it started: the storyline was that a young handsome bloke was having a thing with a married woman, and ended up killing her husband. But instead of staying with that woman he starts up with Brigitte Bardot, which involves them lying on a beach and her taking all her clothes off; all this projected on the old wall in front of the washing with the ancient grannies dressed in black, the kids playing in the dust and the old guys drinking. As this sort of thing (I mean Bardot taking her clothes off) didn't happen in English cinemas – not even in films that you had to climb through the window to see – I was first of all amazed by Brigitte Bardot and then amazed that there was no reaction in the courtyard. The audience went on watching, chatting and playing. I felt a little embarrassed that Mum and Harold were watching nearby, with Bertrand. I thought they might be embarrassed that I would be embarrassed. But after it was over, Harold was killing himself laughing over some other moment in the film altogether, when the husband furiously calls the young bloke '*une ordure*' –'scum'. With a long-extended last syllable, *orduuuuure*, it became his favourite term of joke-abuse for the next forty years.

After that Bertrand told me that the Laurac fête was coming and between me and him, he was very interested in the *oiseaux* (another literalist gag like *oursins*, *oiseau* meaning bird). Over the next day the bunting went up. A team of men shouted and swore at each other as they put up the platform. The bars filled up, and old ladies sat at the tables overlooking the square as folks arrived. A band of accordion players and guitarists played a kind of music I hadn't ever heard before – jazzy, folksy, jiggy – and people danced and clapped. Bertrand said that I should dance too. I said I can't, and don't. He was appalled. He disappeared from sight.

The next day, Mum said that she was really fed up with Bertrand. He and his brother sponged off their mother, she said. The poor woman did all the shopping, cooking and cleaning, while they just sat about drinking. And on the night of the fête he was running after girls at least ten years younger than him.

'He's a superannuated teenager,' Harold said.

Bertrand was fast shrinking into a non-person. Brian knew about this process: he had spotted a pattern. There were people who our parents were dead keen on at first, until all of a sudden something happened or something was said and they became non-people. Brian was right. After the fête, Bertrand was never seen again.

Before his exit, he told us about *les gourdes*. These were pools in the rivers where you could swim. They were deep and cold, and I started swimming underwater across these too. I had read Jacques Cousteau's *Silent World* and was fascinated by underwaterness. Any water as big or as deep as a pool or a river gave me an urge to get in, to plunge under the surface. I didn't have goggles but I loved staring into the foggy space there. Maybe I'd skip being an actor, or a *Beyond the Fringe*-type comedian; I would become an aqualung-ist, gliding about on the sea bottom a hundred feet down ...

Some French kids my age came to the gourde that we went to, and one of the boys in their group, holidaying at a Colonie de Vacances, had the underwater bug too. I got the impression that I was being set up for a challenge – and took it. Soon we were diving in and swimming to and fro underwater in the gourde.

While we mucked around, Mum and Harold talked to their *moniteur* or supervisor, called Maurice. The kids were all from Lyon, he told them, the children of workers at a big chemical plant. Harold was excited to hear that workers in France had won these Colonies as part of their labour conditions. After all, the workers' annual holiday didn't match the school holiday, so the Colonies offered a refuge for their children ... or was it more than that? Something educational?

After a day or two of these swims at the gourde, Harold said that he had been speaking to Maurice, who he had discovered was a teacher and a Communist, and they'd arranged for me to stay at the Colonie for the last few days of our holiday. I couldn't understand how, given that they'd left the Communist Party (and given how irritated he was, say, with Malc's mother Peggy for 'talking like a gramophone record'), someone like Maurice could appear like an instant hero of progress and socialism.

Despite being younger, I was in a tent with boys of fifteen, sixteen and seventeen. I quickly understood that far from being the happy-go-lucky group they appeared to be at the gourde, they were deeply into being pissed off. For a start, they had to spend the afternoons making 'lavender bottles': going into the fields, picking lavender, bringing it back, cutting it into lengths, bunching it, bending back small groups of stems and plaiting red ribbons through them. I joined in. We made hundreds. Then there was the float, a giant swan assembled from thousands of white paper roses. Each rose you constructed by cutting a strip of paper, cutting slits into it, scraping the paper so that it curled and then rolling it round so that it looked like a rose.

Lavender bottles and paper roses took hours; but rebellion was in the air. It was led by a tiny guy who hadn't grown, called Ben Zizi. His parents were Algerian, and he was not only a leader, he was a comedian. He had perfected take-offs of French or American pop stars, where he would strike a pose, run his hand through his hair and flop his hands about as if he was rocking the joint. His big mate, Gaudemarre, seemed much too old to be at a Colonie. He looked like the old-style Teddy Boys I had seen on the streets when I was six or seven: greased-back hair, quiff at the front flopping forward. The enemy was Blanchard, who Ben Zizi, Gaudemarre and the rest despised because they said he was a *mouchard*, spying on them and snitching to Maurice.

The workers started their protest by slowing down the output of lavender bottles and white roses. In response Maurice delivered a long lecture. He said that they were a bunch of *je m'en foutistes* (don't-give-a-shit-ists). He was amazed and disgusted. Did they have any idea of what their parents had been through, the sacrifices and dangers they had experienced? And how hard they had fought to win the right for their children to attend a Colonie de Vacances? 'And now all you're doing is sitting around moaning.'

Back in the tent, Ben Zizi said that they were going to go on strike; was I with them or against them? This was tough. For a start, could you strike against a Communist? And then, I was a guest. How could I strike against somewhere that had invited me to stay?

They went on strike. No more lavender bottles. No more paper roses. Mouchard went off and talked to Maurice. I sat with the workers.

Then Madame Goetschy, the camp director, came to the tent and she gave a long speech too. She was not much taller than Ben Zizi, and wore plastic sandals and a black swimming costume all day and every day. In fact, I got the impression that everyone had come to this Colonie with one swimming costume, one T-shirt, one pair of plastic sandals and one pair of flip-flops. Neither plastic sandals nor flip-flops had arrived in Pinner yet.

Madame Goetschy was less confrontational than Maurice, who sat in the camp office fuming. Madame struck a deal: we would put on a play for the younger (and seemingly tiny) kids at the Colonie. Maurice was hauled back and he proposed that it should be *Don Quichotte* (*Don Quixote*).

Maurice explained that the only props would be stuff that we could find around the camp: brooms, colanders, plates, soap containers and the like.

They put *Don Quichotte* on at night, lit by the outside bulkhead light and lanterns, next to a big fig tree, while the cicadas chirped from the trees further off. Mum and Harold came. Don Quichotte (played by a guy who looked like Jacques Tati) charged to and fro on his broomstick. My striped towel was part of his outfit, and he wore a colander for a helmet. Ben Zizi was Sancho Panza. The little ones squealed and screamed.

Afterwards Harold said that it was bloody terrific. He said it was one of the best bits of theatre he had ever seen. And Brechtian. Mum loved it too, and said how magical it looked with the lanterns, sitting out, and all the children laughing so much.

'Maurice is one in a million,' Harold said, 'and what a rapport he's got with them.'

'Mm,' I said.

I didn't tell him about the strike.

The next day, on the way back to England, we stopped by a river and I jumped in. A girl was there with her grandmother. She jumped in too. As we swam in the river she started talking to me. When we got out, we sat and talked in French; her grandmother said that she should ask me for my address. So I gave it to her. She gave me hers. Mum asked me if I wanted to stay longer. Did it seem like I wanted to stay longer? I said, no, that was fine. A month or so later, I got a postcard and on the card it said (in French), 'Sun, water, an hour by the river …' and a signature.

I tried to imagine cards and letters between us in the future, stretching away over months, and I thought how she would want to come and stay with us and wasn't our family too odd for people like her to come and stay, she wouldn't like it, and I would have to stay with her and her grandmother, and I didn't know what to say on a card or a letter anyway. But then, wasn't she dark and beautiful? Yes, she was … but was that enough? Were looks like hers reason enough to write? Oh, hang on, what if it was just a tease? I didn't like it that it was her grandmother who got her to ask for my address. For days and weeks after, I tormented myself over whether I would or wouldn't write, and the moment where the grandmother got her to ask for my address kept bothering me.

It reminded me of how in *Great Expectations* Miss Havisham sits behind Estella, telling her how to treat Pip.

I didn't write back.

# 8

## Eng. Lit.

My father said, 'I think it would be best if you did your Eng. Lit. with me.'

Translated, that meant: instead of my doing the English Literature O-level course at school, he would inform the school that he would teach me at home, but would they please enter me for the exam anyway?

The school agreed. So every Sunday morning, after breakfast, Harold would say, 'Right, let's start,' and we walked out of the kitchen, down the corridor to the front room, closed the door and spent two hours going through *Henry IV, Part 1*, *The Trumpet-Major* and *The Pageant of Modern Verse*: Gerard Manley Hopkins, D. H. Lawrence, A. E. Housman … Each week he set me an essay to write and a few pages in 'Brooks and Warren' to read – real title, *Understanding Poetry* by Cleanth Brooks and Robert Penn Warren.

'Brooks and Warren' was one of his US Army text books but, more than that, I now know it was an early example of the 'New Criticism': close textual examination of poems, one by one, with no reference to the poet, to any of the circumstances of the poem's making, or to the poet's life or times. Instead, this criticism was a method of looking at how parts of the poem produced 'effects'. There was no means of checking whether these parts of the poem really did produce these 'effects', on yourself or on anyone else. You just learned that they did. You might say things like 'the repetition of the short lines in the poem have the effect of breathlessness' but you nearly always got that from the teacher before you had noticed anything breathless going on. Then, no matter how much you described these different parts, the method said, in the end (and in the beginning) the parts form a whole and the meaning is made through the whole acting on us.

The best poems, this method of criticism said, were those where there is a unity between all the parts. The job of the critic (or the pupil being examined) was to find the parts and show how they combined to make a meaning. This 'proved' that the poem was good. Where there wasn't unity or where some or all of the parts were unoriginal or sentimental, this proved that the poem was bad.

In Britain, this came to be called 'Practical Criticism', thanks to a book of that name by I. A. Richards, and led to the introduction into the exam system of the 'unseen', the question on English exam papers about a poem you haven't seen before. All this produced a routine that examiners, pupils and teachers had to go through when faced with a poem. It became the thing-to-do-with-a-poem. (Other things you might do with a poem, like, say, work out a dance routine to go with it, would not be the thing-to-do-with-a-poem.)

Ironically, as Harold knew only too well, this method started out from a theory that was very different from this idea of fixing the one and only true meaning. It was originally meant to encourage people to feel free to come up with a wide variety of thoughts about what was going on in a poem they hadn't read before, or couldn't 'fix' as being by a 'great poet', and whether they liked it or not. Instead, however, this critical method once geared up for exams treated poems as if they were plumbing problems.

There was another irony. This particular apprenticeship in poetry was very much at odds with the kind of Marxist literary criticism that Harold had read in the 1930s and '40s, which claimed it should place poems and poets 'in history', in relation to the circumstances of their production. And yet more irony: the 'Brooks and Warren' criticism came largely out of America, and for him, out of his time in the US Army, of all places.

Moving on to Shakespeare, all his emphasis was on what he called the 'process'. The play was a play, which meant its meaning came out through scenes being enacted one after the other. It did not come through 'character'. In fact Harold despised 'character'. I was banned from using the word. The job he set me instead was to describe 'interactions'; the dynamics of staging; how protagonists talk about each other; how one scene contrasted with the one that came before; what it felt like being an audience to these processes; and the outcomes of all these aspects – were they expected, unexpected?

He set me to read *The Fortunes of Falstaff* by J. Dover Wilson, a scholar who, Brian pointed out looking at the shelves in our house, had written a book called *What Happens in Hamlet* which was longer than *Hamlet*. Harold seemed surprised that this was a joke. 'Of course it's longer,' he snapped, which made it even funnier.

With Thomas Hardy's *The Trumpet-Major* he repeatedly steered me away from talking about the people in the novel as if they were people. It's not them who are making the choices, he said, it's Hardy deciding what to do with them. A scene wasn't in the book because the characters had reached this point in their lives, but because Hardy had something to show or say. So the scene when Bob comes back and uses up all the eggs in one go was there because Hardy wanted to contrast Bob with the Trumpet-Major, not because Bob likes eggs. As with the Shakespeare, he tried to divert me from talking about Bob's 'character' towards questions about why such a scene was in the book.

The great example that he always came back to was the moment in *Far From the Madding Crowd* when Troy shows off his fencing skills with Bathsheba. 'It's not just what it is,' he said, 'it's symbolic of how Troy enthralls Bathsheba. Hardy creates a believable symbol.'

Did I understand all this? I don't think so. What's odd is that I remembered these conversations all the same. It was as if they hung about in my mind, un-understood or only partly understood, until subsequent reading and talking turned them into sense, a sense that, later, I could take or leave.

I was never great at finishing homework on time, and I wasn't going to change a habit just because it was my father. He had always been a homework-harrier – more of Brian than of me – winkling out of us when we were 'loafing', delay-ing or getting behind. He was very good at stop-and-search methods: 'Did you finish that essay on the development of the Rhine as an industrial waterway?'

Or it could be more root-and-branch than that:

'What work have you got coming up?'

'Oh, nothing much.'

'What kind of nothing much?'

'Oh, stuff ... you know ...'

'No, I don't know.'

'History, I think.'

'History? What history?'

'I think it's something to do with, er ... the Chartists.'

'The Chartists? The Chartists? That's really interesting.'

'Is it?'

'So? What are you doing with the Chartists?'

'It's something to do with "How Chartism Failed".'

'Failed? Failed! Chartism didn't fail. Come here, let me show you ...'

Then, exactly the thing that you desperately hoped wouldn't happen, happened. He went to the shelves, got out a book – A. L. Morton's *The People's History of England*, or one that fitted the topic exactly, like *Why Chartism Didn't Fail Even Though Michael's History Teacher Says It Did* – flicked through to the right page and said, 'It's all there, lad.'

And a week or two later he would be there ready to dole out an on-the-spot verbal fine, if we hadn't finished the essay now subtly renamed 'Why Chartism Failed – or NOT'.

'Getting on with things' was like a great life force inside him and, perhaps more than anything else, he longed for us to take this force from him. We could see him at it. He might be sitting with Mum doing anything from solving the world's problems, talking about tent poles, or doing the crossword with her, when he'd look up and say, 'Must get on, Con.' And he would go off and put his nose in a book. As Mum would say: 'Once your father has got his tukkhes on a chair with his nose in a book, he doesn't do anything else for hours.'

But what was this 'getting on' thing? What was he 'getting on' with? Lectures, talks, articles, marking, reports and, round about now, his Ph.D.

Many people who have this kind of work to do at home, turn a bedroom or a corner of the home into a study. They go off to the study to 'get on'. Instead, Harold did all his reading and writing in *mit' an' d'ring*, in the middle of everything. If we were in the kitchen, he did it there. If we moved to the front room, he followed us and did it there. He trailed after us with his notepad, papers and books, perching them around him on the arms of chairs, on the edges of tables, mingled with ashtrays, toast, pickle jars and the *Radio Times*. Mum said that this was because when he was a boy he was worried that his mother was going into hospital.

And the getting-on wasn't silent. It was a noisy getting-on. As he read another book – *The Meaning of Narrative* or *The Narrative of Meaning* – he would call out: 'The man's a *meshuggener*!' (crazy), as if we knew the man he was talking about or understood what the man was saying. In between there was a lot of tutting, clapping of hand to forehead, slapping down of book, and loud scribbling.

Sometimes he would exclaim, 'Let me read you this,' and without waiting for us to say yes or no, he would read out something from one of the books, or something he had just written. He didn't notice whether we were busy talking about something else, reading something else or dreaming of something else. Ghostly figures from the world of linguistics, literary theory and philosophy loomed up into our kitchen and front room, as heroes and villains, without any of us knowing exactly why. New swear words appeared: 'behaviourist', 'reification', 'mechanistic', interspersed with the old Yiddish ones. One moment someone could be 'reductive' and the next '*verkakhte*' (literally someone who's shat his pants, but metaphorically meaning 'pathetic').

Now Harold was taking classes with a mythic figure called Halliday, and we started living with the spirit of Halliday. Halliday says that language is behaviour. Halliday says that every linguistic act is a choice. Halliday says that you don't know what language is until you learn another one. And a mythical term came to dominate mealtimes: the 'T-unit'. Some mommza had invented 'T-units'. Harold's PhD was going to be a demolition of the T-unit. I had no idea whether this was an important thing to do or not. I didn't know if there were or were not thousands of people somewhere duped by the evils of the T-unit that Harold was going to save them from, but I think I trusted that he would.

In the meantime, I had my Harold homework to do. And, come Saturday night, I usually hadn't done it. I thought, tomorrow morning at ten he'll be saying, 'Right Mick, let's get on', and we'll sit down and he'll say, 'Essay!' and I won't have it! What then?

So, sometimes as late as ten or eleven at night I would start on the Harold essay. This is fine (or just about) when the place you deliver the essay is in school or college, physically separate from your bedroom. My problem was that my bedroom was open and available for Harold to visit, inspect, and probe – and he did. He would walk straight in, go over to my desk, pick up books, open school exercise books, examine my shelves. Not only would he be marking my essay, but he could, if he wanted to, know how I was 'getting on' with it before it was finished. I think most of the time he pretended not to notice that I wasn't getting on. And I pretended that I didn't know that he pretended that he hadn't noticed. But at about ten o'clock on the night before the lesson, it was that much harder to keep the pretence going.

The door opens. I'm sitting at the desk. He strides towards me.

'What you up to?'

I do speed-shuffling with the books so as to disguise 'D. H. Lawrence: Internal and external narration in "Snake".'

'Not doing tomorrow's essay, are we?'

'Just finishing off some stuff with it … Had a kind of extra thought thing that I thought I'd kind of add on … sort of … sort of stuff …'

Amazingly, sometimes, just sometimes, this kind of bleary fobbing-off fooled him. Or he pretended it fooled him. Or – most likely – Mum had said, 'Leave him alone, he's tired.'

*My father Harold's mother and father, Rose Hyams and Morris Rosen.*

*Morris in a garden in the US in the 1940s.*

*Rose on the* SS President Harding, *1922, returning from the US to live in England with (from left) Harold's sister Sylvia, brother Wallace, and Harold.*

*Harold in his US Army uniform (1945–1947).*

*My mother, Connie Isakofsky, and Harold.*

*Connie, aged seventeen.*

*Harold and Connie getting married with Rose on Harold's right and 'the Westons' on his left.*

*Harold, top left, with one of his classes at Greenford County School in the early 1950s.*

*Harold in his US Army jeep in Germany.*

*Tyneholme Nursery*

*Seventh from left on the back row: me. Fourth from left: Mrs Gallagher.*
*Fifth from right: Hornby Teacher.*

*Miss Goodall's Class, West Lodge Primary, Pinner, 1955/56. I'm at the very back. Brian Harrison is in the second row of desks from left, 3 desks back, on the left.*

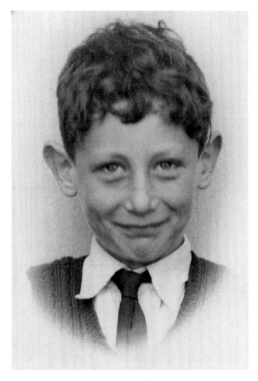

*Me, aged 7.*

*Harold and me at Butler's Farm, Skenfrith, Monmouthshire.*

*Malcolm Aprahamian and me at a Woodcraft Folk Camp, in the Mendips, Somerset.*

*Unter den Linden, Berlin 1957, Mum and me with the 'Hitler' woman on Mum's right and the woman's friend.*

*Len Goldman and me.*

*The International school. Top left, Peter Wright; my mother wearing scarf with Dorothy Diamond to her right; second to Mum's left, Len Goldman; possibly John Holly below Len. Rose Betts is five people to Mum's right.*

*Brian and me with 'the girls' in the Thuringian Wald – no names remembered.*

*On far left, me; four people to my right, Peter Wright; then Mum, yawning.*

*Harold and Mum in Grosvenor Villas, Rickmansworth.*

*Mum*

*Bernard (behind) and me at 'La Chaise' on the Ardèche River, 1962.*

*Taking a break from building a ford. Standing from left: me, Henri, [???], Bertrand, Pink Nicolas. Crouching from left: Lucien le blond, Bernard.*

*The girls at the Colonie in fancy dress.*

*Me at Harrow Weald County just before moving to Watford Grammar School, 1962.*

*The beer bottle sketch, Oxford Playhouse, 1967(?).*

*Chief Weasel, in the gardens at Magdalen College 1968(?).*

*'The Plebeians Rehearse the Uprising'. Left to right: Stalin (!), Nicholas Arnold as Brecht, Donald Macintyre, me, Mike Gwilym, Chris Barlas.*

*Oxford. Me trying to bend the notes on my 'harp'*
*(harmonica).*

*'Proctors must go now.'*

*The March 1968 anti–Vietnam War demo.*

*Harold in 1995.*

It wasn't only through 'Brooks and Warren' that the Englishness of Eng. Lit. was Americanised by my home life: in 1962, *Catch-22* came out. Like *Great Expectations*, the connection between what was described in the book and Harold's own life must have been so powerful that the only thing he could do with it was let it bubble out and affect anyone within earshot. What he did was read it out loud. He didn't even mind if we got up, went out the room and came back in. He just carried on. It was his own US Army life re-enacted, turned into fantasy, inverted, ridiculed and shared with the world. When he read it to us, he seemed to know these people: Yossarian, Major Major Major Major, Orr, Lieutenant Scheisskopf ('It means "shithead", you know'), Milo Minderbinder and the rest. And as he did the accents and called out the military voices, he had two years of his US Army service to call on. Sometimes he shook his head as he read, saying, 'This is what it was like.' Or, 'I knew ten Milo Minderbinders ...' It felt like a gift that Joseph Heller had given personally and specially to him. A new set of quotes and phrases came rushing into our lives:

> 'Yossarian? What the hell kind of a name is Yossarian?'
> 'It's Yossarian's name, sir.'
> Lieutenant Scheisskopf had the facts at his fingertips.

That interchange became a portable comment on any name we heard on TV, radio or in conversation – whether it was a rare or common one.

'Robertson? What the hell kind of a name is Robertson?' one of us would say, and straightaway the other would come back with, 'It's Robertson's name, sir. Lieutenant Scheisskopf had the facts at his fingertips.'

It was a rerun of what he'd done with *Catcher in the Rye* a few months earlier, reading it to us in American accents. The moment when Holden Caulfield leaps on to the college jock, Stradlater, and tries to pin him down – and fails miserably – was one of many that survived into our daily lives: 'Liberate yourself from my vice-like grip.'

In son-dad wrestling, of which there was an enormous

amount, 'Liberate yourself from my vice-like grip' (in an American twang) served us well.

Quite apart from the great power of these two books, there was a way in which they worked another kind of subversiveness. As I went through the Eng. Lit. system over the next few years, these American novels, characters, scenes and quotes were so strong in my mind, they undercut the implied superiority that came with the whole package of 'English literature'. They were, if you like, a cultural resource in my head which the more they were ignored by education, the more attractive and necessary they were to how I saw myself.

Meanwhile it was war at school. Not seriously violent; more like a permanent state of surreal contest. Before 'Happenings' had happened, a group of us discovered how to do Happenings. When the newspapers were full of a US preacher claiming that it was the end of the world, we took it 'seriously' and created a mass End of the World ceremony on the school field. Within seconds it attracted hundreds of younger children. We wailed and prayed on the cricket pitch, with our trousers rolled up and our uniforms turned inside out. A squad of teachers rushed out of the school. It had to be stopped. The head teacher's end-of-term comment in my report said, 'I don't mind him celebrating the end of the old world, I just hope he enters the new one a little more soberly.'

The routine of school dinners was livened up one day by a guerrilla banquet: we arrived at our packed-lunch table with bags full of gear. At the signal, we spread several of the old school trestle tables with tablecloths, napkins, candlesticks, glasses and framed pictures of the Queen, and we started toasting the Duke of Edinburgh and Winston Churchill. The deputy head furiously reminded us that the job of a grammar-school pupil was to conform.

We invented the chair-moving task. We chose a classroom, picked up all the chairs and walked round the school with them. We 'explained' to on-duty teachers or prefects that the caretaker had asked us to do this. He hadn't. We walked on and on, in a long line, all round the school, the playground, across the field, back into school, round the school, each of us with a chair telling people, 'We're moving these for Mr Tyndall.' It became a slogan to 'explain' a lot of things.

Someone invented a kid called Furd, who was supposedly in class '5C'. Kids less well known than me deliberately committed a crime so that they could be given a detention and could then give their name as 'Furd 5C'. Furd 5C would naturally not turn up at his detention and so, according to the school rule, had his name read out in a whole-school assembly the following day. Solemnly, the duty teacher would announce to the whole school:

'The following pupil failed to attend Tuesday's detention: Furd 5C.'

Loud cheers.

'No need for that.'

I was glad to have got that small part in *Much Ado About Nothing*, but when Mr Jones tried to sort out rehearsals, a problem cropped up. He wanted me on Tuesdays.

I said, 'Sorry, I can't do that night, sir.'

'Why not?'

'I do detentions on Tuesdays.'

It got to the point where there weren't enough detention days for me to be doing detentions on. Our reports came in a book (with the number of detentions served clearly marked), which had to be returned to the school after our parents had signed. I drew a detention graph on the back of mine, to show the increase. Harold refused to sign my report and threw it across the room. Mum did it later – secretly.

At lunchtimes, a group of us met up on the school field to re-enact the previous night's TV programmes, dramas, series or game shows. One of them was an adaptation or extension of H. G. Wells's *Invisible Man*. In the real series, several actors perfected ways of looking as if they were being attacked by the transparent hero. Day after day, we worked fanatically at trying to imitate these, practising being tripped up, wrestled to the ground, hit in the face or bundled into cars with no one actually doing it. We took it in turns to stage a fight in front of the others, rather like street dancers take turns to show off their moves. If you had asked me at the time if there was something I was really proud of, I would have said, yes, it's acting like I'm being beaten up and killed by the Invisible Man.

After a session where we barricaded the doorway of one of the rooms with chairs, a teacher we didn't know was summoned to deal with us. He said, 'You lot think you're hard, don't you?'

I didn't think any of us thought we were hard.

'I've got some guys who really are hard. My scout troop. We're going to challenge you lot to a night hike. We'll see just who is hard, won't we?'

It was all a bit odd. Why would we want to go on a night hike racing against his scout troop? Apart from me, none of us ever walked anywhere. Running through the boys who were there, our interests were: Thelonius Monk, clarinet, impasto (and gouache), Magritte, the Church of Christ the Scientist, the Invisible Man, Chuck Berry and *Wisden*. Even so, we agreed to it, so we met at Princes Risborough Station in the Chiltern Hills, at ten o'clock at night; there was about eight of us, and eight of the hard guys from the scout troop. The teacher gave us some clues to follow, and the first pair back here in the morning would be the winner.

I was with Dave. Somewhere in the middle of a beech wood, at three in the morning, Dave said that he had a bellyache. I said, 'Just keep walking, it'll wear off.' Dave had once asked me if ever when I was sitting on the toilet, did I get a pain that was so bad, I could hardly breathe? I said no.

We kept going.

The clues were OK, till we got to the last one. The sun was coming up over the escarpment, and the clue was something to do with 'Old Joe'. We couldn't do it. I said, it doesn't matter, let's keep going.

We kept going.

We were first back. We had beaten his hard guys. All of them.

He looked at our clues. 'You haven't solved the last one,' he said. 'It's the Old Red Lion pub.'

'Why?'

'Lyons tea rooms,' he said, 'Old Joe. Get it?'

I looked at him. He was smiling.

I said, 'No, I've never heard of Lyons tea rooms as Joe Lyons. I just know them as Lyons.'

I thought of the Lyons tea room next to Trafalgar Square where we used to go after demos. The smell of damp hot woollen jumpers, stacks of banners and posters leaning against the walls. I thought of the one at South Kensington Tube station where Harrybo and me used to go after we had been with the Junior Naturalists' Club at the Natural History Museum, behind the old mahogany doors where no one else goes, drawing birds and mounting pebbles onto card using PVA glue and cotton wool. No one had ever called them Old Joe Lyons.

'If you haven't done the clues, you haven't won, have you?' he said.

After about half an hour, the first pair from his team arrived, two guys a couple of years older than us.

'How did you get here first?' they said to me and Dave.

I shrugged.

'Wow, you must have really legged it,' they said.

'They haven't won, Derek,' he said, 'they haven't got all the clues right.'

He looked over their clues sheet. 'You're the winners.'

I looked at him saying this, his eyes gleaming. It hadn't worked out as he wanted it to. We weren't supposed to have walked it faster than his best two. But he had found a way to make it look like we weren't as good. I did my heavy eyelid act.

A couple of the poems in *A Pageant of Modern Verse* and the 'Brooks and Warren' were 'Bat' and 'Man and Bat', by D. H. Lawrence. After I had read them, I had a strong sensation of wanting to write a poem like that. It felt like an itch I had to scratch. This didn't come totally out of the blue. Poetry had status at home. My parents read it, they listened to poetry on the radio, they taught it. They played gramophone records of Dylan Thomas reading his poems, Richard Burton reading Dylan Thomas, the Barrow Poets performing medleys. At the same time, Mum had started to present BBC Schools Radio programmes about poetry, in the same slot occupied by C. Day Lewis, Ted Hughes and Jimmy (their friend and hero from the London Association for the Teaching of English, who always called Harold 'Johnny').

Both Harold and Mum had many poems or parts of poems hanging about just behind their eyes, and verses, lines and phrases would appear at odd moments. Mum liked Stevie Smith, and would sometimes say in a cracked Stevie Smith sort of a voice and for no immediately obvious reason, 'I am a cat who likes to gad about.' Brian and I spent some time perfecting absurdly exaggerated performances of Burton doing Dylan Thomas's 'Fern Hill', or our own version of '"Is there anybody there?" said the traveller, knocking on the moonlit door'.

A colleague of our parents, Geoffrey Summerfield, had started coming to the house to ask them about some school anthologies he was producing, which went on to become *Voices* and *Junior Voices*, two of the most influential poetry collections ever to have gone into schools. These two volumes combined poems with hundreds of photos and pictures. The poems in the collections were the most diverse that had ever been seen in schools – ranging across many countries, many styles, taking in poetic utterances as well as poems: speeches, proverbs, and translations of folk songs and oral poetry from all over the world.

When Geoffrey came over, he brought bundles of poems and pictures that he laid out on the front room floor. He, Mum and Harold walked round them, picking them up and putting them down, arguing about them. Sometimes he came over with his tall, spidery-legged editor at Penguin Education, Martin Lightfoot, and it became clear that this was much more than just another collection of poems.

This was a group of people who wanted to change the way poetry was taught and read in schools. Geoffrey wrote a handbook for teachers to go with the collections, in which he laid out ideas about encouraging children to make their own connections between poems, and then again between the poems and the pictures. He wanted the books to be reasons for children and teachers to want to read and write poetry on their own, but also to branch off into other activities, too:

drama, painting, photography and dance. It wasn't that there weren't primary schools and lower secondary schools doing this sort of thing. It was that these books would make it easier for them to do it. And with all those pictures, the poems were presented in what was then a new format.

'You've got to hand it to the Leavisites,' Harold said, meaning Martin Lightfoot who had been taught by F. R. Leavis: 'When they put their weight behind something like this, they never let go.'

'Old Leavis' – someone Harold never met, we never met or even saw – became another ghost in the home. It was nearly always 'Well, at least old Leavis says …', meaning, as far as Harold was concerned, that while this abrasive literary critic was wrong about most things, at least he did something right on this occasion. This 'something' was what, though? He liked books? He read books? He was good at getting other people to like books? He believed in 'the book'? There were no answers to these questions, other than that 'old Lightfoot' (who wasn't old) was a result of something good about 'old Leavis' (who was old).

So when I read 'Man and Bat' and 'Bat', it wasn't a surprise that I thought I would like to have a go at this. I was standing in my room, a moth flew in through the window and I ducked. Lawrence's poems came to mind, and I thought, I could write about a moth, in the way that Lawrence wrote about a bat in 'Man and Bat'. I called it 'Moth'. Not 'The Moth', or 'A Moth', or 'A Moth in My Bedroom', just 'Moth'. That was my tribute to Lawrence.

I borrowed the plot line: dark brown thing comes into your room, you scrabble about trying to kill it, you think about it, The End. I also borrowed Lawrence's technique of being in the moment and outside of it within the same poem. One moment Lawrence describes what it was like at the moment of contact with the animal, and the next he's reflecting on himself and how he reacted – a little bit like someone watching a film of himself and commenting on it. I did the same with my moth. It was published in the school magazine:

Last night a moth was frantically drumming
Above me on the cold hard window;
His browns and ochres merging and blurring
Above me on the cold hard window.
I cursed.
He had intruded.

The poem goes on to say how it flitted and rushed around
me, then landed on my bed; I trapped it in my pyjama-jacket:

In his own dim thick world he lay there twitching
I threw him out
Crushed and dry

By this time, I had also read *Sons and Lovers* and *Lady
Chatterley's Lover*, which was published openly, legally
and excitingly for the first time just as I hit puberty. One kid
brought it to school covered it with brown paper and wrote
'Black Beauty, by Anna Sewell', on it. We all read his edition
of *Black Beauty*.

In both books, I remember Lawrence's narrators and characters seeing things in desperately intense ways, and – as with
the bats – being disgusted. One thing bothered me about *Sons
and Lovers*: it was when Paul starts to dislike Miriam because
of the way she looks at flowers. Why, I thought, would you
break up with a girlfriend because of the way she looks at
flowers? Not that I had a girlfriend.

Many, many years later I arrived at a school to perform my
own poetry show, and the deputy head was jigging about and
pointing at himself, as if I should have known who he was.
I didn't. He told me: he was Paul, the brother of someone in
my year, and somehow or other at that time we had ended
up working together at a builders' supply depot in the holidays. We had found a way to skive off by hiding in an open
attic space above the stores. But then we thought we'd chuck
things from where we were hiding. This deputy head – as he
was now – also reminded me that it was him who had got the
sack for chucking stuff, not me. I said I was sorry but I really
couldn't remember it at all.

I did my performances and then he joined up with me again and said that one class had been writing poems and wanted to show them to me. Would I come and have a look? He took me into the room and said, 'Is there anyone here who would like to show Mr Rosen their poem?'

There was a child on the front row doing that shooting-up of the arm thing and squealing, 'Me, me, me' like they're desperate for the toilet.

'Carol,' he said, 'show Mr Rosen your poem.'

The girl put it in front of me. As I read it, I thought it looked really familiar: the sound of it, the subject matter, the way it was written. I got it: here was a kid who had been reading 'Snake' or 'Bat' and was imitating the style.

I said, 'I don't want to be rude, but this looks familiar; have you been reading any poems by someone called D. H. Lawrence?'

'No,' she said.

'What did Mr Rosen say?' the deputy head asked.

'He says it looks familiar.'

'There'll be a good reason for that,' the deputy head said, and he whipped out a copy of our school magazine from the time we were there. It was open at 'Moth'. The poem the girl had shown me was also called 'Moth'.

'I got Carol to copy out your poem from our old school magazine.'

I was embarrassed that I hadn't recognised my own poem, and embarrassed that I had so obviously written something that was really not much more than a parody of 'Man and Bat'. The deputy head could see that I was embarrassed.

'That'll pay you back for the time you got me the sack,' he said, 'gotcha!'

The next writing moment came when I read James Joyce's *Portrait of the Artist as a Young Man*. I read it several times, and then read the first draft of the book that was published as *Stephen Daedalus*. I became fascinated by how writing was something you could do by creating a style which of itself said something about who was talking or what was being said. In the case of these books, it was the way Joyce evoked the age of a young person by expressing it in the style of speech. When he's very young, the style is that of a young child, and as he gets older the style ages with him.

I thought I would like to have a go at that, and I wrote some sketchy pieces about my earliest memories, of sitting on the beach at Margate when I was two. I wrote in short, disjointed phrases like a child who didn't know how to say whole sentences. I was rediscovering stream of consciousness, fifty years late.

So now I had two styles, Lawrence and Joyce. Then one week Harold and I looked at Gerard Manley Hopkins and I went off on a Hopkins trip, trying to write poems packed full of alliteration, with words shifted from their usual life as adjectives or nouns and turning them into verbs, or turning verbs into adjectives and nouns. I walked about saying, 'I am soft sift in an hour glass.'

I decided Hopkins was a revolutionary. In order to say new things about seeing everything in the world in a new way (it didn't matter to me that this was to do with God), he created a new way of writing. And it was violent. The kind of language that I had to use in exams, sentence after sentence after sentence, was no use to Hopkins when he was writing poems. He had to break words out of their usual habits and put them into runs that were nothing like usual sentences: 'dapple-dawn-drawn Falcon, in his riding of the rolling level underneath him steady air ...' There was a jazzy, jerky feel to it, with moments of regular beat, broken a second later into something quicker with more syllables squeezed in to fit the same beat. I wrote about trees or wind or sea or rivers as if I was Hopkins.

And there was Carl Sandburg. Geoffrey Summerfield had included some of Sandburg's free-verse, 'proletarian' poems, full of dialogue, proverbs, slang and everyday sayings, in *Voices*. Harold had many more in one of his US Army books. I liked the way some of Sandburg's poems were lines of conversation. These lines, it turned out, were part of an experimental work, a montage of hundreds of these conversations and popular sayings collected together to give an oral impression of America, called *The People, Yes*.

I started to think that I could do something similar in

relation to our family life: I could assemble lines of family dialogue as short poems, and then another and then another and then another and together they would make a totality out of the parts, without any of the D. H. Lawrence-type commentary.

So now it was Lawrence, Joyce, Hopkins and Sandburg. I realised that poems could be at war with each other, one saying, 'This is the way to get to the essence of a moment, a place, a person or a thing!' And another poem butts in and says, 'No, you're wrong, this is the way to do it.' And it could be your own poems being at war with each other in that way … as if there was a struggle going on inside your own head.

At this time I gave 'being Jewish' a second go. I had already opted out of school assembly on the grounds of being an atheist. Harold had often explained that the 1944 Education Act included a clause that allowed parents to withdraw their child from assemblies and religious lessons; I had said to him that that was what I wanted.

'That's so that you can get to school late, without getting a late mark for it, is it?' he said, but he wrote the letter anyway and I sat in an empty classroom reading a book, being an atheist instead of going into assembly. Then Mr Adams, the maths teacher, 'came out'. He said he was Jewish – which none of us had guessed – and offered a morning Jewish assembly. Dave said that he was going to it. I said I wasn't interested. But then a girl I fancied said she was going and would I come, and I thought this would help my chances. So it wasn't exactly an interest in Judaism.

Anyway, from then on, I sat in the Jewish assembly each morning as Mr Adams said the prayers in Hebrew. At lunchtime, some of us who went to this Jewish assembly discussed why and how we didn't believe in God – as if our atheism had nothing to do with the fact that every morning in Jewish assembly we said and did things connected with belief. I don't remember anyone at school, or at home, asking me the simple question: 'If you're an atheist, why do you go to Jewish assembly?' If they had, I would have been forced to admit that it was so I could improve my chances with Lynne Fridkin.

It worked.

Her father was a hairdresser, her mum was the receptionist at the hairdresser's, and Lynne worked at their salon every Saturday morning. The first time I went to her house there were people from the hairdressing trade talking about perm mixture. Her mum was telling a disaster story:

'You've never seen anything like it. It's all over the garage floor. I said to Harvey, "Whatever you do, don't put it in the garage." He says, "What's wrong with the garage? We don't want it in the house." I said to him, "You go ahead, Harvey. Do it. Don't mind me. I'm not here." So all the tins of perm, he leaves in the garage. In the morning they've burst. All over the floor. "I'm not clearing that up," I said. It was green. It had all gone green.'

Harvey was sitting there, nodding and smiling along, like he had done really well. After they had finished the perm story, they turned to Lynne.

'So this is Michael?'

'Yes, Dad.'

'What does he want to do in life?'

'Ask him. He's standing there.'

'Lynne says I'm to ask you what you want to do in life?'

'I didn't say that you're to ask him. I said: if you want to know, ask him.'

'I will. Thank you, young lady. Michael, what do you want to do in life?'

'Maybe I'll be a teacher.'

There was an explosion. 'A teacher! What's the good of that?'

'Dad, don't embarrass yourself,' Lynne said.

When she came to our house, Harold said, 'Ah, Lynne Frumkin.'

'My name's Fridkin,' she said.

'That's what I said,' Harold said.

'Where did you get all these pictures from, Harold?' she said.

'Some from Germany.'

'How can you bear to have things in the house from Germany?'

'We manage,' Harold said.

At school, Lynne said it was fine if people knew we were going out together, but that didn't mean that we had to do that thing other couples did, walking round together all the time. She said she wanted to be with her girlfriends.

When a new boy arrived, her girlfriends got very excited. He was brought in front of the class. He had done so well at the local sec. mod. that he was going to do O-levels with us, they said.

Lynne's girlfriends mouthed to each other across the room, 'Is he Jewish?'

They looked at him. 'Yes,' they mouthed back.

This made him eligible. Though it was complicated. One of Lynne's girlfriends was Jewish and the other two wished they were.

The teacher announced the boy's name: 'Sunil Das.'

The girls stared at him again.

It turned out his parents were Indian, but it didn't seem to make any difference. The Jewish one went out with him. Multiculturalism 1961.

It wasn't the only way we mixed. Dave came in one time and said that his dad had told him a joke:

Harry and Solly meet in the street.

'How's things?' says Harry.

'N-n-not s-s-so g-g-good,' said Solly.

'Why's that?' says Harry.

'I w-w-w-ent for a j-j-job as a n-n-news annnnn-nouncc-c-c-cer at the BBBBBBC.'

'And?' says Harry.

'I d-d-d-d-dn't g-g-g-get it.'

'No?' says Harry.

'N-n-n-n-o,' says Solly, 'th-th-they d-d-d-on't t-t-take, Jews.'

Chris (who wasn't Jewish) came in the next day and said that he had told his Mum the joke. He said that his Mum listened very carefully and then said, 'But he wouldn't have got the job anyway.'

Lynne and I went to see the film of *West Side Story*. She got teary, but I said that I thought the bloke playing the lead, the one who sings, 'I once knew a girl called Maria' was awful.

It wasn't the right thing to say. She said she was really disappointed in me for that. I found that I was disappointed that she loved Helen Shapiro and 'Walking Back to Happiness'.

Me with Blind Lemon Jefferson, her with Helen Shapiro: it wasn't going to work.

By spring, things were getting tense. In June were the big exams, the first public exam we had sat since the Eleven Plus. Teachers talked of struggling to squeeze the whole syllabus in on time and then, in the blink of an eye, we camped out for days and days in the school hall with no company other than small pink printed sheets headed 'University of London'. We sat in rows, grimacing at each other as we coughed up piles of facts.

In English Language lessons we had spent day after day after day doing 'adverbial clauses'. We had charts and matrices of the different kinds of adverbial clauses: adverbial clause of time, of condition, of concession … And each with their different subordinate conjunctions: when, after, because, if, although, etc. 'Just learn those,' Mrs Turnbull said, 'and you'll be able to handle the grammar question.' We learned them.

We went into the exam, and flipped the paper over to see what the grammar question was. It was a question about adverbial clauses. Quick, check the subordinate conjunction. But it was a word – a phrase, actually – that none of us had ever seen heading up a subordinate clause: 'no matter'. What? 'No matter'? What's that? Our heads popped up and we looked at each other, eyes questioning. We shrugged. Hours and hours of lessons on adverbial clauses, and none of it any use for this question. I thought, hadn't someone once said that exams are about what you don't know, rather than what you do know?

In the German exam, I wrote an essay about liking the theatre and how I had just seen *Chips with Everything* by Arnold Wesker. I couldn't think of the German word for 'chips', so I wrote, '*Kartoffel mit alles*' – potato with everything. Wesker wouldn't mind, I thought.

In Eng. Lit. I wrote about how the dynamic of the relationship between Hal and Falstaff changes. I was so absorbed by that, I pretty well wrote the whole paper on that one question instead of the three they asked for. No problem I thought, they'll be so impressed by the Hal–Falstaff job, it'll make up for the short answers to the other two.

Geography – I'd spent days learning the towns and cities along the Rhine from Basle to Rotterdam, in the right order. A question on the towns and cities along the Rhine didn't come up.

Biology – I had learned to be a red corpuscle. The question every year was, 'If you were a red corpuscle, starting out from the right auricle, make a list of the blood vessels you go through on your way to your foot and back to the right auricle.' Every year it changed slightly so that you might, say, start out from the left ventricle and go to your hand. Yep, that one turned up. Sorted. I loved being a red corpuscle.

At the end of a whole week doing nothing but write answers to questions in exams, I decided that I would take up race-walking. I would train for the School Sports Day mile-walking race. I was an athletics fan, spending hours watching it on TV, and going to White City to watch national championships. I had discovered that I couldn't run fast enough or long enough to compete; I could chuck a discus reasonably but not well enough; now, suddenly, I found that walking very fast was something I could do. I practised every day. I did it in bare feet, sometimes with a competitor number sellotaped to my bare chest.

Almost everyone I knew – and many I didn't know – thought that because there's all that bum-wiggling, I was doing it as a joke, another one of our Happenings. But I wanted to win. I thought of Abebe Bikela, who had won the Rome Olympics in bare feet. Oh, that moment as night fell and no one knew who would appear first at the head of the marathon … and out of the dark came this lone figure! Who was he? Which country? What? An Ethiopian? How come? That's impossible. But it wasn't impossible. It was a glorious and total arrival onto the world stage. Maybe I could be Abebe Bikela.

Come the day, I lined up with the previous year's champ, and several guys all older than me. Round we went. Then I did something I had seen the world's greatest athletes do:

wait my time behind the leader, and then with about 300 metres to go, pull out, overtake and hold the lead.

I won. I surprised myself by how much it mattered to me. So I could be Abebe Bikela! Mr Richards the maths teacher came over. I thought he was going to congratulate me. He looked at my bare feet.

'Last time I saw feet like that was in Malaya,' he said.

I told Mum.

'He didn't mean he was on holiday there, you know,' she said, 'we'll never know the atrocities they got up to there …'

As summer approached Harold said that he had been writing to Mme Goetschy and, if I wanted to, I could spend the whole summer on my own at the Colonie de Vacances.

It sounded like a good idea to me.

There was just time for a class trip to Stratford and Coventry before the year ended. In Stratford, Lynne and I hired a boat and rowed up the river and down the river.

'I like looking at you rowing,' she said.

We all went to Coventry Cathedral and on to the Belgrade Theatre, to see *Arms and the Man*.

On the coach back, as it got dark, we snuggled up together. She took hold of my hand and put it down the back of her knickers. As we all got off the coach, I said that maybe this was the last time I would see those of us who were leaving school, as I was off to France in the morning.

'Shuttup, Rosie,' they said.

I was right, though.

# 9

<hr>

# In the Colonie

Brian was off and away. I hadn't seized my threshold moment yet. OK, I had 'run away' to the Aldermaston March, and one Easter I did walk across Wales with Malcolm and without parents. In the end I didn't jump, I was pushed.

'Six weeks,' Harold said, 'you'll come back speaking like a French kid.'

He was going to take me to the station, Mum had to go to work. I said goodbye to her. She didn't leave and went upstairs again. Harold waved his hand at me.

'What?' I said.

'Your mother. Go to her. She's upset.'

I thought, what's she upset about? I've been away before, Brian's been away before. Perhaps now, thinking back, it was because I was the child who came after. The thing she never spoke about.

I went to her but she said not to fuss. I thought maybe it was the journey that worried her. I would have been the only sixteen-year-old she knew who had to get themselves from London to the Ardèche by themselves. I was the only one I knew, too. Harold thought he'd make it safe by going through the journey as if it was a list: 'Dover, Calais, Gare du Nord, metro to Gare de Lyon, Valence, and Aubenas where you'll be met by Madame Goetschy.'

I wondered if the same crowd would be there, Ben Zizi? Gaudemarre? Maurice the *moniteur*? Alice the Moroccan girl? Mercedes the Spanish nun (not really, she just looked like one)? The guy who played Don Quichotte who looked like Jacques Tati? Blanchard the *mouchard*?

There had been a lot of details. Money – into the maroon Moroccan-leather wallet.

'What's he going to wear, Harold?'

'He's got his anorak.'

'It's too small. It doesn't fit.'

'Alright, alright. He can wear mine.'

His? The East German anorak? Bought in Weimar. Or was it in Berlin? I'd always loved that anorak, with its soft tartan lining, and the outside: faded blue. I loved that faded blue.

'And you can put your wallet in the front pocket. Then you'll know where it is.'

I also made sure that I had shorts and flip-flops. Not that it had been easy convincing Mum and Harold that I had to have them.

'What's the matter with your sandals?' Harold had said.

'Yes,' Mum said, 'your sandals are good. Everyone's wearing sandals like that.'

'They're not. No one bloody wears sandals,' I said.

'So they call you pisher!'

He meant: what was the worst thing that could happen to me, if I wore sandals? They might call me 'pisher' – a pissy little person, a nothing. In its own way, it was a very protective thing for him to have said. It forewarns and forearms. At the end of the day, being called a pisher is not the worst thing that can happen to you.

Even so, I really couldn't bear to spend six weeks with the kids asking me why I wore strange things. I wanted to fit in.

Paris was hot. The Gare de Lyon was hot. Look at me: sitting in a cafe in Paris on my own, drinking *jus de pomme*. Out of everyone I know at school, I must be the only person who's ever drunk *jus de pomme*.

At three minutes before midnight, the train groaned out of the station. I stood in the corridor, looking out at the waves of apartments and I thought of the thousands and hundreds of thousands and millions of *petits pois aux lardons* sitting in their tins in the cupboards of the buildings. I thought of how school had ended with that coach trip and the sad snogging, and then I realised that I had left the anorak with the wallet in it, hanging from a door handle in the cafe.

Madame Goetschy was there waiting for me at Aubenas Station, still in her swimsuit. 'It's going to be a good Colonie this year,' she said, and reached up to hug and kiss me.

'*Comme t'es grand*, Mike. You're so tall. One metre eighty? Everyone's here. This year we're in a different place. You can't drive there. Or walk there. You have to go over the river. You have to pull on wires.'

She took her hands off the steering wheel and pulled on imaginary wires. I slid about on the metal floor in the back of her 2CV van, bouncing up into the mountains. 'Oh, it's marvellous you've come. You remember Alain? Maurice?'

I said I did, but there were several people called Alain and Maurice ... which Alain? Which Maurice?

Next to her on the front seat was Jules: dark Jules, dark skin, black hair, long muscular neck. Wasn't he the kid that the others said they didn't like, and there was a fight last year when someone said that his bed smelt of wee? At least that's what I thought they said. 'Pisse-en-lit,' they called him, though it also means 'dandelion'.

We drove down a long path alongside a river till we got to the wires. Yes, this year we would reach the Colonie on a chariot with wheels attached to wires slung across the river, like a little wooden cable car, but open to the air. Everything and everybody would get to the tents, the shower and the cooking blocks by chariot. There was no other way. The 2CV van couldn't go any further. We stopped on the bank.

'You stand on the platform of the chariot and pull on the wire, Mike,' they said, and I could see from watching Jules that as he pulled on one wire, the chariot's wheels ran round above his head, locked on to the other wire.

'*Vas-y*, Mike,' Jules said, and Mme Goetschy laughed.

I climbed up on to the chariot. Mme Goetschy watched from my side of the river; a baby, Mme Goetschy's sister and Jules watched from the other. In the middle it lurched and invited me into the water below.

Over the next six weeks I grew to love the lurch of the chariot above the river, in the shadow of limestone cliffs. We would get up onto the chariot in twos and threes: me, Ben Zizi, Maurice the footballer, Pink Nicolas. We would sit on the hot wood of the chariot's platform and dive or fall or bomb off it into the water below, over and over. We would sit with our legs dangling, looking down; then, we would nudge and shove till we plummeted, flailing about in the air before smacking into the river. We could pull the chariot fast and allow ourselves to fall off the back. You could hang like a cowboy on a cliff edge. You could take off screaming or roll off dead as if attacked by the Invisible Man. I tried to explain the game we played at school but my French wasn't good enough to make it sound funny. We sat there in the heat, pulling our sunburnt skin off and dropping the flakes into the water, and talked about the girls in the Colonie, one by one, every single one of them.

I rehearsed a phone call home. How would I tell them about the wallet, the money, and the anorak? It was a disaster. I rang and told them about how the journey was fine and Mme Goetschy had been there to meet me and this year we were in a place by the river, surrounded by high limestone cliffs. That it looked like Lone Ranger country, and you can only get to it by a chariot over the river ... and that I left the anorak at the Gare de Lyon.

It was Harold on the other end, and I could hear his look. It was the one he did when he looked across the room at Mum. And I could hear her look back. And her doing the lips. If things weren't going well, they were both very good at lip work. It was soundless tutting.

'You're not to worry, lad,' he said, 'If it's lost, it's lost and we'll claim it off the insurance. You make sure you have a good time. And write. Tell us how it is.'

Mme Goetschy said that she rang the Gare de Lyon, but nothing came of it.

It felt as if I had lost my last link with home. I was on my own now. And there was a difference about everything in this place. I had never felt before that what was going on around me, every minute, every day, every week was so different from what I was used to. There were times when it would start to feel as if I would never get back.

Ben Zizi hadn't grown at all. I thought this year he looked like a Brazilian footballer. I noticed now that he collected guardians, though the oldest and biggest boys treated him as their leader. Gaudemarre – the Elvis look-alike – walked around after him saying on his behalf, '*Qu'est-ce que c'est ce boulot?*' which means something like, 'What's the point of all this bloody work?' and, '*Ça va, la foule?*' meaning how you doing, you lot? Maurice the footballer was strong and loud and spent hours doing keepy-uppies and singing, '*Allez l'O.L., allez l'O.L., allez …*' in honour of Olympique Lyonnais, their local football team.

One day Ben Zizi announced that he was in love with Françoise. He said she was a '*belle femme*'. (Woman? Weren't we boys and girls?) I thought she was beautiful too, but didn't say a word. This year the girls wore a bikini that was like a swimsuit with the middle cut out. Apart from Nicole, that is, who wore what looked like three tiny blue hankies.

The girls now poured Nivea cream on their arms and it was beyond belief to think that as they sat on the stones by the river, their nakednesses were only seconds away. I had never been so close for so long to so many girls wearing so little. And they all seemed completely and calmly uninterested in any of us. They seemed to love each other instead, smoothing in the Nivea, washing and brushing each other's hair, painting each other's nails, moving each other's bikinis and T-shirts into the right place, swapping jeans, telling each other what they looked like from behind, going off to the shower-room, locking the door and laughing in there for hours.

This year our *moniteur* was Henri who told us he wasn't *croyant*, not a believer. He had his beliefs, but it was a long story. For the whole six weeks he wore the same pair of leopard-skin nylon boxers. He looked like a Brazilian footballer, too. As he lay on the army bed next to mine in our tent at siesta time, I looked at his hair. It looked like black lamb's wool.

Alain, the trainee electrician, rigged up a record player outside and strung the wires up between the fig trees. Ben Zizi played Les Platters, four Americans who sang 'Sixteen Tons', and Ray Charles who sang 'Georgia' and 'Let me hear

you say "Yeah!"'. Ben Zizi sang them all, and when he did his
Ray Charles act, he said that I ought to be able to sing them
too and then went off to jive with Françoise who stood at
least two foot taller than him.

Henri interrupted Ray Charles with the jazz cabaret big-
band singer, Léo Ferré, who sang about a girl called 'Jolie
Môme'. Another song was about Paris, which Ferré didn't
call Paris. He called it 'Paname' which seemed strange, and
yet another was about a hard-labour prison camp on the Île
de Ré where the men sang 'Merde à Vauban' – shit to Vauban,
who, Henri explained, was a famous seventeenth-century
civil engineer. What?! Why would you have a modern song
in which prisoners shout 'merde' to a seventeenth-century
civil engineer? Ben Zizi rocked his head back, hung out his
little hands in an Elvis way and sang, 'Let me hear you say,
"Yeah!"'

I thought, why am I more interested in Ferré than in Ray
Charles? He thinks I should be raving along with him and
instead I'm trying to figure out 'Merde à Vauban'. And not
getting it.

Our brown tent with its rows of army beds stood on an old
vine terrace where a few vines still grew. Maurice the footballer raided the branches, grabbing at bunches, holding them
above his mouth and running his lips over the grapes like a
camel would, pulling them into his mouth. He laughed at me
trying to eat them one by one, spitting the pips out. 'Just scoff
them, *bouffe-les, bouffe*,' he shouted at me. Even grape-eating
was different here.

Our tent smelt of armpits, grit, hot canvas and old comic
books. Nothing covered the ground apart from a few old
duckboards, *caillebotis*, so our beds slowly worked their way
into the earth. When we lay on our backs on the beds in the
afternoons, we'd watch the sweat well out of our chests. Above
us, we looked out for the beasts that ran over the roof: the
plastic-green praying mantis stalking the flying grasshopper
with her egg-laying spike sticking out of her rear; horseflies
as big as your thumb, planning their next plunge into your
arm, ants climbing the struts and tent poles. We used to argue
over what they were for, these beasts, and concluded that

they aren't 'for' anything. They just are. And they're all bigger than the ones at home.

One day someone left a lit cigarette end in the rubbish basket while we were hanging round the river. Dark Jules spotted the smoke while he was coming away from the shower-block. As he ran towards the tent, it burst into flames and he started yelling and yelling. He got there first and ran into the tent, grabbing our stuff and throwing it out into the vines. By the time we got there, he was crying and choking. Soon Henri the *moniteur* had a chain set up and we were hurling water at the burning canvas. As I helped I wondered if the praying mantis was being burned at the stake.

Mme Goetschy's husband arrived at the camp and said the boys from Berliet would be joining us. Berliet was the truck factory, and these were the sons of workers there. That was why Lucien *le blond* turned up with two tall white boys, 'Bernard et Bertrand'. Lucien was white too but that was because he was nearly albino, white wavy hair that he was always patting, and white hairs on his legs. He said he had won the Marseille under-seventeen 200 metres race. He wore running shorts all the time and once when we camped out by the side of the river, he danced in front of everybody singing Little Richard: 'Balamm bamm tutti frutti oh rooty' in a French accent. I thought of back home and couldn't remember any of our mob living so much with the sounds of Ray Charles, Little Richard and bands like The Platters in our ears.

Bernard et Bertrand said that they were the kinds of guys who like to do things. Ben Zizi looked round at everyone with a meaningful, big-eyes look. Bernard et Bertrand would have to learn that in this Colonie, when it came to doing things, they should talk to Ben Zizi first.

Bernard et Bertrand organised the building of a ford across the river. Every day, we lifted rocks and boulders and laid them in the river. I had never sweated like it. M. Goetschy came and stood on the bank. He was short, stocky and tanned with slicked-back silver hair and a growly, tangy sort of a voice. He saw my back under the sun.

'*Jolie écrevisse!*' he called out. Nice crayfish.

We moved hundreds of stones. Henri loved it. He called us *bagnards*, hard-labour convicts, and sang 'Merde à Vauban' at us.

Gaudemarre said, '*Qu'est-ce que c'est, ce boulot?*'

One day, after moving more boulders, we sat down to eat. Henri said something about how maybe even if we finished the ford, we probably wouldn't be able to get cars over it and Bernard exploded. He shouted about how it had been his idea and that we hadn't helped him, and Henri had never taken it seriously and we could all go fuck ourselves and he was fucked if he was going to eat the rest of this shitty dinner. Bertrand (who was the only French boy in shorts I had ever seen who wore socks at the same time) put his arm round him, but Bernard shrugged it off. I said, if he wasn't going to eat his ice cream, I would have it and I pulled his plate over and sat eating his ice cream.

Ben Zizi, Gaudemarre, Pink Nicolas, Maurice the footballer and Alain the trainee electrician looked at me. I went on eating the ice cream. Ben Zizi said, 'That sort of thing's not done, Mike. We don't do that sort of thing.'

I was on my own again, different.

Henri said we were going to go for a night walk on the plateau. We would hike until dawn.

We crossed the river in the dark, but there was enough light from the stars for us to see ourselves in the river. Up on the plateau we saw glow-worms and toads. We alerted dogs and got lost.

Once we had got ourselves beyond lost, more like abandoned, Henri said, 'We'll make a fire.'

So we made a fire and we cooked *petits pois aux lardons*. Henri stamped on the flames to turn the wood to embers and threw strips of meat on them. We sat under a bluey-white roadside light, eating. Nicole and Giselle said we would never get back to the camp and everyone asked Henri if he knew where we were.

'No,' he said, '*allons-y*, let's go.'

A few hundred yards down the road, he stopped. He got out his torch and shone it on a stone by the side of the road. There was a list of names. Henri said that there had been a village here and during the war the Nazis had killed all the men of the village.

'Bastards,' Ben Zizi said.

'*Dégueulasse*,' said Alain the trainee electrician. Disgusting.

We stood in the road. A big sky above us, one or two trees scattered around, Henri holding his torch still and the men's names caught in the light. I tried asking Henri what had happened but he couldn't speak and Ben Zizi put his hand on my arm to shut me up.

I was meeting moments like these again and again where I understood something but not everything: things being said or done which seemed to have a background that I couldn't reach.

At the mid-point of the six weeks, this sense of difference grew to where I realised that I needed my fellow campers more than they needed me. They knew each other well, their mothers and fathers worked together, they shared the same schools and streets and shops. They talked about meeting in the market, going to football matches together, hanging out together in the street. I wanted to be them, I wanted to be part of them, but I was infuriated and saddened that I wasn't and couldn't be. There didn't seem to be anything they wanted from me: there wasn't anyone English they wanted to know about, there weren't any English words they wanted to hear. They didn't need to know why I was annoyed that the deputy head had said that her notion of the ideal grammar school boy was one that conforms, nor why the ones who didn't agree with her were the ones who liked Charlie Parker and Blind Lemon Jefferson. They didn't really want to know about the Invisible Man, and no one cared about mile-walking or Arsenal.

Once someone asked me something about Prince Charles and I said that I was a republican, which set up a running gag: every other day someone sitting near me would sing 'Godde seve ze quinne' and leap to their feet. I said that I thought Brigitte Bardot was *incroyable* because the previous year I had seen her on the old wall with the ancient grannies and the toddlers playing in the dust.

'You know,' I said, 'they cut the naked bit out when they showed it in England.'

'Ah, that's you Anglo-Saxons again,' said Henri.

I wondered what the Anglo-Saxons had to do with it, them with their axes and Thor's hammer? And anyway, '*Merde, je suis pas anglo-saxon, moi, hein?*'

I kept trying to say that I wasn't the kind of English boy that they thought I should have been, but saying that seemed to make the difference between us even bigger.

There was a tree I found that I liked sitting under. A cicada laughed all summer there and the fat red ants worked on me and my feet. It stood on its own by the side of the stone path that ran from the shower block down to the river. There were times there, on my own, that I let myself think about the last day of school and what was going to happen to all the people that I had spent so much time with. One of us was off to be a fridge mechanic, one a travel agent, another was heading to art school; some were planning to be secretaries, or hairdressers, or students.

Lynne wrote to me saying that her parents wouldn't let her stay on at school, even though she was better than me at several subjects. Her parents said they needed her in the hairdressers but she said that she wanted to study, so they reached a compromise and agreed that she could study to be a secretary. She wanted to use her languages, so they said that she could train to be a bilingual secretary.

It all seemed too far away and nothing to do with me at this moment. So I wrote to say that I didn't think we should go on together. Maybe I was thinking, but didn't like to admit, that I didn't want to get into any more arguments about *West Side Story* or Helen Shapiro and 'Walking Back to Happiness'. It was my Trabb's boy moment, in *Great Expectations* when Pip is spotted being a snob. If I'd mentioned Helen Shapiro, Lynne would have said, 'It's just a song, Michael, don't make it more important than it is.' But even as I was writing to her, thinking that I was far away and in another world, I wasn't really in this 'other world'. I was in it but apart from it.

There were other differences working their way through the camp. I was beginning to understand that the boys from Lyon despised the people from the Ardèche as *paysans*, peasants. Local people worked for the Colonie, cooking our food, and gave us lentils every Thursday. The boys from my tent refused to eat it. 'Peasant food!' they said, 'food for peasants. Only peasants eat this stuff.' I loved it. Not just loved it, adored it. I ended up eating bowlfuls of it. They couldn't believe it. The *anglais* likes lentils. *Incroyable*. How was that possible? So, now I was the peasant.

Bernard et Bertrand (who came from Saint-Étienne, not from Lyon like the others) discovered that the old boy who looked after the place when the Colonie wasn't there made his own pastis, the liquorice-tasting drink. I 'discovered' it comes as brown in the bottle, but the moment it hits water, it goes whitey-green. The story went round that the old boy's pastis was like no other, none of your shop stuff like Pernod. Henri pretended he hadn't heard us whispering about it, and Bernard et Bertrand led a late-night excursion to raid the pastis. Everyone who went had some and we were soon grinning and giddy. Every sip of it was powerful. Bernard drank more than some.

In the morning we had headaches and Henri said that people who drink it die. It kills them. The old boy looked like he was doing fine on it. His grandson helped in the kitchen, and one day he said he had the key to the stores. A group of us followed him in there and there was a bucket full of apricot halves.

'*Couilles de singe*,' monkey's bollocks, he said, and the Colonie kids loved that.

He opened some bottles and they started drinking.

'Mike,' he said, 'I've got a special one for you.' He opened another bottle. 'Drink!' he said.

'No,' I said, 'it's a trick.'

Ben Zizi tried to reassure me. 'No, Mike, no no, he's not joking.'

I smelled it. 'It's vinegar,' I said.

They fell about at that. 'Mike said it's vinegar! No, it's *pinard*,' the slang for cheap red wine.

'No, it's vinegar.'

Every time I saw him after that, he would say, 'It's vinegar!'

I was getting used to this way of talking, *pinard* for wine, *flotte* for water, *godasses* for shoes … none of it French I had learned at school. Even the French was different here.

Every afternoon at four, no matter where we were – by the river, up on the plateau, walking to town, playing volleyball – it was time for bread and chocolate: a torn-off chunk of bread and six squares of *chocolat à croquer*, a strong, hard, plain chocolate. I started to love it and looked forward to that time of the day. How could something so simple taste so good? At home I had 'invented' honey and raisin sandwiches; now I had something else. I would ask Mum if she knew where we could find *chocolat à croquer* and French bread so that it would taste exactly the same. It would have to be exactly the same. If it wasn't exactly the same, it wouldn't be as good.

With ten days to go before the end of my holiday, M. Goetschy came to us and said that we were going to go on a canoe trip for several days, down the Ardèche river from Pont d'Arc to the Rhône. There was a buzz around the Colonie. I picked up from the chat that this was a big thing. Massive. I thought M. Goetschy meant canoes like kayaks, but a day later a truck arrived and we unloaded fat-bellied wooden canoes with single paddles. One of us would sit in front pulling while the one in the back had to pull and steer, with the same kind of single paddle.

I could see that this was all very, very important for him. It was serious training. He was being a real youth leader. I wondered if it was something to do with them being Communists – if they were Communists. Was there a whole agenda here for guys like him, advancing the working class through this kind of training? For hours and hours, he worked us on our river, shouting '*Appel!*' and '*Écart!*', teaching the one in the back to do what I thought only Hiawatha knew: how to paddle and steer a canoe on your own. Only boys could do this, he said, and Nicole spat into the river and said girls could have done it, *merde!*

Once the trip had started, we put the boats into the water

at Pont d'Arc, and fanned out over the river. 'We're paddling,' shouted M. Goetschy, 'under the biggest natural bridge in Europe, guys.' It arched over us, a limestone cliff with a gaping hole in it. I was with Bernard and we were the last in the line of ten red canoes pushing along on water that glittered in our face. We called out to each other across the river and our voices bounced down the gorge. It was stunning. More thrilling than anything I had ever done before.

At a site called La Chaise, we tried to handle white water with our paddles buried in the foam. At night we slept on thyme and smelt of it all through the next morning. We sucked Mont Blanc condensed milk out of tubes that looked like they ought to be full of toothpaste. Coming round one cliff, two naked women kneeling up in a canoe skimmed towards us. 'Keep your eyes on the river,' shouted M. Goetschy and he laughed into the air.

I couldn't believe these things were happening, and both wanted and didn't want Harold and Mum and Brian to be there to see me doing them. This was my stuff and I was proud of it.

Later we sat under the Cathédrale, a pinnacle of rock, three or four hundred feet above us. It rose in three distinct spires and we watched an eagle gliding between them. Bernard, giggling during his turn in the back, levered his paddle against a rock and snapped it. For the last five miles, he used my paddle and I lay in the belly of the canoe taking the sun full on. Lucien le blond cursed my luck.

And we reached the Rhône. We did it! We had canoed all the way from Pont d'Arc to the Rhône. We looked at each other as if we were heroes. M. Goetschy looked as if he had done a good job with us and for us. Now, more than at any time since the Colonie began, I felt that I had joined them. I felt less different.

When we arrived back at the Colonie, the girls seemed to know that they should be there to greet us, and they told us how brown we were and we showed them our blisters before they went back to their Nivea and adjusting each other. In the days we'd been away they had become even more beautiful, the way their arms reached forward and away from their bodies making a space that we were never allowed into.

I was never sure whose idea it was to invade their tent. Without any lavender bottles or flowers for a float to complain about, it was this year's revolution. It had to be secret so the plan was whispered. The idea was that we would come down off our vine terrace, cross the field and get down to the bamboo thicket by the river that sheltered the girls' tent. We would go after the evening meal, when the *moniteurs* sat in the office drinking wine and the mosquitoes and moths fried themselves on the purple killer light. They would think we were under the fig trees talking about Les Platters, but we would be flying across the field to the girls' tent.

'Are you with us, Mike?' they said.

I wasn't sure what I was with or what I was against. What were we going to do when we got there? What were we going to say that we didn't say when we were with them? But, since the canoe trip, how could I not be with them?

We crept away from the fig trees, along the vine terrace, and then across the field. There were about fifteen of us, hopping over the rocks and thistles, swearing under our breaths as our toes scraped the stones. We got to the bamboo round their settlement, past the washing-lines hung with their jeans and T-shirts. The light was on inside their tent but it was quiet. Not a sound. We looked at each other. What was the plan? That we would rush the tent? Then what?

Ben Zizi pointed to the path through the bamboo thicket and we tiptoed along it and just where it opened out in the space in front of the tent, we saw Henri and Mme Goetschy sitting in deck chairs waiting for us. '*Salut!*' Henri said. His face was lined with false smiles. 'What a good evening for a hike. You should have told me that you fancied going on one more before the end of the Colonie. We could have gone up on the plateau again.'

The irony was painful.

Mme Goetschy said it was sad, sad, sad. Soon everyone would be back in Lyon, back at school, the Colonie would be over. Let's not have a sad end.

Mme Goetschy saying this did make it sad, though. The

with what's going on inside you? Really? Really? 'Well, do you know what you could do? You could be a doctor.'

They looked at each other: it was a brainwave. Of course he would like to be a doctor. He would love being a doctor. And he would be so good at it. He would make a marvellous doctor.

'Let's talk to Chick.'

In a second, Harold was on the phone to their old Jewish ex-Communist ex-East Ender friend – and doctor – Chick, to find out about how to become a doctor. Within a day we were at his house, and Chick was explaining to us how there was some special route to being a doctor, involving Arts A-levels for two years and then Medical School. Once you were there, you did a special course that was like science A-levels but specially geared to becoming a doctor and crammed into one year; it was called 'First MB'. After that, you did what every-one does: 'Second MB' – anatomy, physiology, biochemistry. Finally you're allowed on the wards doing your 'firms', and you take your final exams. And you're a doctor. Easy peasy. I was getting carried along with this. A doctor? People respect you, they rely on you. You're knowledgeable about all sorts of clever stuff and because you know that stuff, people come to you for help. And you help them. And they're grateful. What could be better than that?

Chick then told Mum and Harold to go out the room, so they talked in the back room with Chick's Jewish ex-Communist ex-East End wife, Gertrude, who came from a line of East End doctors. Chick asked me about biology. I told him what I had said to Mum and Harold about the outside and inside and the secret code. 'Good, very good,' he said, 'I'll write you a reference.'

That's how I ended up applying for Medical School, and indeed, getting in. I had a place at Medical School. I was going to be a doctor. Mum and Harold were over the moon. Ecstatic. 'That way,' Harold said, 'you won't end up reading books about books, which is all I ever bloody do.' I got it: being a doctor was something sacred for him.

Then another change came lumbering over the horizon. estate agents below our flat closed and a new shop

canoe trip had been a high, and now we had ruined it. What did we think we were going to do when we reached the girls' tent? I thought, Gaudemarre and Maurice the footballer seem like guys who've spent years being told that they are the ones who spoil things. Come to think of it, hadn't I been told at school over and over again that I had spoiled things? Is there some kind of permanent way in which some of us are locked into spoiling the things that teachers and *moniteurs* do with us?

And then the Colonie was over. It seemed as if the oldest ones were the happiest that it was the end. They were desper-ate to get back on the streets of their neighbourhood.

In the coach back to Lyon, Nicole cried and cried but no one knew who or what she was crying for. She couldn't say. We looked at her. Coming down off the mountains, Maurice sang, '*Allez l'O.L., allez l'O.L., allez …*' for the thousandth time. Ben Zizi shouted that the coach was on fire. We looked down and the wooden floor was burning. There were flames round the bottom of Pink Nicolas' seat. The driver stopped the coach and pushed his way towards us. He stamped on the floor and the flames went out under his foot. He waved his hand and said it wasn't a big thing, '*pas grand-chose*'. Seemed like a pretty big thing to me.

As we got into Lyon, they started cheering like crazy. The place mattered so much to them, but not to me. I felt envious of their big homecoming. I was separate from them again. The coach pulled up under the walls of Gerland, the giant chemical works where their parents worked. Some of these parents were there waiting for them. Not Gaudemarre's, not Ben Zizi's. Nor Alain the trainee electrician's. Nor Maurice the footballer's. They were men now. I wondered if I was a man yet. No, probably not. I shook everyone's hand.

'Let's write,' we said.

Mme Goetschy said that she would take me to the station, the Gare de Lyon.

The Gare de Lyon? Lyon's Gare de Lyon? Yes, she said. Was this the Gare de Lyon you called to see if they had found my anorak? I asked. Yes, she said.

I felt again that I had trapped myself in my lack of French. I hadn't even been able to sort out which Gare de Lyon I meant. How typical. Yet another thing where I got the surface but missed the whole truth. It frustrated me that it could feel one moment as if I was 'getting' everything, and the next that I hadn't 'got' the bit that mattered.

At the station, she hugged me and kissed me and said that it had been a good Colonie. I nodded and nodded because I couldn't say it all. Of course I couldn't say it all, I thought. That's the point.

On the way home, I was thinking: this trip has made me into someone different. I don't know how exactly, but it must have done: I've been with people who don't fit with anything or anybody in London and I haven't spoken English for six weeks. I've been thinking in French. There are things that I only know in French. Apricot halves are now *couilles de singe*. You paddle a canoe using *appel* and *écart*. But I'm not French. I was different over there, too. And now, back home, with all that in my head, I'm going to be different again.

Brian and Harold were waiting for me at the station.

'In the end, you wrote good letters,' Harold said, 'we started to get the picture. You're not as brown as I thought you'd be. Did it rain?'

'No,' I said, feeling tired that this kind of abrasive interrogation was about to start up again. 'It didn't rain once. For the whole six weeks, we had sun. It was very hot.'

I got into the car, I sat in the back, Brian in the front.

'Don't you want to know about your exam results?' Harold said.

He told me as I looked at London going past. It was a row of Bs and Cs.

'So, what do you think?' he said.

'Not bad,' I said.

'Not bad?' he said. 'Not one A. Not even for English Literature.'

Brian was killing himself sitting in the front. He had been there before: the results inquest. How he loved it now that it was me in the dock. He sat there mouthing, 'Not one A,' shaking his head, doing Harold's sad disbelief thing, creasing

his cheeks like Harold did and then breaking off from being Harold, becoming himself again, looking back at me and laughing and laughing.

'Have you got a present for your mother?' Harold said.

'Have you got a present for your mother?' Brian said.

If I thought I had done enough change and difference for the time being, I was mistaken. There was a lot more to come.

The new term began in just a day or so. I had opted for English, French and History A-levels, and I could see them stretching out in front of me for the next two years. For reasons I can't excavate now, instead of immediately immersing myself in literature, French and historical stuff, I started thinking about something else altogether. What was it going to be like not studying the other subjects, the subjects I was dropping – Geography and Biology? Yes, Biology! I thought of what it would feel like not doing Biology.

Why exactly had I liked Biology so much? In the Colonie, hadn't an old zoologist guy turned up one day and taken us on a trip to find scorpions? And we did find some. He grabbed them with his dark brown fingers and put them in little see-through boxes so that he could explain how sting penetrates the skin and injects poison. 'Look,' he said, 'the little sac, full of poison!' I had been fascinate that. At school, there was the time we stuck photo neg to geranium leaves to see if we could get them to gro pictures of ourselves on the leaves. I remembered how felt to know how things worked inside me. From th there was no way of knowing how blood pumped body or what was in the blood being pumped. W Biology, you knew. You found out what's going was like discovering a code. That's exciting.

I talked about this with Mum and Harold. have done that. I didn't realise it at the time, fided those things it was as if I was luring long-lost place which, if they could return their greatest, most dearly held hopes. The the butterfly kit and Questors rolled into stuff to do with biology, eh? And especi canoe trip had been a high, and now we had ruined it. What did we think we were going to do when we reached the girls' tent? I thought, Gaudemarre and Maurice the footballer seem like guys who've spent years being told that they are the ones who spoil things. Come to think of it, hadn't I been told at school over and over again that I had spoiled things? Is there some kind of permanent way in which some of us are locked into spoiling the things that teachers and *moniteurs* do with us?

And then the Colonie was over. It seemed as if the oldest ones were the happiest that it was the end. They were desperate to get back on the streets of their neighbourhood.

In the coach back to Lyon, Nicole cried and cried but no one knew who or what she was crying for. She couldn't say. We looked at her. Coming down off the mountains, Maurice sang, '*Allez l'O.L., allez l'O.L., allez ...*' for the thousandth time. Ben Zizi shouted that the coach was on fire. We looked down and the wooden floor was burning. There were flames round the bottom of Pink Nicolas' seat. The driver stopped the coach and pushed his way towards us. He stamped on the floor and the flames went out under his foot. He waved his hand and said it wasn't a big thing, '*pas grand-chose*'. Seemed like a pretty big thing to me.

As we got into Lyon, they started cheering like crazy. The place mattered so much to them, but not to me. I felt envious of their big homecoming. I was separate from them again. The coach pulled up under the walls of Gerland, the giant chemical works where their parents worked. Some of these parents were there waiting for them. Not Gaudemarre's, not Ben Zizi's. Nor Alain the trainee electrician's. Nor Maurice the footballer's. They were men now. I wondered if I was a man yet. No, probably not. I shook everyone's hand.

'Let's write,' we said.

Mme Goetschy said that she would take me to the station, the Gare de Lyon.

The Gare de Lyon? Lyon's Gare de Lyon? Yes, she said. Was this the Gare de Lyon you called to see if they had found my anorak? I asked. Yes, she said.

I felt again that I had trapped myself in my lack of French. I hadn't even been able to sort out which Gare de Lyon I meant. How typical. Yet another thing where I got the surface but missed the whole truth. It frustrated me that it could feel one moment as if I was 'getting' everything, and the next that I hadn't 'got' the bit that mattered.

At the station, she hugged me and kissed me and said that it had been a good Colonie. I nodded and nodded because I couldn't say it all. Of course I couldn't say it all, I thought. That's the point.

On the way home, I was thinking: this trip has made me into someone different. I don't know how exactly, but it must have done: I've been with people who don't fit with anything or anybody in London and I haven't spoken English for six weeks. I've been thinking in French. There are things that I only know in French. Apricot halves are now *couilles de singe*. You paddle a canoe using *appel* and *écart*. But I'm not French. I was different over there, too. And now, back home, with all that in my head, I'm going to be different again.

Brian and Harold were waiting for me at the station.

'In the end, you wrote good letters,' Harold said, 'we started to get the picture. You're not as brown as I thought you'd be. Did it rain?'

'No,' I said, feeling tired that this kind of abrasive interrogation was about to start up again. 'It didn't rain once. For the whole six weeks, we had sun. It was very hot.'

I got into the car, I sat in the back, Brian in the front.

'Don't you want to know about your exam results?' Harold said.

He told me as I looked at London going past. It was a row of Bs and Cs.

'So, what do you think?' he said.

'Not bad,' I said.

'Not bad?' he said. 'Not one A. Not even for English Literature.'

Brian was killing himself sitting in the front. He had been there before: the results inquest. How he loved it now that it was me in the dock. He sat there mouthing, 'Not one A,' shaking his head, doing Harold's sad disbelief thing, creasing his cheeks like Harold did and then breaking off from being Harold, becoming himself again, looking back at me and laughing and laughing.

'Have you got a present for your mother?' Harold said.

'Have you got a present for your mother?' Brian said.

If I thought I had done enough change and difference for the time being, I was mistaken. There was a lot more to come.

The new term began in just a day or so. I had opted for English, French and History A-levels, and I could see them stretching out in front of me for the next two years. For reasons I can't excavate now, instead of immediately immersing myself in literature, French and historical stuff, I started thinking about something else altogether. What was it going to be like not studying the other subjects, the subjects I was dropping – Geography and Biology? Yes, Biology! I thought of what it would feel like not doing Biology.

Why exactly had I liked Biology so much? In the Colonie, hadn't an old zoologist guy turned up one day and taken us on a trip to find scorpions? And we did find some. He grabbed them with his dark brown fingers and put them into little see-through boxes so that he could explain how the sting penetrates the skin and injects poison. 'Look,' he had said, 'the little sac, full of poison!' I had been fascinated by that. At school, there was the time we stuck photo negatives to geranium leaves to see if we could get them to grow with pictures of ourselves on the leaves. I remembered how good it felt to know how things worked inside me. From the outside, there was no way of knowing how blood pumped round the body or what was in the blood being pumped. When you did Biology, you knew. You found out what's going on inside. It was like discovering a code. That's exciting.

I talked about this with Mum and Harold. I should never have done that. I didn't realise it at the time, but when I confided those things it was as if I was luring them into some long-lost place which, if they could return to it, would fulfil their greatest, most dearly held hopes. Their reaction was like the butterfly kit and Questors rolled into one: you like all that stuff to do with biology, eh? And especially the biology to do with what's going on inside you? Really? Really? 'Well, do you know what you could do? You could be a doctor.'

They looked at each other: it was a brainwave. Of course he would like to be a doctor. He would love being a doctor. And he would be so good at it. He would make a marvellous doctor.

'Let's talk to Chick.'

In a second, Harold was on the phone to their old Jewish ex-Communist ex-East Ender friend – and doctor – Chick, to find out about how to become a doctor. Within a day we were at his house, and Chick was explaining to us how there was some special route to being a doctor, involving Arts A-levels for two years and then Medical School. Once you were there, you did a special course that was like science A-levels but specially geared to becoming a doctor and crammed into one year; it was called 'First MB'. After that, you did what everyone does: 'Second MB' – anatomy, physiology, biochemistry. Finally you're allowed on the wards doing your 'firms', and you take your final exams. And you're a doctor. Easy peasy. I was getting carried along with this. A doctor? People respect you, they rely on you. You're knowledgeable about all sorts of clever stuff and because you know that stuff, people come to you for help. And you help them. And they're grateful. What could be better than that?

Chick then told Mum and Harold to go out the room, so they talked in the back room with Chick's Jewish ex-Communist ex-East End wife, Gertrude, who came from a line of East End doctors. Chick asked me about biology. I told him what I had said to Mum and Harold about the outside and inside and the secret code. 'Good, very good,' he said, 'I'll write you a reference.'

That's how I ended up applying for Medical School, and indeed, getting in. I had a place at Medical School. I was going to be a doctor. Mum and Harold were over the moon. Ecstatic.

'That way,' Harold said, 'you won't end up reading books about books, which is all I ever bloody do.' I got it: being a doctor was something sacred for him.

Then another change came lumbering over the horizon. The estate agents below our flat closed and a new shop

opened there, Babette Baby Clothes. The man running it –
who Mum and Harold only ever called Babette – was a tall
Jewish bloke who looked like Dennis Norden. I could tell
that he knew we were Jewish, as the odd Yiddishism dropped
into his speech when talking to us: if a delivery didn't come
in, he'd be in *shtuck*, that sort of thing. Maybe it was just to
soften us up: one day Harold came up from chatting to him
in the back yard, looking sickened. 'Bloody Babette is going
to evict us,' he said. 'Bloody Tories.'

I could tell from Mum's face this wasn't a joke. But was
the point that Babette was a Tory? No, the point was that the
Tories had 'decontrolled' rents. For decades, tenants had been
protected by rents fixed according to the 'rateable value' of
property, and if that rateable value was below a certain level
you had security of tenure. But then the Tory government
said that there had to be a national review of rateable values.
This changed the status of thousands of flats and houses
overnight, making it possible for landlords to evict tenants
and raise rents. And that suddenly and definitely included
us. Babette – for all his suggestion that we and him were
chaverim (friends) – was going to kick us out of the flat we'd
been living in for fifteen years.

'Oh he's very sorry about it,' Harold said, 'oh terribly
bloody sorry.'

'Now what?' Mum said.

Their first thought was to find another flat to rent somewhere. But they looked at rents and were alarmed. Up till
now, they had spent very little of their joint income on rent.
Controlled rents had worked very well for them. Their one
big spend was the holidays. Then someone in Mum's school
pointed out that because she taught in Hertfordshire, and
because she had a few quid in the Teachers' Providential
Fund, a professional savings society, Mum was entitled to a
mortgage with them.

'Mortgage'? Mortgage was a completely new word to
come into our home: 1962 was the year mortgage happened
for us. We could go through all our friends and say which
ones rented and which ones had mortgages. Harold wasn't
happy about it. He made various speeches about it just being

a way of 'them' getting you where 'they' wanted you: in debt for the rest of your life. It's not a mortgage, it's a millstone. 'Rent, profit or interest. That's how they do it.'

Mum said, 'Never mind that, Harold, we've got to find somewhere to live.'

Nonetheless, things started to move fast. They found a little Victorian gardener's cottage that was the twin half of another, in a detached building with the ludicrously grand name of 'Grosvenor Villas'. It had been built for garden-ers on the Moor Park estate, in around 1850. It came with a garden – the first time Harold and Mum would have a garden – but only an outside loo, and a makeshift bathroom. It seemed to me to be damp and dark, with small, low rooms, like the Fidlers' house on their tenant farm in Skenfrith in Monmouthshire. Even less handy, the nearest stations were more than a mile away, the nearest regular bus stop was half a mile away, and the house itself was on a lonely stretch of road between Northwood and Rickmansworth, two places I had not the slightest reason or wish to live in, or near.

And another thing: it was going to happen in six weeks' time. We were moving. Life was moving fast. I wailed to myself, why couldn't we live in Ealing? I liked Ealing, with its shops, and Questors. Or better still, why couldn't we live in Crouch End or that 'foreign' country, Muswell Hill? The more I went over there to see Malc, the more exciting a place it seemed to be. There was also a whole gang of people my age – boys and girls – I knew from Woodcraft and Aldermaston, who hung out together, playing guitars, going to folk or jazz clubs; they knew cinemas that showed foreign films and the secret places round Alexandra Palace, Highgate Woods and Hampstead Heath. The smell of Granny Aprahamian's house, with the gramophone horns looking at me, was much more alluring than a place with no name and dark rooms, halfway between Northwood and Rickmansworth.

Then Harold said that there wasn't much point in me staying at Harrow Weald, it would be a right old bloody journey every day. Why didn't I go to Watford Grammar School for Boys? It's just down the road. I said, 'It might be just down the road for you, because you've got a car. For me, it's a bus and a train.'

'Well go by bike, lad,' he said. 'Mind you, you'll have to stay awake.'

'I was tired. I'd been on a long cross-country run ...'

Here, he was talking about the time I arrived home late with a bump on my head, the crossbar of my bike bent back on itself and no memory of how it had happened. We pieced together that I must have fallen asleep while cycling down the road where Harrybo lived, came off the bike, smashed my head, half knocked myself out, and wheeled the bike home. Not that I recalled any of it. I should have taken it as a warning of things to come.

So, we started packing up, and for me this meant leaving the only home I could remember. It wasn't easy. At Harrow Weald, I said goodbye to the people who had stayed on. It meant leaving halfway through rehearsals of Thornton Wilder's *Our Town*, too – I was the narrator in the play, so the sudden announcement that I was pulling out didn't go down too well. The Latin teacher who had knuckled my head, and told me that it would have been better if 'we' had been on the side of the Germans in the last war, stopped me in the corridor. I wondered what sneer he was going to see me off with: he looked me in the eye, said, 'Don't get rubbed out,' and walked off.

Weirdly, it's about the nicest farewell that anyone has ever said to me. It feels like it's the most tuned in to whatever it is that makes me do what I do. I have some idea of why no one wants to get rubbed out, but no real idea of why I have spent so much of my life making marks I don't want to see get rubbed out. I guess he could tell that that's what I was doing, and unlike the ones who thought the priority was to conform, he thought I shouldn't give up.

On a very different scale, but around the same period, the world was going to come to an end. Not like the time we rolled up our trousers and danced about on the school field. This was for real. America said it didn't want Russian missiles in Cuba. Everyone said that these missiles proved that the Russians wanted war with America. The Russians pointed to the American missiles in Turkey and in Italy. Everyone said that this proved that the Americans were doing their utmost to defend us against the Russians. The papers were full of it day after day. The TV and radio raged about it. There was going to be a world war. Never mind that I was going to be a doctor. Never mind that we were moving into a house with no loo. Never mind that I was going to switch schools. There was going to be a world war. It was exactly as Bertrand Russell and Canon Collins had predicted. It was going to be hundreds of Hiroshimas. One evening, it felt like a crunch point had been reached. We went to bed wondering if the missiles were going to be flying over Pinner that very night. In the morning, Harold got up and said that he had felt the room move and the house start to tip over on its side. When he discovered that it hadn't moved or tipped over, he couldn't figure out why it hadn't.

And it didn't. The Russians took the missiles off Cuba. The papers and the TV were exultant: America has won the Cuba Missile Crisis, they said, because the good, strong Americans made Russia stand down. In the small print, out of sight, America withdrew its weapons from Turkey and Italy and signed a deal with Russia saying that it would never invade Cuba without direct provocation.

'It's a game,' Mum said, 'it's all about how they tell the story. For all we know, they arranged the whole thing beforehand.'

'Who?'

'The Americans and the Russians.'

'Really?' I said.

'You won't hear a dicky bird from Gaitskell about that,' Harold said.

I wondered if we were still on the side of the Russians, or whether they had changed position so that now they saw it more as an even-sided punch-up, and the big deal for them was that we were always being told the story with the West as angels and the Russians as devils. They were turning, I was turning, where we lived was turning, the world was turning. And like the Shakespeare code I had stumbled across when I had been in *The Merchant of Venice*; like the biology code going on inside our bodies; like the French code I had picked up in the Colonie; here was another code, a political code, another story behind the story.

# 10

## The Politics of Culture

I was going to start at Watford Grammar School for Boys, straight after the half-term break in the autumn term.

'You'll love it,' Harold said, 'the head's a great bloke, I've known him for years.'

This was Harry Rée, war hero and known radical educationist.

'They've got a wall magazine,' Harold said, as if that was a clincher. By the time I got there, it had been banned.

There's a way of talking about 1950s and '60s grammar schools as if they were all one kind of school. There couldn't have been two more different institutions than the ones I was moving between, and the contrast kicked off a train of thought that's stayed with me ever since: how different one kind of school is from another, how these differences appear to be about education itself but are also about the purpose of different kinds of education, and how that purpose ultimately concerns class. The English education system, then and now, was finely tuned to produce layers in society.

Since this time of going to Watford, I've never stopped wondering how it was that I could grasp most of what was put in front of me, and how ironic it was that this ability to access what the school offered came largely from parents who were dissidents. Then, because I spent so much time on out-of-school activities that mattered as much – if not more – to me as the schooling, I also spent a good deal of time trying to figure out the cultural differences between the two areas, out-of-school and in-school, and what the politics was of all these differences.

The moment I went to Watford, I could feel the contrast in every minute of the day. Harrow Weald had been a 'mixed county grammar school'. Watford was a 'grammar school for boys'. Harrow Weald seemed to have appeared in around 1933. Watford was 'founded' in 1704. At Harrow Weald, the grammar-school apparatus was much less grand, much less formal. Though Harrow Weald decreed grey uniforms, the school uniform police looked the other way if someone's grey was lighter or darker than the precise stipulation. Girls worked a hundred variations on their skirts, striped summer dresses and hats. School assemblies at Harrow Weald involved a bit of standing up and sitting down.

Arriving at Watford, my first time in an all boys' school, my first impression was that it really was the St Custard's of Geoffrey Willans and Ronald Searle's *Down with Skool*, but deadly serious with it. The teachers – nearly all men – were older, greyer, more solemn, all in gowns all the time, and the entrance and hall areas reflected the school's sense that it had a history, stretching back centuries, and a continuous presence as a site of national achievement and status. In important places, there were cups, noticeboards for head boys, war memorials, paintings of past head teachers, and wooden panelling; and every boy was in immaculate uniform, black shoes, white shirts. Here, assembly began with a military march-in from the prefects, right the way down the lateral aisle. The head ('great bloke, Mick') emerged from a room at the side of the hall, gown flowing, grave-faced, and the school leapt to its feet in absolute silence. The whole staff sat in rows on the stage behind him, like a museum of owls.

Had every one of them been shot at or bombed on, or, just as likely, bombed or shot someone in the Second World War? Andy, one of the first people to admit me into his circle, explained that Harry Rée had got dropped into France and joined the French Resistance. War hero. But terrible things had happened in his life: his wife had died and his son had had a motorbike accident that damaged his brain. He walked about the school wrapped in heroism and tragedy, with a melancholy grandeur never matched by anyone at Harrow Weald.

In my first few weeks at the new place I struggled to place Andy and the other boys. They didn't seem like any of the guys I'd met either at school or in my lives away from school. I tried to locate blues enthusiasts, or Aldermaston marchers, or surrealists, or jazz types, walkers, campers, ex-Communists, anti-apartheid marchers, French-speakers, actors, comedians, or people who would love to roll all over the floor being beaten up by the Invisible Man. I myself was met with a bit of surprise, curiosity even. I quickly gathered that I was an oddity. But I wanted to be the kind of oddity that got laughs, not the kind of oddity that was odd. I couldn't handle it.

One time, I was fetching some paper from the paper store next to the staff room, and on the end of a shelf there was a tray of letters. On top was one with headed notepaper from Harrow Weald. I could see at once that it was from my old head teacher … and it was about me. I scanned it as quickly as I could while pretending to be picking up some station-ery. I saw that he had written stuff about how he had rather hoped that I would have played some kind of leadership role in the school, but as I had persisted in being foolish, he had given up on that. I had some talent academically, but I was disinclined to work.

I felt my face flush. I was furious. No matter how I had goofed or mucked about, why was that old bastard screw-ing up my arrival at a new school? Why was he telling them that I was a no-gooder? He wasn't so good himself. After he replaced the old alcoholic head, the only things he did in the first year he was in charge was rearrange the detention system and pay for some daft light system for his study door, to inform people whether he was there or not. It infuriated me that there was this corridor of authority that ran from my last school to this, expressed in a currency of secret letters.

To make things worse a boy started to give me the verbals, now that I was the new guy. I don't suppose it was all that nasty. He was a good mimic – a comedian even – and exactly the sort of person I would like to be friends with. And his imitations were getting the laughs. I wasn't.

In a whirl of infuriation I stayed behind after school one Thursday night and drew a picture of him on one of the

tables in our form room: not a little cartoon tucked away
in the corner but a huge whole table-top caricature, drawn
in thick ink lines, and labelled with names and descriptions
that I thought were brilliantly on the mark. I did it in a blur
of frustrated and vindictive irritation but when I had finished
it, I realised that it was permanent. I had done it in blue ink
that had immediately soaked into the wood. I knew straightaway I had done something crazy: this was something that
a five-year-old might do, not a sixteen-year-old who only a
few weeks ago had been discussing being a doctor. Far from
purging my feelings about being trapped, I had now trapped
myself even more. I travelled home more miserable than I had
ever been before. I needed to escape.

My first dodge was to bunk off. I said the next morning
that I wasn't feeling well. They were both so preoccupied
with their work or the new house or money that me being
mildly ill hardly registered. They were off and away. The
next two days were the weekend, and I filled it with watching TV, but come Sunday night I knew I couldn't put it off
any longer.

Monday morning I took myself to school and crawled up to
the form room. Our form teacher that year was something of
a hero in the school: Giraldus Hughes, an old Welsh socialist,
history teacher, with thick pebble glasses and worn-out suits;
seemed to love his job, great sense of humour, loved engaging
with ideas and politics and telling us about how he had come
up through 'Labour College' (that sounded interesting – what
was it? Were there secret, working-class kinds of education
that we didn't ever hear about?), and so he was always desperate to help his boys (us) get to university. He looked at me
as I walked in and before I had got more than a few feet, he
said the head wanted to see me. At least I wouldn't have to
face the crowd, or – even worse – the guy I had caricatured.

Harry Rée made me wait. I sat in the sombre entry hall
near the war memorial. The door opened. He ushered me in.
'Christ, you've made a bloody bad start!' he said. He told
me that I had been behaving oddly. He had seen me talking
loudly so as to attract his attention only a few days ago, and
the PE staff had told him that I was not fitting in with the

timetable properly: I had signed up for rugby, but then disappeared on a cross-country run.

I thought he was going to mention Harold, but he didn't. He made no sign that they knew each other or that he had read the letter from my old head. He told me that I'd have to clean the desk, and that he hoped I would sort myself out. He didn't even suggest that he was going to write home about it.

I came out of his study and the fact that he said, 'Christ!' and 'bloody' – no shock in itself as far as the words were concerned, but surprising enough from a head teacher in that situation, in that school, with all its pomp – seemed strange, but in a way comforting. Instead of the encumbrance of a long lecture, a long punishment, a long letter home, a long post-mortem, it was just one short, sharp, slightly vulgar put-down, with a couple of footnotes. But then, if you know you're high up in the social pecking order of schools, maybe it's easy to throw around a few 'christs' and 'bloodies' in situations like that.

Back in the class, Giraldus didn't mention it, and he must have said something to everyone about not mentioning it either. Underneath the solemn exterior there was kindness. I took it.

We had an English teacher who belonged to a previous era. He had a small toothbrush moustache; he only ever marched, never walked; he wore his gown at all times, and spoke like an army general. He called us 'chaps', which was all very friendly, but there were times when he'd hear something outside the classroom, lift his head like an alert bird, then dash out the room. A few seconds later you heard a door slam and him yelling at the top of his voice, though the words were indistinct as they floated off into the empty corridor. There was then a pause, and you'd hear the sound of beating. A few seconds later the military steps came back down the corridor and into the room, and he'd say, 'Now, where were we, chaps?'

The beatings, I was told, were with a gym shoe that he kept in a special gym shoe pocket inside the jacket of his suit.

In his classes we were reading through *Antony and*

*Cleopatra*, and had reached the point where Enobarbus has a lot to say. This teacher stopped the reading and put his foot up onto a chair, carefully giving his trousers a little slide back as he did so, revealing sock suspenders.

'Now, chaps,' he said, 'I want to say a few words to you about Antony and why he can command such loyalty from a fellow like Enobarbus. I want to take you back to 1932 when I was at college in the OTC, the Officers' Training Corps. We were pretty green, I can tell you, but damned keen with it. One morning, the news came to us that we were to be reviewed by the Prince of Wales – later to become the Duke of Windsor – and we were pretty excited about that, believe me. Now, I don't know what it was, but there was something about him, and do you know, every man jack of us would have laid down our lives for him. That's the sort of chap that Antony was.'

He stopped and did some emotional breathing while he thought about this moment thirty years earlier when he was face to face with the Prince of Wales. Then he had a few more words for us. 'Now that's what it's like in the sixth form. We have chats like this. Right, carry on. Who was reading Enobarbus?'

It was a moment that came from another class of person and another era, totally unlike anything I had encountered at Harrow Weald.

I started to hunt for people who might become my friends. There was Terry, whose dad was 'in the print' – working in one of the big Watford print factories. Terry had discovered Johnny Cash and Ray Charles. We did French together, and he was doing German as well. At lunchtimes, along with two others, he went to Watford Station to smoke in the Edwardian waiting room. I started going with them, even though I didn't smoke.

There were a couple of guys two years ahead, Mike and Chris, who were staying on for the beginning of a third year. They wore CND badges, and had something to do with the wall magazine that got banned. They talked about a new socialist group that wasn't Labour and wasn't Communist.

This was the germ of the International Socialists, which would later turn into the Socialist Workers' Party. At the time, it seemed a bit shadowy and they weren't around much, but I caught up with them sometimes.

There was a serious threesome who called themselves anarchists and pacifists, in a scholarly sort of a way, which was interesting but I didn't feel any tug of friendship. With my table-top adventure, I had burnt my boats with the comedian for the time being. As I had opted for rugby there was a friendly take-it-or-leave-it chat that went on around doing team sport, though Terry was utterly baffled as to why someone who was into French, jazz, CND, socialism and poetry would want to hang out with the rugby lot. In the year below, there was a guy who knew the Muswell Hill crowd, played the guitar, and had been on the Aldermaston marches. His dad was 'in the print' too, and both parents were most certainly still in the Communist Party.

I started to nudge my way round all this, trying desperately hard not to do anything that would get me into trouble again. There was a certain bother about me being Jewish, (or kind of Jewish, or what-are-you-anyway-Jewish). As far as I could make out there weren't any other Jews in the sixth form. I was the first one they had ever met, seen or examined.

It was also the first time I met anti-Semitic jokes head-on. A couple of them had some routine about throwing money on the floor and saying, 'You don't want to throw money on the floor, he'll only go and pick it up.' I was so on the defensive, I took the easy way out. I went along with it and adopted a stage-Jew act. It suited them. They could slot me into whatever matrix or hierarchy they had worked out about non-Jews and Jews. I just helped them do it. Because I didn't take that home and share it, I didn't get any tips from Harold or Mum on how to confront it.

Meanwhile the schoolwork was getting serious, and there was a lot of it: essays and translations, the Tudors, Chaucer's 'The Knight's Tale', *Candide*, the Hapsburgs, Matthew Arnold, T. S. Eliot's *Family Reunion*. I was too late to get into the school play, but I got a walk-on as a soldier in *Henry V*.

In the second term, I signed up for a school exchange: it was more education about education, yet another reason for me to question what I was doing and how I was doing it. The headmaster had set up three-way swaps between Watford, Forest Hill Comprehensive in South London, and one of the country's top three private schools, Winchester College. I put myself down for the exchange and started by swapping with a boy from Forest Hill. I stayed with him, and then he stayed with us.

He was keen and kind and his mum was unbelievably solic-itous, making sure that I had a towel and a good breakfast. The lessons were similar to those at Watford, and it seemed like the kind of place I could have gone to and liked. This was at the height of the national furore about whether the country really would put an end to school-selection at the age of eleven. I saw nothing at this comprehensive that made me think we should carry on with selection. I liked it. It seemed to be the best and fairest way to do things. The boy wasn't being 'held back' by attending a 'comp' – which was what the pro-selection lobby said would happen to him. When he came to our house, it must have seemed chaotic compared to what he was used to: Mum and Harold disappearing off in the morning, me fending for myself. I don't know what he made of Watford. He didn't say, but he got on well with Terry and the others.

Then I went to Winchester. I was overwhelmed by every-thing: the way it was a community so cut off from the outside world; the totality of wall-to-wall, midnight-to-midnight boarding; the poshness of everyone, with an accent that no one at Harrow Weald had, and only a few at Watford; the mix of utter formality and utter informality, for instance between the filing into chapel every day and the rowdy chaos of tea-time, with boys fighting over bread and jam; the famous 'notions', the in-group Wykehamist lingo which named every part of daily life and schoolwork; and a style of teaching sixth-formers that felt like something out of a period drama.

What really struck me, though, was the tone and feel of the education itself. One English lesson I went to, a small group of 'men' sat around in the room where they wanted. They were doing Hardy's *Far From the Madding Crowd*, and the teacher looked up at the ceiling and said, 'Hardy. Mmmm. Optimist or pessimist?' and then waited.

Some replies started and he nodded, or made 'Mmm' noises, or murmured 'Interesting!' and it all turned into a chat. I felt very much at home, and chipped in what I thought. The teacher seemed pleased about that. At one point, he put his feet up on the desk. At other times, he strolled around. In some ways it reminded me of Barry Brown at Harrow Weald, but Barry had been an outsider, and we always got the impression that he was frowned on. Maybe Herbert (the one who told us about the Prince of Wales) imagined that he was having a 'conversation' like this, but he wasn't. This Winchester style was so full of ease, of a sense that this was a chat between equals. I knew that there was an anxiety around Watford that they could only compete with a place like Winchester if they crammed as much as they possibly could into our lessons. There was no time to just break off from a course book, look at the ceiling and say, 'Optimist or pessimist? What do you think, chaps?'

On another occasion I went to a debate in a stunning eighteenth-century hall, and again felt overwhelmed. This time I was struck by the fluency of the speakers. How did they carry on for so long without written speeches or notes? How did they know how to do that thing of walking and talking in tandem? How did they manage to lace their talks with little quotes plucked from nowhere? One of them repeated what his opponent had said, but then ridiculed it by saying 'True, O king, true', as if those few meaningless words nullified it.

Then my 'pair' came back to our place. He came from a family of Labour Party grandees, so there wasn't much to shock him about us. Perhaps Mum was a bit of a surprise, but he was much too polite to say anything. Perhaps Harold's swearing might have seemed a bit curious. He fitted in fine at school, he wasn't that different from some of us. Again, perhaps if he'd teamed up with Terry or Howard, people who were the first in their families to stay on at school after the age of fourteen, it might have surprised him more.

I was glad I had done this exchange. It took me back to the Eleven Plus and how we had been grouped for the big test coming up, and how that exam segregated us – people like my best friend Harrybo going one way, me another. It brought home how there were comprehensive schools like the one Harold had taught at, or that boy from Forest Hill went to; how the schools we were put in, though nominally the same if they had 'grammar' after their name, were in fact very different; how, tucked away in the countryside, there were places like Winchester which were creating a race apart. And even though I knew of these layers of schooling, there were yet more kinds that I didn't know about, in other places, like Giraldus Hughes's Labour College.

There was another way the subject of education itself got to me: Mum's progress with her Diploma in Education (what she called her 'Schiller Course') was now preoccupying her in ways that none of us had seen before. She would spend hours staring into the middle distance, or scribbling little notes in files. One time I got in from school and thought that the house was empty. All the lights were out, but when I walked into the kitchen I saw that she was there, sitting in the dark, pondering on something. She started to formulate these thoughts into aphorisms and gnomic sayings which she shared with Harold, who seemed to know what they meant, or she just threw them into the air for anyone to catch.

Out of the blue, related to nothing else, she'd say, 'It's all about doing and talking.'

Or: 'Talking, thinking; thinking, talking.'

Or: 'Thinking and doing – that's it.'

We had been used to her coming up with little slogans in the past, but these had mostly been satirical. One time she came across an eighteenth-century sampler which said: 'Let self-sacrifice be its own reward.' For reasons way beyond our ken, she found this both hilarious and significant, and would suddenly blurt it out when no one was expecting it. Now her catchphrases were 'doing and talking', or 'talking, thinking; thinking, talking', or 'thinking and doing'.

What she was trying to do was find a way to sum up how

children's activity ('doing') can be (should be?) linked to their ability to think, and their thinking can be (should be?) linked to their talk. The reason why this needed so much pondering was because all our educations – hers, Harold's, Brian's, mine, and probably much of what she had done as a teacher before – worked on the basis of instruct, learn, instruct, learn. It was a system that had worked very well for her, Harold, Brian and me, although I've come to think that the vast amount of extra-curricular voluntary activity we did was a profound but hidden motor to all our abilities to make that 'instruct, learn' system work for us. But, while it worked for us – given our propensities to 'get' it – there was a majority of kids, both in their time at school and in ours, who didn't 'get' it. The majority of them were out of the school system altogether by the time they were fifteen.

Mum was trying to link learning – what she was calling 'thinking' – to 'doing' and 'talking'. Sometimes either Mum or Harold would quiz me about how much time we spent at school discussing the subjects that the teachers taught us. The answer was that it varied enormously. The biology teacher who encouraged us to fix photo negatives to geranium plants based her lessons around a mix of what she had to say and what we had to say. That's where the photo-negatives experiment came from. Others, like some of the teachers I had at Watford, treated lessons as sixty-minute lectures. Kindly Giraldus had wodges of browned notes on the Tudors and Stuarts which he unfurled and monologued from. Our European History teacher, young military Neil, had sharp new notes on the Hapsburgs and produced a rapid-fire spiel from them. Harold said, 'Why don't they just give them to you as handouts?'

I didn't have an answer to that, and didn't dare ask them.

For Mum, all this was changing her, but at around this time she was seriously knocked back: she tried to become a head teacher. The more she was excited by these ideas about children's language and development, the more she wanted to put them into practice. She heard that the local authority she had worked for throughout her career wouldn't appoint women to be head teachers. The new head at her school who had been appointed over her, was kind and friendly enough but too reliant on her, she thought, to come up with new ideas about teaching and learning. In and amongst the gnomic sayings, there were now elaborate stories about how the head had said this-or-that (which only showed that he didn't know what he was doing), and that she had recommended that-and-this (which was fine, but she wasn't the one being paid to take that kind of leading role). Of course, had she been working in Central London there would have been no block on her being a head at that time, and she knew that. Sitting in that no man's land between Northwood and Rickmansworth was a constraint on her, too.

I started to put as much energy and time into non-school stuff as into schoolwork. It was the beginning of my teaching myself the politics of culture. Terry and I decided to start a folk and blues club, playing music at lunchtime. I brought some tapes and records around the theme of 'hard times' and played Woody Guthrie's 'Hard Travelin'' along with Sonny Terry and Brownie McGhee, Leadbelly, Cisco Houston, and some Ewan MacColl, Peggy Seeger and Enoch Kent, who I was beginning to go and see perform in the Pindar of Wakefield at King's Cross. This felt like a world of great lyrics, music, meaning and feeling, nothing to do with what we were being taught.

Terry started coming over to mine, I went to his and met his mum and dad and sisters. It was a bit like Dave's place, in that his dad quizzed me closely about CND and why my parents had left the Communist Party and what did I think of trade unions, while Terry tried to get him to stop talking. Terry liked telling the story of how his dad would watch him getting out of his school uniform and putting on a pair of jeans.

'It was the other way round when I was your age,' he said, 'the moment I got home from work, I got out of my overalls and put on a decent pair of trousers, like the ones you go to school in.'

In 1962 in Watford, a pair of jeans was becoming something to be figured out.

Culture of a different kind: just before Christmas, I had to go back to Harrow Weald to get my exam certificates at a presentation evening. Lynne was there. I hadn't seen her since the coach journey back from Stratford on the day before I left for France. She waited for me. She was done up in high heels and a posh dress. She looked at me with a smile and a raised eyebrow. 'Why did you write to me like that, Michael?' she said.

I flailed about and said something about how I thought we couldn't get on, we weren't alike enough.

'And you couldn't have said that to me, to my face, instead of leaving me to read it in a letter?'

She was angry.

I said I was sorry. She laughed at me.

'Sometimes you're so full of yourself and other times I just look at you and think, *nabbech*!'(poor little thing).

I nodded.

'How's Harold and Connie?'

'They're fine, very busy. How's your mum and dad?'

'They've opened another shop. We could still go on seeing each other, you know. It wouldn't hurt you.'

'Yes.'

'Do you still go to that acting place in Ealing? You come through Rayners Lane, don't you?'

'No, I don't do that anymore. And we're living way, way out in Rickmansworth now. It's miles away.'

'OK,' she said, 'tell Harold and Connie I miss them. They changed my life, you know. I'll tell you some other time. Kiss me goodbye.'

I thought, how did they change her life? She didn't know them all that well, did she? I remembered them quizzing her about her life and she quizzing them about theirs. I remembered her looking at the books in the house, and the pictures. That changed her life?

Instead, at that time, I met Janey and we started going out because I thought she looked like Catherine Deneuve. I know there should have been a better reason, but that was the main one at the time.

It turned out that her father was Polish but ended up in

the French Resistance. He was picked up by the Nazis and taken to Dachau – the camp primarily for political prisoners – because they never realised that he was Jewish. He survived, but only just, and Janey's mum (who wasn't Jewish) met him when she went to Paris as one of the medical team sent over to nurse ex-camp inmates back to health. She said that he was nearly dead, just weighing a few stone. Now, he was strong, fit, with a crew cut and French T-shirts. His hero was Camus, he said, and there were copies of Camus's newspaper *Combat* in the house. None of this should have been any more reason for going out with her than thinking she looked like Catherine Deneuve. I really needed to have reasons for why I went out with someone, but didn't know how to ask myself.

Now there was a new routine for me. To get to her place, I had to take buses and trains across London. It was another reason to be fed up that we weren't living in Muswell Hill or Crouch End. Why were we stuck in Rickmansworth?

Seeing Janey meant that if we went to things, we went into the West End. Meanwhile, most of my school friends went to things in Watford. I realised that I'd done it again: I had made something separate from school and separate from my friends at school. It also meant that I missed things I would have loved. Terry came in one Monday morning and said he had seen Sonny Boy Williamson at the weekend. That was in Watford. Janey and I had been at the Academy Cinema in Tottenham Court Road seeing a Godard movie. That was fine – but still, only just down the road had been a great blues harmonica player and singer and I'd missed him.

I did get to see *This Sporting Life* in Watford, though. In one week, I read the book and saw the film. I loved the total immersion where you could live books and films for days on end. I was utterly convinced by it: Rachel Roberts was so twisted and hurt; Richard Harris was so sure he could reach her and have her, even though he was reduced by the system to being no more than a chunk of muscle owned by the Alan Badel character. I acted out the moment Harris kills the spider on the hospital ward wall.

It was a good time for things coming out, and I went in for it all in a hungry kind of a way. Seeing *Oh! What a Lovely War* took me back to the Theatre Royal, Stratford, on Joan Littlewood's patch: actors who had been in the children's shows and *A Taste of Honey* turned up again in this production. Now, I got this: this was Brechtian. This time nothing on stage was pretending to be real, it was about truth. It was funny, sexy, catchy, tragic, historical, political ... I thought I would love to be in something like that, inventing it, being part of it.

It was also the time of Dylan's *Freewheelin'* second album. I played it a hundred times. There was a moment early on when I was a Woody Guthrie snob, and thought that he was just pretending to be Guthrie. But once I was listening to the songs, occupying them, I wanted to be part of them. And how had he invented a way of singing that sounded as if he was talking?

Of course, none of this was like the culture they taught us in school, and yet I knew it was just as valid, just as important.

The holidays offered something else. Dave, who I had hardly seen since moving, got in touch and said, why don't we hitch-hike round France? I leaped at the idea. The Colonie de Vacances had left me with a sense that I wanted to know about France, I wanted to live France and, yes, be French. If we went to France, I could research it, study it, *be* it. Would that be possible? What would France throw at me?

We quickly exchanged suggestions of what to do, what to see. I said that the French *assistant* at Watford was a funny guy called M. Vitse who lived in a place called Montauban, and he'd said that any of us could drop in anytime ... Though there had been one nasty moment when we were discussing Camus and *L'Étranger* and he said that Arabs were ugly and we had yelled at him, saying you can't just say things like that. Dave mentioned there was an Ingres museum near there, and he was just discovering Ingres at Art School. I suggested heading further south, and going to Albi to see the Toulouse-Lautrec birthplace and museum. Dave replied that he was going to say that anyway. I said we could go on further to a place I had been to when I was a kid, Perpignan. He agreed. That was that. My self-imposed course in Frenchness was on.

When we made it to Montauban, we knocked on M. Vitse's door but the moment he saw us he looked horrified.

'Hi,' I said, 'we're hitching round France, came to Montauban and, like you said, thought we ought to …'

He interrupted in a panic: 'No, you can't come in. There are friends and family in the house. Absolutely not. No.' And he shut the door.

'What's happening?' Dave said, as he didn't understand much French.

'He says he's got friends and family staying there and that's it.'

'Well that didn't work out, did it?' Dave said. 'What sort of bloke is he?'

'I thought he was friendly enough. He said if any of us were passing we should look him up. He sounded as if he meant it, but maybe he didn't.'

'Did you get on with him OK?'

'He said we were all mad Communists and we said he was a Fascist.'

'Is he?'

'I'm just thinking. At the time I thought it was a pose to provoke us, but he did say he thought Arabs were ugly, and he was all for Algérie Française.'

Dave laughed. 'Then why the bloody hell have we come all this way to see him? And you're the one who talks like he knows all about France!'

'Yes, doesn't look so clever now. We might have done better going to see the German assistant. He was much more radical.'

'Where does he live?'

'Hamburg,' I said and we both laughed. We weren't going to hitch to Germany just now.

'He's a very good 200-metre runner,' I said.

'Let's go and see the Ingres paintings,' he said.

The museum wasn't far, but when we got there it was shut for the summer. Dave was furious. He said that he had been told by one of his tutors at art school that if he had the chance to get really close up to an Ingres picture, there was a lot he could learn from the skin tones that Ingres created. But we weren't going to get any nearer to them than looking through the gate.

So, next stop Albi, for Toulouse-Lautrec. On the way, Dave said that he had broken up with the girl he had drawn naked in charcoal. 'I didn't tell you before, but it ended really badly. We were sitting in a life drawing class and she slashed her wrist and ran out of the room and down the stairs. There were tutors and everyone running after her. She splashed blood all the way down. For the rest of the term, you could see the dried blood on the stairs.'

'Jesus H. Christ.'

'You're sounding like *Catcher in the Rye*.'

'Yep.'

(Jumping ahead thirty-five years, Dave was at home and there was a knock at his door. A woman was standing there. She said, 'Do you remember a woman called Anna you were at art school with?'

'Yes.'

'I'm her daughter and you're my dad.'

He hadn't even known that she had a baby.)

The Lautrec exhibition was overwhelming. What was he actually doing in the brothel? Was he like a little toy man for them? Or were they flattered that he wanted to paint them? It was one woman after another, half-dressed, not dressed, a bit dressed ... and every now and then, caricatures of Lautrec himself, looking like a mini Marx Brother. It seemed an odd thing to fill a gallery with in the middle of a town so dominated by a cathedral. When Dave looked at the pictures, it was as if he was drinking them. I liked the way he did that.

I said, 'Let's try Perpignan next.' So we started hitching our way there. Usually I sat in the front with the driver and talked, while Dave sat in the back drawing. One time, a young woman stopped in her little 2CV car. She looked like the German girl Brian stayed with in the Thuringian Wald: short blonde hair, glasses. We chatted about who Dave and I were. I said how Dave wanted to be an artist and I was going to be a doctor, and she dropped us off about thirty kilometres from Perpignan.

Dave started yelling about how much she fancied me. I told him to shut up, we were just chatting. He said I was blind and how she was really up for it. I banned him from saying that stuff. We camped the night, and next morning got a lift from a priest. He said he was a priest in a tiny, tiny, tiny village called Espezel, high up in the Pyrenees. It was so mountainous there that the peasants tie themselves to a post at the top of the mountain and lower themselves down on ropes in order to cut the grass. He said that the thing about peasants in small villages in the mountains, is that they have a death cult: that's why they go to the cemeteries every week. It's not like religion in the towns. They have little shrines on the roads. These are part of their cults.

'I just go along with it,' he said. 'I would say it's paganism, really.'

Before dropping us off in Perpignan, he invited us to come to Espezel. He would show us the kinds of places we had never seen before. I was translating for Dave and he seemed interested. Never mind him, I was interested. This was more like the course in Frenchness I had in mind.

As we came into Perpignan, I was trying to remember it from when I was seven but nothing surfaced from then. We went into the Youth Hostel, cooked our food and then sat with others in the open area. There was a group from one family there, and I got talking to them. It turned out that their mum was a lycée teacher and their dad was a professor of Italian at the Sorbonne. I told them my mum was a primary teacher and my dad a university teacher. There were two brothers, two sisters and a cousin. Dave got seriously fed up with all this chit-chat in French, which he couldn't understand, and stomped off to bed. I carried on and in the end they said, why didn't we come and see them in their parents' place in the mountains? It's in a village, they said, where Papa was born and brought up before he moved to Toulon and then to Paris. They said that sometimes they got bored up in the mountains, so they'd come down to Perpignan for a few days.

I replied that Dave and I had agreed to go to a tiny village called Espezel, so how would it be if we went there first and then came on to your parents' place. 'Espezel?' they said, 'we know Espezel. It's the other side of the mountain we're on. It's so steep there that the peasants tie themselves to a post and lower themselves down the mountainside to cut the grass.' I said that the priest wanted to show us around, so they said that they would come and meet us in three days' time at midday at the church. I said, 'How do you know there's a church in Espezel?'

They thought that was very funny, and before I let on that I hadn't originally meant it as a joke, I laughed too.

Upstairs in the dormitory I explained all this to Dave, and he got even more fed up and said that he was OK about coming to Espezel but after that he wanted to go home. For me, it was all working out. I was getting into France.

We managed to hitch our way to Espezel and met up with the priest. It was, just as he said, high up in the mountains, at a level where there weren't many trees. He lived in a large, ancient stone house in the village, which only had one road branching off in stony, grassy tracks. Inside his house were massive flagstones.

He said we could stay as long as we liked, and an old lady brought us food. Apparently young people often came to stay. He took us out and showed us the village. People seemed to like him. He explained to us that there was no running water, everyone gets water from a pump. In winter, some of them bring the animals into the houses. They sleep above the animals. It's how they keep warm. A woman walked towards us down the road with a huge bundle of hay, wrapped in a cloth, sitting on her head.

The next day he said he was going up to the lake, did we want to come? Dave said, no, he would do some drawing, but I went. Once we were there, he said that he was going to sunbathe. Did I want to? I said no.

'Do you mind if I take off my clothes?'

'No, no, you go ahead,' I said.

He took off all his clothes and showed his chubby pink body to the sun. I walked about, throwing stones, trying to

catch flying grasshoppers and rubbing thyme into my hands.
He said he was going to read some Teilhard de Chardin. Had
I ever read any Teilhard de Chardin?

'No,' I said.

'You would be very interested in him,' he said, 'he is both
very modern and very ancient in his thinking.'

I listened without looking at him, and mooched off again.
I was wondering how long this was going to go on for. Then
he put his clothes back on and said that we would go back
now. In the car, he asked me if I was shocked that he had got
undressed.

'No, no,' I said, 'it was fine.'

The next day I said goodbye to the priest, goodbye to Dave,
and waited by the church. The group from the family turned
up at noon, and off we went to their parents' place on the
other side of the mountain.

Papa was in Romania, leaving Maman to look after everybody. She was the calmest person I had ever met. She listened
to people, watched them as they spoke, left a pause and only
then spoke. There were six children in all, but only five of
them were there, one of them with his wife. Down the road
lived their cousins, the children of Papa's brother.

They showed me photos of how the house used to be –
an old house like the ones in Espezel, which they had spent
years making habitable. There was a little field that led up
to a wood and down to a stream. Above us loomed a big
peak, and way down below in the valley you could see more
peaks, forests, outcrops of naked rock. The people here speak
patois, they said.

I told them about my family, and they wanted to know how
I had ended up in a Colonie de Vacances. We played table
tennis for hours, and I met some of the people in the village,
many of them very old and brown and bent, born when there
had been no electricity, no cars, no metalled roads. Some of
Papa's relatives still lived here, though others were in Toulon,
near Marseille. What happens, they said, is that the people
who went away come back in summer.

It felt like France was unfolding in front of me, its past, its
present, its countryside, its cities, its layers, its language.

When it was time to go home they drove me down to the nearest station, in Ax-les-Thermes, an old spa town that whiffed of sulphur. In the square, the water in the fountain or in pools gave off wisps of steam. It was hot to the touch.

I desperately wanted to come back to all this. I wanted to know more and be a part of it. That would have to wait till next year.

For now, I had my dates worked out. If I caught the right trains, I could get to Valence where I knew Janey would be on her way home from her aunt's house in the Vercors. It would be a surprise. I got there the night before and bedded down in the waiting room. Trouble was there was an old woman in there who wasn't going to go to sleep. She sat up all night, sniffing. It wasn't just sniffing, it was what Mum called 'shnorkling', the sound people make when they sniff back everything that's in their nose and you can hear it all gargling and snorting in the back of their throat. She did it all night.

In the morning I saw Janey arrive with her aunt, and I nipped on to the train out of sight. Once it was moving, I walked through the carriages and said, 'Hi.'

She stared at me. It was a surprise. A bad surprise. She said, 'How come you're on this train?'

I said I'd worked it out, and thought it would be nice.

'Why didn't you tell me?'

'Surprise.'

'Did you see me come into the station?'

'Yeah, I was in the waiting room.'

She didn't like that. She didn't like it that I was on the same train. She didn't think it was anything clever or romantic. We talked for a bit about how her holiday was. I talked a bit about mine.

I said, 'Maybe it'd be better if we didn't travel together, then?'

'Yes,' she said. (I wanted her to say no.)

I went off to another part of the train. I thought, I'm not very good at this relationship lark, am I?

In Paris, I bought the Léo Ferré and Georges Brassens records that Henri in the Colonie played. I found a book of Georges Brassens' lyrics, *Poésie et Chansons*, and tried to teach myself '*Il pleuvait fort sur la grand-route* …' I bought Mum and Harold some brandy. As I was going through the customs at Dover, I declared it. The customs man said it was too much. It was a three-quarter bottle. I was only allowed a half-bottle. He started to take it off me.

I said, 'What if I tip away the extra? I can pour it down this drain, you just tell me when to stop.'

'OK,' he said.

I started to pour.

A guy further back in the queue said, 'Hey, hang on, I could drink that.'

'Is that allowed?' I said to the customs man.

'I think so,' he said.

So the guy from the queue came over with his camp cup and I said to the customs guy, 'Say when?'

I poured.

A few seconds later, he shouted, 'When!'

The queue guy lifted his cup and knocked it back.

The customs man looked at my rucksack. 'Have you got anything else in there?'

'Yes,' I said, 'an old nail.'

'I'll have a look at that.'

I got the old nail out. It was a huge handmade cast-iron nail I had found in the Pyrenees. Probably a hundred years old or more. 'What are you going to do with that?' he said.

'I'm collecting it.'

'OK,' he said, 'carry on.'

I put the nail on my mantelpiece and told everyone the story of pouring the brandy down the drain. I did the voices and the actions.

Back at school, once the new term had started, a new, very tall English teacher introduced himself to our group. He said that he was sorry, but our A-level text was Milton's masque, *Comus*. He'd never read it, and to be absolutely honest, he had no idea what it was about. This meant, he said, that he wasn't going to teach it in the usual way. We would explore the poem together and see what we could make of it; we'd help each other find out.

Seemed a good plan to me, and I liked his honesty. I told Harold and he said, 'Very good. Very cunning. That's a good strategy. Because it's an obscure poem, he pretends that he doesn't know what it's about and you all feel more confident about analysing it.'

'No, no,' I said, 'he really meant it: he doesn't know the poem and he doesn't understand it.'

'If you want to believe that, that's fine,' he said.

So, that year we looked at *Comus* and it was strange, and occasionally implied sexiness in ways we weren't expecting: 'What hath night to do with sleep?' or someone wanting 'to please, and sate the curious taste'.

Many years later I bumped into the same teacher – he was a head by now – and he said, 'Do you remember that year we did *Comus*? You know, I didn't have a clue as to what it was about. Not a clue. But then you and that class set about making sense of it. It was quite extraordinary.' Somewhere in that one moment is a whole theory of teaching not always being about the transfer of knowledge from teacher to pupil.

Bits of the official culture of schoolwork were growing clear to me. Matthew Arnold, who we had started the previous year, got under my skin in a way I liked. Was he the Forsaken Merman? Was he Sohrab or Rustum, or neither? And what did he really dread as he stood on Dover Beach?

'A revolution, probably,' Harold said. He was amused that I had started to like Arnold.

'Yes,' he went on, 'mostly when these nineteenth-century chaps start dreading strange, destructive forces I reckon you can take it they mean the Great Unwashed rising up.'

That was like Shylock and the code behind the surface all over again.

The politics of school carried on too. At the beginning of term, the head stopped me in the corridor and offered me to be a prefect. I said, no thanks. He looked startled.

'It's an honour, you know.'

'Yes,' I said, 'but no thanks.'

'Do you want to say why?'

'No, I don't think so.'

That evening, I told Mum and Harold.

He said, 'Why didn't you tell him why?'

I said, 'I wasn't going to go on about it, but I don't want to be in charge of other people, handing out detentions to kids only a couple of years younger than me.'

In French, Mr Emmans had us read some stunning books. We read Sartre's play *Les Mains Sales* aloud, sharing the parts in the class. I realised that it addressed something of the life Mum and Harold had led; even so, the word 'Communist' in France meant something different from anything they had experienced: it involved millions of people. Many had been in life-and-death situations and taken part in the Resistance, which had turned into an uprising, a civil war and a liberation – but then, what?

I was used to reading about how the Soviet Union had 'gone wrong', but I was new to the idea of people like Sartre who reckoned the Communist Party in France had got progress and socialism wrong too. I realised that, up to this point, I had put Soviet Communists on trial, but not British or French ones. And the interesting thing was that the way into this was through a piece of culture, a play – and even more interesting that Watford Grammar, with all its pomp and circumstance, was showing us this. Maybe there was a bridge after all between the stuff I cared about out of school and some of the things they gave us in school.

Janey's dad had been in the Resistance, but he wasn't a Communist. He was amused when I told him that another of our books at school was *L'Étranger*. '*Aujourd'hui, maman est morte.*' Mum died today. What a way to begin a novel! He loved Camus – but what was there in *L'Étranger* that you could ally yourself to, I wondered. It was more like a feeling than a position, wasn't it? He said, 'Read *La Peste*!' It was very hard to argue with him. I had been warned off talking to him about Dachau. He had survived. Don't ask how. That was the point.

In class, we also went back over *Candide*. I decided that this was the most brilliant book ever. I wanted to turn it into a play or a film, or write a *Candide* for now. I loved the contrast at the heart of the book: how in the face of disaster and cruelty someone was saying that this world was the best of all possible worlds. For as long as I could remember, people had told me that the kinds of beliefs that my parents or I had were impossible because of 'human nature'. In other words, we lived in the best of all possible worlds. Wars, famines, natural disasters could come and go, but it was still the best of all possible worlds.

And there was *La Symphonie Pastorale*, André Gide's story of a village priest in the mountains (I thought of the curé of Espezel) who looks after a blind girl. She recovers her sight and realises that his care for her was more predatory and sexual than she had known, and, by implication, more than he himself had known before, too. It was disturbing: outward goings-on – conversations, acts of kindness – might not match what was really being thought and felt. You might have desires you don't know about, that are disguised, and you might even be the one who disguised them. I read the Penguin English translation, to check I hadn't missed some tiny hints and suggestions. I was loving this stuff.

In History, we were told there was going to be an exam paper at the end of the year that involved a specialised topic, a close examination of one short period which would involve reading original writings by people involved. The subject was the unification of Italy, the 'Risorgimento'. We would have to read books by Mazzini, Trevelyan's account of Garibaldi and the Thousand, and other documents. This started to seem like a film, with characters: Garibaldi, Mazzini, Cavour, Victor Emmanuel, King Bomba, each taking up a position with regard to progress, revolution, nation and society. I wanted Garibaldi not only to be brave but to be great and right. But why did he let himself be talked out of carrying on marching north? Why did he let Cavour take over? I loved this stuff, too.

For our lessons on English history, Giraldus Hughes had moved on from the Tudors. We were doing the English Civil War. There was a writer we might like to read, he said, called Christopher Hill. I bought Hill's *Century of Revolution*. Harold got some of his old, orange Left Book Club volumes off the shelf: *The People's History of England*, and *The Left in the English Revolution*. One serious puzzle: how was the

Milton who Hill talked about, the same Milton who wrote *Comus*?

It was a time of trying to make connections. This felt new. And fascinating.

The course in European History had finally left the religious wars behind (how the hell was I going to remember all that stuff for the exam?), heading fast for the 1848 revolutions. Harold gave me Hobsbawm's *Age of Revolution*. At first I was uncomfortable with his way of telling the story. At school, each topic was neatly contained by its moment and place. In contrast, Hobsbawm mucked it all up by writing 'across' Europe, making connections between countries.

'Look here, Hobsbawm,' I said to myself, 'we're not doing Hungary, so why bring Hungary into it?'

And then, even more oddly, he started going off on one about Beethoven. What did Beethoven have to do with anything? Ah, yes, there was the time I'd listened to his music with Brian and he'd said: 'Listen out for the next bit, it's where Napoleon comes in again ... Same theme, Mick ... But when he got fed up with Napoleon he changed the name of the symphony ... still great though ... Here comes the theme, Mick ...' Still, what did Beethoven have to do with the school subject 'History'? Hobsbawm was saying he had a lot to do with it: more politics of culture here, then. I stopped being uncomfortable with it. I wanted more. Much more.

Another English teacher arrived. It was his first job and he had just come off the course taught by Jimmy, Nancy and Harold at the Institute of Education, so he was about as close in age to us as a teacher could be, maybe five years older at the most. He asked us how we had been reading *Antony and Cleopatra* and what work we had done. When we told him, he didn't say anything, but in retrospect, I can see that he must have thought we'd been wasting our time.

We started again. It was as if we had changed schools, or embarked on another kind of education. We read it line by line, making sure through discussion that we understood everything, and then at the end of each scene exploring how we thought the play had advanced – what more did we know? Somewhere in the quiet probing, and occasional provocative questioning, I got something I hadn't ever got before with Shakespeare: that you shouldn't trust the view expressed by any character as being 'the truth'. People express views of others because of who they are, from their perspective, in line with their interests. Before we see Antony, two men stand at the side and say, 'See the triple pillar of the world turned into a strumpet's fool'. It deflates the pomp of Antony at that moment, but are they right that he's a strumpet's fool? They want Antony to stop lingering over Cleopatra, so of course they're saying that. And this reminded me of Brecht: you get 'distance' on characters in the plays because you see people from different perspectives. Now that connected with my out-of-school stuff.

A few of the boys had the idea that we should produce an underground magazine – all articles to be anonymous. In its own way, it was my first taste of 60s counterculture. They called it *Keyhole*. I was asked to contribute, so I wrote a monologue in the style of Giraldus. The magazine took the mick out of the school and the new head went ape. A great search went on to find the culprits. They had their suspicions, and the guy who was the editor thought we ought to confess, so we trooped into the head's study and told him it was us.

The head said he wasn't having it. (Of course he did.) We were to stop straightaway. I remember there was some effort on his part to get us to explain why it was no good – as if he would have been pleased had it had been well written! I made the mistake of saying that I thought some of it was better than other parts, and was told how typical it was of me to imply that my bit was good, and the bits the rest of them had written weren't.

When the application forms for university came in and everyone started filling them in, I realised that it was absurd that I was going to do Medicine. I didn't know anything about medicine, and I wasn't in touch with any doctors or doctoring. The anticipation in the other boys' voices made me envious. They talked about guys they knew from the year above who were already at Leeds, Manchester, Sussex, Keele, doing Economics, History, Politics, Sociology, American

Studies. It all sounded so bloody new and exciting. I decided that I'd give up on the Medicine. I'd apply to Sussex to do History or Sociology or something where you could combine a subject like that with French. As soon as I could, I talked to Giraldus about it. He said that he'd half expected me to do this and gave me a form, I filled it in and went home with it.

There was an explosion. It was out of the question. I had put them and Chick through a big shemozzle, hours of talk and help. I'd got a place at university already. This was a brilliant opportunity to do something really worthwhile. If I was so interested in all these other cultural things that I seemed to think were so bloody important – theatre, history, French, France – I could carry on doing them. Hadn't I seen how Chick has marvellous interests, like his photography and 8mm films? Doctors could be like that.

OK, I said to them eventually.

Though they knew and I knew that my real interest was in the politics of culture, I agreed to study something that had nothing to do with that. And it would be life-changing. Deep down, I knew it wasn't right; I knew there'd be trouble further down the line, but I still said, OK.

Big mistake.

# 11

## International Connections

Mum and Harold were by my bed. Mum sat next to me, her face with the dark look that spoke of pure anxiety. Her fingers drummed up and down my forearm. They asked me who had been to see me. I said I didn't know and I couldn't remember. They told me what had happened. I'd forgotten that too.

That night, I got out of the 'sling' and tried to walk out of the ward. But they caught me, the Chinese nurse laughing as she lifted me up and put me back into the sling. She was so small.

The guys in the beds next to me told me I'd been saying all kinds of things, talking about rugby and a dress rehearsal. On this side of the ward they were all young like me, but they were in plaster casts and in traction. On the other side, because it was a split ward, they were all ancient guys, with urino-genital problems, one of them sitting all day in his dressing gown with his First World War medals pinned to the top pocket. Apparently I'd come into the ward in the middle of the night. I had broken my pelvis.

Mum and Harold told me the story again. I had been walking along the road to the house, the dark stretch, on the wrong side, not facing the oncoming traffic, and a car had hit from me behind. The guy driving the car didn't stop, but went into Rickmansworth Police Station a mile or so down the road. He said that he thought he had knocked someone down. The police came back with him to the spot, but couldn't see anyone. His speech was rushed and they wondered if he was drunk. They were just about to leave when they heard someone talking. The voice was coming from the ditch a few yards down a slope, away from the road. They went to look and it was me.

I was lying on my side, talking. They picked me up and took me to the hospital. I answered every question, told them the name of our doctor – wrong one, the old family doctor from Pinner not our new one – and they got Mum and Harold in. I was peeing blood so they wanted an X-ray. I lay 'on the slab' (as Harold put it), chatting away till four in the morning, when the X-ray people came. They found that I had broken my tibia and my pelvis had come apart at the front. Women's bodies are equipped to do this in childbirth, but it wasn't usual in men. Apart from the tibia, nothing was actually broken but the body had to be helped to knit back together, that's why I was put in a sling. I would have to stay in it for at least eight weeks.

'What about *Twelfth Night*?' I kept asking. The production was bothering me more than anything else, as it was less than a week before the first night.

When the chemistry teacher who was directing turned up, he enquired whether I'd be able to do the part in crutches. Everyone was very sorry, but no: I was out of the show. I had lost Toby Belch. I was unbearably sad that I had lost Toby Belch. I still am.

Everyone who came to see me wanted to know if I remembered anything of what happened. Nothing at all. I did discover, however, that I had lost the feeling at the back of my right thigh. So I lay in bed playing games, running my finger up and down my leg: feel it, feel it, can't feel it, can't feel it, feel it.

Harold said that the man who knocked me down had been in touch and wanted to see me. What did I think? I said fine. He was young and red-faced; he apologised over and over again. I kept saying it was OK. I could see he wanted me to say that, so I did.

Stories started to come out of the others in the ward. All the smashed legs and arms and amputations were motorbike accidents. Young guys, same age as me, had spun out of control, hit walls, gone under buses. Their lives would never be the same again. Would mine? Where had my memory of those moments gone? It made me worry over whether I would be able to remember my A-level work. And now I was going to miss several months. The exams were only six months away.

'You'll have plenty of time on your hands, lad,' Harold said, 'you can spend all day studying.' He brought me my school books and stuffed them in the locker beside my bed.

But I spent all day talking. We told jokes, shared our life stories, argued, played tricks and waited desperately for visitors. Sometimes my bed was surrounded with as many as twenty people. Other times it was just me and Janey. The nights were long.

The fellow with the First World War medals, 'Peachy', told us First World War jokes in his gravelly Cockney voice. 'Once, the adjutant come round and he says, "What kind o' place you got here, then?"

"Very friendly, sir."

"What do you call yer generals?"

"We call 'em our chums, sir."

"What do you call yer colonels?"

"We call 'em 'chum', sir."

"What do you call yer sergeant-majors?"

"We call 'em our chums, sir."

"And what about yer privates?"

"We call 'em bollocks, just like anyone else, sir."'

He told us we didn't know what war was like. Meanwhile I lay in bed worrying about A-levels, but I couldn't work. The books sat in my locker and I couldn't bear to look at them.

On Christmas Day the ward was invaded by students from the London College of Divinity, which was just down the road. Unannounced, they rushed in, and one by one stood by our beds. A vicar started talking to the whole ward. He had the same high-pitched sing-song voice that Alan Bennett imitated in *Beyond the Fringe*:

'Do you remember, I wonder, the Thomas the Tank Engine stories? That one where Gordon the Big Engine went down the wrong line. He should have been on the main line but off he went down the wrong line. James the Red Engine arrived and said to Gordon, "Have you lost your way?" It's a very good question, because, you know, it happens to so many of us, doesn't it? We lose our way. I wonder, have any of you been stuck on the wrong line? Have you ever said to yourself, "I've lost my way." If you have, then, you know, Jesus had an answer. Jesus said, "I am the way."'

When he stopped, the Divinity student standing next to my bed said, 'What did you think of that?'

I said I didn't think it was for me.

'Why not?'

'I'm a Jewish atheist.'

He didn't reply to that, just stood by my bed in complete silence for the next five minutes while the rest of the students chatted away to the other patients. Then the vicar said that we would now sing 'O Come all Ye Faithful' and he said a short prayer. After that they all swept out.

In the long hours of the day, evening and night, conversations dwelled on the body, pissing, shitting and sex. On our side of the ward, we were young men bashed, mangled and chopped up by roads and machines. The old boys in other half of the ward could often be heard to groan: 'Ooohh, it's like pissing broken glass …' They were dying from the inside. One went off to the loo and never came back. Peachy had seen it all before. 'I saw 'em die like flies,' he said.

The nurses, cleaners and women who brought the food round were endlessly scrutinised and discussed. They came from all over the world, and stood by our beds saying we would get better. One of the men on our side was a champion swimmer who said he had a broken neck. It didn't seem to stop him walking about the ward and, he claimed, having a thing with the Indonesian nurse. Pete, the loudest of the bikers, with one leg off, was engaged to Sue, and his story was that prior to the accident he'd been spending most of his time with her 'doing it'. He was allowed home over Christmas on the strict condition that he lay in exactly the same position as he was lying in hospital. He was sent off with a volley of jokes about the 'same position', giving us the thumbs-up from his wheelchair.

The routine of the ward meant that we were woken up every morning at half-past five by the 'polisher'. Maria from Italy came in to clean and polish the floor. She hardly knew any English, and every morning I tried to think if I knew any Italian. We once did six weeks of Italian with the long-lashed Latin teacher, Mrs Young, who explained how Italian was very like Latin but that was all to do with an *agricola* ploughing his field and the Gauls being stuck in a *fossa*.

Then it came to me: in *Candide* there is a passage where the Old Woman is telling her story. When she was young and beautiful, she found herself in the midst of some awful carnage and a heap of bodies. She falls into a trance, but is woken by a young man leaning over her saying, in Italian: '*Che sciagura d'essere senza coglioni.*'

'You'll find the meaning in the notes,' Mr Emmans said. And there it was: 'What agony it is to have no testicles.' '*Sciagura*', he said, 'is a bit of a poetic word, though.'

I thought, as Maria comes past my bed with the polisher, why don't I say that line? It was half-past five in the morning, dark outside. Maria switched on the polisher and came towards the bed. I did a sideways lean out of the bed and groaned out, giving it the full agonised performance, '*Che sciagura d'essere senza coglioni.*'

I thought she would think it was funny – rude, yes, but funny too. Perhaps I wasn't thinking of what I looked like, suspended above the bed with a sling around my middle. She wasn't on the medical staff, how would she know what had actually happened to me? Why could it not possibly have been something related with my *coglioni*? And it didn't occur to me that my dying act might have been at the very least somewhat convincing at that time of the morning. I hadn't thought it through.

She screamed, dropped her polisher and ran out the ward. I heard shouting outside and a moment later the matron came running in. She was a very small Danish woman, who marched up to my bed and said with real menace in her voice,

'What have you just said to Maria?'

By now everyone was awake. 'I said something from a book we're reading at school.'

'What, though?'

'I don't know. I don't speak Italian. It's a famous, very famous, classic French book I'm studying for my A-levels and there's one bit where it's in Italian. But I don't know what it means. I just thought I'd say it to Maria to see ... to see if ...'

'I don't believe a word you're saying. Not a word,' she said. 'If ever you say or do anything like that again, if you do anything to annoy or frighten my cleaners, you'll be out of here. Believe me, you'll be on your way home.' And she stormed out.

Everyone else was on to me: 'What did you say?' 'What happened?'

I told them the whole story – what it meant, where it came from – and pleaded with them to keep it to themselves. They did. Maria came in the next morning and I apologised to her. I said I was very, very sorry. I told myself that I could see a flicker of a smile on her face. I have imagined since, that there have been times when people have asked her about her work and she's told the story of the big silly English boy leaning out of his hammock crying about his poetic agony.

Pete came back. Thumbs up. But then, a few weeks later, disaster: Sue was pregnant. Pete lay in bed singing the new Frank Ifield hit, 'Don't blame me'. Peachy could hardly contain himself: 'Who else should he bleedin' blame?'

Beatlemania was now gripping Britain. The tide flowed over the hospital, we all knew how to sing every number on the album with 'All My Loving' on it. It became our soundtrack. As a treat, the nurses got hold of a film of the Beatles in concert and were going to show it in the hospital cinema, usually used for training purposes. So, they levered us out of our beds, put us in wheelchairs and wheeled us off to the cinema. There, on a very raw, oddly coloured film were the Beatles singing, a bit of tuning up between numbers and us in our wheelchairs and plaster casts watching. There was even a bit of Beatle banter going on. I loved their banter.

Part of the thrill of the experience was the way the Beatles talked. Radio and television were up until then arenas of politeness. The cross-fire repartee of everyday speech was almost entirely excluded. We had heard snatches in films like *Saturday Night and Sunday Morning*, but that was safely corralled as fiction. But when the Beatles were interviewed, something happened that was altogether unprecedented. Sometimes they didn't even bother to answer the questions; sometimes they talked to each other instead of talking to the interviewer; and of course they said all sorts of flippant things when they did answer.

And it wasn't a one-off. It kept happening. We've got so used to it since then, it's become the cliché: the interview with the 4×100 relay team, the dance troupe, the hen party or the boy band, where interviewers positively encourage the anarchy of everyone talking at once and making jokes at each other's expense. But the Beatles invented it. Back then, rather than being a staged routine, it clearly discomfited and bewildered some of the interviewers. It disrupted their scripted flow. For a brief moment the people in control had lost control, and those of us watching, we knew it.

After eight weeks I was allowed out of the sling, but I had forgotten how to walk. I was taken into the corridor in a wheelchair and told to stand up, but then I just stood there without moving. Mr Adams, the charge nurse, was having none of it. He was a very brisk, openly gay man from Lancashire. He always had stories of people who were just like us; he'd seen it all before. In our blue hours of missing wives and girlfriends he'd laugh and say they were all 'hospital romances'. 'They won't last.' He pretended to be a hard-hearted, cynical bastard but we heard that the only reason Peachy was there was because Mr Adams was wangling something for him. Peachy had no family, no one knew where he lived, all we knew was that he was dying.

'Now come on, Michael!' Mr Adams shouted at me, 'we want to get rid of you, boy!'

But there was no connection between my head and my legs.

He shoved my leg. I moved it a little. Then it was the other one I couldn't move.

'Look ahead of you,' Mr Adams said. The corridor went on forever – I will never walk that far again.

Every day they took me out into the corridor and, bit by bit, I got it. I thought of my brain sending messages to my legs and feet, telling them to do things. They said that I needed to be rehabilitated and I should go to Garston Rehabilitation Centre.

I said goodbye to all the people on the ward, and we said how we would stay in touch. 'You won't,' said Mr Adams, 'just go.' He was right. Even though I went past Mount Vernon Hospital nearly every day for the next six months, going to and from school, the only one I bumped into was the swimmer who said he had broken his neck. He said that the thing with the Indonesian nurse was unbelievable, but he was coughing up spinal fluid.

At the Garston Rehabilitation Centre they put us in dark blue tracksuits. We were given a routine in the gym or on the playing field outside. The people running the place were like the rugby teacher at school, muscly guys in shorts who liked doing star jumps. The trainer said I was the fittest person who had ever come to the Centre, and he expected me to be doing circuits and one-mile runs by the end of the two weeks.

He sent me out on to the playing field and told me to run 400 metres. But I had forgotten how to run. I lifted one leg but couldn't get the other to do what it was supposed to. I was on my own this time: it was a cold March morning, the field still damp.

Again, the others in the centre were a mix of young and old. People had been sent there from all over Britain, often after industrial accidents and diseases. In the gym there were two miners and they did a bit of exercise. Then they sat down, and a guy rubbed and banged their chest, and they coughed and spat into a spittoon. Again and again and again.

I sat at mealtimes with someone my age. He had left school at fifteen and was doing an apprenticeship to be an electrician. He had been up a tower scaffold working on a beam when the tower started to collapse, so he had grabbed hold of the beam. The tower fell away and he was left holding the beam, thirty feet up. They ran about not knowing what to do, and he hung on for as long as he could but then let go. He broke his legs and smashed his feet. He walked about with an aggressive shuffle in a pair of big floppy black leather clown shoes.

I told him how one holiday I had worked in a factory, painting the ceiling. They had sent me and another guy up on a beam with no duckboards or rail to hold on to. We had to slap white gloss paint on two big sloping ceilings that were really just the inside of the roof. Outside it was hot, the sun was shining directly onto the roof. I started to feel blurred. Things were getting near and far, near and far. I looked across to the other bloke. 'You OK?' I said.

'No,' he said, 'I'm feeling fucking weird.'

I shouted down to the foreman, 'The paint's getting to us. It's hot up here. We're coming down.'

We clambered off the beams, down the ladder and rushed outside for some fresh air. We stood grinning at each other. It was like a sick feeling but instead of being sick, it made you grin.

The guy at Garston heard me out, but I knew and he knew that I'd survived my time on a high beam. I had survived whatever happened to me on that road. And I was already beginning to run again. He wouldn't ever run again.

About the time it was all over, and I was back home, the first Stones album came out and I was caught. At first the blues snob in me thought they were just a bunch of suburban boys, same as us, who knew the same Mississippi and Chicago Blues songs as we knew and were doing them, but not as well as the real thing. Why not listen to the real thing: Howlin' Wolf, John Lee Hooker, Mississippi John Hurt, Fred McDowell, Sister Rosetta Tharpe, Elmore James, Muddy Waters, Robert Johnson – even Chuck Berry and Bo Diddley? OK, the backing was neat – I suppose – but the singing! It was so feeble, and sounded off-mike half the time. I watched them on TV. Why did people think they were so good?

But then I had a much bigger problem: why did I think they were so bloody good? Before I knew or could admit it, I thought they were great. The fact was, I loved the Stones's first album. I wanted to be in the Rolling Stones. I bought a 'marine band harmonica', the same as theirs, and tried to teach myself to play 'blues harp' as it's called. I bought two EPs of Gus Cannon's Jug Band from the 1930s and listened in awe to one of their line-up, Noah Lewis, who played the harmonica like it was a clarinet. The sound of a harmonica blues over the top of an electrified Chicago blues backing became the most exciting sound I'd ever heard. I taught myself how to bend the notes, to turn the wheezy concertina sound of the harmonica into the blue note, so that it sounded like an American train hooter dip as it speeds past. 'That's the Doppler effect,' Brian said.

Brian had taught himself to play the guitar, and when he came back from university we would have 'blues-ups' and try to sing Big Bill Broonzy numbers or tracks from an album we had of Sonny Terry, Woody Guthrie and Cisco Houston:

> Me and a man was working side by side,
> This is what it meant
> They was paying him a dollar an hour
> but they paying me 50 cent
> They said, 'If you'se white, you'se alright.
> If you'se brown, stick around
> but if you'se black, get back, get back, get back' ...

And:

> Down in the hen house
> on my knees
> thought I heard a chicken sneeze.
> Only a rooster sayin' his prayers
> thanking God that the hen's upstairs
> We shall be free – in the mornin' ...

And:

> Jackhammer man all day long ...
> I been doing some hard travelling ...
> Vigilante man ...
> This train is bound for glory, this train ...
> Some will kill you with a shotgun, and some with a
> fountain pen ...

One day I could do this ... be in a band and play harmonica.

For the time being, I had to get on with A-levels. There were whole books I hadn't even read, let alone studied: Mauriac's *Nœud de Vipères*, Conrad's *Nostromo* and – Jesus – what about the Restoration following the Civil War? I started waking up in the night and sweating. It was like the Eleven Plus exams all over again. Though this time I came out in a row of pustules round my chest. I was a 'spotty bastard' in my late teen years anyway, but I had never had them on my ribs. The doctor said it was shingles, was I anxious about anything? 'Not really,' I said.

Harold said there was going to be an insurance case, and I would be interviewed by a doctor from the company who insured the car of the bloke who knocked me down. There'll be some money involved. Neither he nor Mum seemed bothered about it. I thought it was odd, even wrong, to earn money from an accident. In the back of my mind, I thought of the guy standing next to my bed, red-faced and sorry.

The doctor who examined me was older and posher than I expected. He did all the usual stuff, pulse, reflex, say 'Ahhh'. I said that I felt a twinge of pain in my groin and I had lost some sensation on the back of my right leg. He did what I had done with my finger, but with a pin. 'Say when you can feel it.'

'Anything else?'

I said that I didn't think I got an erection the way I used to.

He said, 'How do you know? You're not married.'

I said I did have a girlfriend.

He cleared his throat and said it wouldn't last.

The whole session went on for about ten or fifteen minutes. Later we heard that they were going to give me £400. Mum took me to the bank and got me to open an account and put it in. She said, 'That's yours. Spend it on something you really want.' I couldn't think of anything.

At school, the serious CND-ers (who I suspect thought that I wasn't serious enough because I had broken the rule of serious CND-ing, which was 'You can't be a CND-er and play rugby') invited Colin Ward, the famous anarchist, to come and talk to us in the new Sixth Form Common Room. He gave a short talk on anarchism – which was new to me – and then opened it up for discussion. He was calm, quiet and very good at answering a question with a question. 'Why do you think you need leaders?' he said. 'If there are things that you think need changing, why not get together with other people who agree with you and do what you can to change things?'

Was I an anarchist? The head teacher thought so. One day he stopped me in the corridor, pointed at my chin, and said, 'Off!'

A few days later, I hadn't shaved it 'Off!' and he said, 'Do as I say or you'll be chopped.'

I told Mum. 'What could he possibly mean?' she said. 'What a bizarre bloke,' Harold said.

Maybe Janey's parents thought I was an anarchist too. I said to Janey, why don't we bunk off school and go to Hampstead Heath? We each leave home looking as if we're going to school, but instead we meet at Hampstead Station, go to the Heath, and then each go home and make like we had been at school? She was nervous but liked the idea. We spent a day in what seemed like a secret location, not far from where the water sits round the viaduct. It was hot and sunny; the grass and trees were lush. For a few hours, we pretended we weren't attached to anything other than ourselves – though amazingly enough, I think we did some homework. We were both interested in what we were studying, and worried about exams. Then we went our separate ways home.

Someone must have squealed, or maybe Janey couldn't bear to lie to her parents, and next thing, I was summoned to her house. Janey's mum thought I had betrayed all the trust they had put in me. Janey's dad thought I was a bastard and had ruined her chances of doing well in her exams and if I ever did anything like that again, he'd kill me. As we had thought for years that Janey's dad was one of the world's expert killers, this had a scary edge to it. The only relief was Janey's half-brother, who thought it was bloody funny. Not that he dared admit it in front of his step-dad, who regularly explained to him why he was no good.

In the lead-up to A-levels I devised (or thought I had devised) a way of revising I called 'reducing': write out the thing I was supposed to be learning, reduce it to 'points', and reduce those to single lines, phrases and mnemonics. It worked for everything apart from the books I hadn't read. I was running several different motivations in my head: I thought revising for exams proved that exams were pointless, plus, for the first time in my life I didn't need to do well in a set of exams, because the Medical School had only asked for two passes. Even so, I wanted to do well. So I beavered away with a sense of freedom. When it came to the exams themselves, I had an exhilarating sense of everything flowing easily on to the page. My 'reducing' system worked. But, I kept thinking, what was the point? What was the point of knowing how to 'reduce' and 'expand' it back up again, just for an exam? It was a technique that fitted the system, but surely it wasn't any good for anything apart from exams?

After we had all finished them, a bunch of us came over to our place and we sat on the lawn that Harold had become obsessed by. Not content with the satisfaction that this was the first lawn in his life, he spent hours prodding and poking it, and discussing dandelion roots and clover with anyone he met. We sat on this much loved turf and devised a manifesto for a new kind of sixth form. We wrote this up as a booklet, an agitation for better education. We spent a week devising new kinds of syllabus, new ways in which subjects could be combined, and how portfolios of work could be submitted. Rather than just choosing three subjects, you could do less of one topic but more topics, to make up for it. Teachers would circulate their notes instead of dictate them. Schools would get sixth-formers to set up 'study groups' outside of class, to meet and discuss things. You were to be told the questions before you went into the exams – just as we had done for the special History subject, the Risorgimento. The list of demands got bigger and bigger, more and more utopian, but we didn't ever write it up. It still sits in my mind, like the memory of that day on Hampstead Heath with Janey: full of sunshine and hope: a bit heady, a bit dizzy.

A nd that was it. We'd all be at university in September. I would start doing the equivalent of Biology, Chemistry and Physics A-level all crammed into one year. But I had already developed a dread of it. I had no sense whatsoever of being on the verge of an exciting change.

Before that began, however, I planned to spend the summer with my French friends in the Pyrenees. I wanted to pick up from where I had left off the previous summer, and deepen my self-imposed immersion in Frenchness. What would I absorb this year?

The long overnight train journey from Paris to Ax-les-Thermes turned into a Godard film. Two arty girls – chic in an unruly way, uncombed hair and silk shirts – who were in my compartment stood in the corridor with me, asking me where I was going and what I was doing, long before I asked them anything. After I had told my life story and why I was heading for the High Pyrenees, I quizzed them. They were sisters, they said, daughters of an ambassador. I made sure several times that they really did mean an ambassador – the real thing, a real-life ambassador? I asked where their father had done his ambassadoring. New York.

As we sped through the French countryside, I fitted them into a panorama of dinner parties and dances (culled from TV and Pathé News), swanking with the Kennedys, five-star generals napalming Vietnam, Latin American juntas with Boeing epaulettes. And we were standing in a train corridor. Couldn't dad afford a couchette or two for them? They were going to Ax-les-Thermes too, a little un-chic town in an un-chic part of the Pyrenees. Dad lived there now. Sometimes. And why had I put in the effort to get the white-sock plus gym shoe look? They wore black socks and brown leather shoes. And yet looked French. Better to not even try.

At the house in the mountains this year, it was Mum and Dad (M. and Mme Miquel) plus Dad's ancient mother, Mémé, one of the sons, François, and the two daughters – Annie with her school friend, Geneviève with her future husband, Giovanni. Dad had been Professor of Italian to Giovanni, who himself had an Italian father. He wore something I had never seen at close quarters before: one of those floppy hats with a little peak and a cloth button in the middle. People like Charles Aznavour and Sacha Distel were wearing them too. I thought about buying one, but censored the thought. There were limits to the extent to which I could kid myself I was French. The matelot T-shirt maybe, but not the floppy peaked hat. Giovanni and Geneviève didn't stay long.

I soon discovered that M. Miquel was not only a serious academic translating Cesare Pavese into French, but also a comedian. What with him being of humble origin, working as an academic in the arts and being the same age as Harold, the analogies became closer by the minute. He told set-piece jokes – or rather taught them to me, as they often involved specific points of context, like this: the word for beautiful in German is *schön*. The word for a fast in French is *jeûne*. When Germans speak French, French people think they pronounce the 'j' sound as 'sch'. That's the explanation, now for the joke. The great German cardinal of Cologne and the great French cardinal of Paris are walking along the road together in Paris. The German cardinal catches sight of a beautiful woman. The German cardinal says, '*Schön*', and the French cardinal replies, '*Et abstinence.*'

I didn't laugh. M. Miquel had a bit more explaining to do: '*jeûne et abstinence*' is like a slogan of the Church clerisy. Ah, yes, got it.

He tried me on another. Context: it's during the war; there is severe milk rationing. Every morning the women queue in the town square in Ax-les-Thermes to get their ration. The government has imposed a rule that there should be two queues. One for pregnant women, who receive a larger ration, and the other for all other women. As a result, the non-pregnant queue was full of vigilant women forever checking for evidence that the pregnant ones really were pregnant, staring very closely at bulges, looking to see if women had stuffed cushions up their blouses and so on. One day, one of the non-pregnant women is suspicious and says to a woman in the other queue (here M. Miquel moved into a perfect imitation of the local southern accent, where the 'r's are all rolled and the final 'e' sounds are sounded out, making it sound a bit like Spanish): '*Vous n'êtes pas enceinte, vous!*' (You!

You're not pregnant!) The other woman replies, '*Presque!*' (Nearly!)

I got that gag.

François had a new joke. This one needed the context of Franco's Spain, reputed to have the world's largest percentage of military and ecclesiastical personnel in relation to total population of any country in the world. The space race is on. Who will be first on the moon, the Americans or the Russians? In the end the Americans get there first. The American astronaut opens the door of the spaceship, climbs down onto the moon's surface and sees that there's a bloke sitting there.

'Wow!' says the American. 'Where are you from?'

'Spain,' says the guy.

'But how?'

The person telling the joke now has to do a gesture, banging the ends of his fists together as if piling them one on top of the other. '*Curé, militaire, curé, militaire … jusqu*'à la lune!' (priest, soldier, priest, soldier … all the way to the moon).

I started going out for walks on my own, climbing the lower hills, exploring the forests, getting over the mountain to see into the neighbouring valley. It was stunning; I had never seen anything like it. When it came to harvest time I was asked to help. I had helped with harvests or haymaking before, and recalled golden fields, stooks of wheat, beat-up old tractors, carts full of hay. On one occasion in the Jura I had sat with a French boy on a hay cart pulled by oxen, and I remember us giggling our heads off when the ox in front of us shat.

This was different. The field was on a slope and in place of golden wheat, there was grey-looking rye; we were going to do *battage* – a form of threshing. While men and women cut the rye with billhooks and scythes, another chap manned a juddering thresher that was no bigger than a sideboard. He took bunches of rye and poked them into this machine, where it bashed the heads of the rye. My job was to fetch bunches from the people who had cut them and take them to the chap doing the threshing. They all talked to each other in patois, not French. In fact, they talked to me in patois too, and the son from the family translated. The first phrase I learned, born of necessity, was '*N'y a prou*' – meaning 'Enough!' I was handing him the bunches too quickly for the machine. The second, also from necessity, was *'Soun gantsat'*, 'I'm tired'. This old language was M. Miquel's original language, and it belonged to a place he had migrated from. Another overlap, with Harold and Yiddish. These connections grabbed me.

Afterwards, all the people who worked the harvest were invited to a feast laid on by Mémé's sister, an ancient woman who had never left the village. She was very small and brown-skinned, wore a headscarf and a dark dress down to the floor. She must have been born in the 1880s. She had cooked the feast in a pot over a fire, and it was a stew of many meats, mostly game birds. We sat round tables that had been shoved together, ate and drank, drank and ate, while the harvesters talked in patois. I tried out *'N'ya prou!'* and *'Soun gantsat!'* I felt I was lucky to be taking part in a bit of old Europe. My Frenchness studies were progressing.

A few days later it was the village fête. Everything was going well at first, with a band similar to the one in Laurac three years earlier, and the lead singer singing about pétan-que, the game of bowls played in every village square in France – *'Une partie de pétanque, ça fait plaisir, tu la tires et tu la manques'* (A game of pétanque, what fun, you throw and you miss) – but then I heard some shouting. There was a rushing-together of men, women screamed, fisticuffs broke out and a group of men huddled round the village mayor and pulled him away. Some others walked off jeering and throw-ing obscure gestures back at everyone, stroking the underside of their chins, clenching fists and wiggling little fingers and such – mostly meaning things like 'You're rubbish' or 'You've got a little dick.'

I got the story later, back at the house where everyone had an angle on what had happened. Young men and kids had come from the next village, Sorgeat, less than two kilo-metres away, and had made fun of the pétanque song. The village mayor, a man in his eighties, told them to lay off. They mocked him and he tried to thump them while shouting about one of them, in his bass voice and full southern accent: *'Il me casse les couilles, ce type-là'* (literally, 'He busts my balls, this guy' but meaning 'This guy really pisses me off').

Then Mémé said her piece. There had always been a problem with Sorgeat. Once when she was a girl (that would have been around 1900), it was Christmas and Sorgeat was getting snowed in. So the people from her village invited some of the Sorgeat people to come over. The children arrived wearing red socks. That was the story.

She repeated, they came wearing red socks. Bit by bit we got it that red socks was a cheek. Red socks was insulting to the people who had invited them. And then she kept repeating '*Ça ne me regarde pas*' (It's no business of mine), a phrase that she must have held with her for more than sixty years: that people thought red socks was wrong, but put on a show of it not being their business. At least that's how I understood it. She sat there shaking her head, saying it over and over again, '*Ça ne me regarde pas*,' with her 'r's rolling in the southern way. M. Miquel repeated the village saying in patois: '*De Sorgeat, ni buon vent, ni buon gent!*' (From Sorgeat, neither good wind, nor good folks.)

'Exactly,' Mémé said.

M. Miquel was carrying on with his translation of Cesare Pavese and got stuck on a line where Pavese had written in English, 'Ripeness is all'. What does it mean, he asked me. I talked about fruit being ripe, how 'ripeness' wasn't really a word that people use very much and I had no idea why it was 'all'. He said he would leave it in the English but translate it in a note. I thought of Voltaire writing '*Che sciagura d'essere senza coglioni*' in Italian in a French book. I was a bit mystified by it. I didn't find out it was a quote from *King Lear* until about three years later.

I got back in time to receive my A-level results, which involved going up to school and walking into the head teacher's study where he had a master sheet in front of him. He took his time, ran his finger along the line and read them out: History, A, English, A, English S-Level, A, General Studies, A, French, D. 'Very good. Down on the French, but very good,' he noted. 'You've got the best mark of the year in History and English. You can't have school prize in both, you'll have to choose. That's it. Goodbye.'

And I left.

Mum and Harold were on holiday and had said they'd ring me from a call box. I waited in. I said, 'I've got As in everything except French', and waited for him to say, 'So, you couldn't get yourself an A in French, eh?' but no, as he relayed the results to Mum he got more and more excited and kept saying, 'And to think you were in hospital all that time. Bloody amazing.' He was clearly delighted. To tell the truth, it was me who was disappointed about the French. I had devoted all this time and effort to knowing France, being as French as I could, and here I was showing I wasn't much good at it.

It mattered. It irritated me. Yes, there was the fact that I hadn't read the books, but it seemed like a feeble excuse. Then, when I thought about the English and History, I worried about being about to stop doing them. Because they were things I could do, liked doing, was good at doing. No, there was more to it than that: studying English, French and History was how I thought. It was all how I was. Since the Colonie de Vacances I had gained a taste for internationalism and making connections: patois–Yiddish, Rolling Stones–Muddy Waters, Voltaire–Pavese, Garibaldi–Cromwell …

I rang round the others, and they had all got what they needed to go to university. Terry was in at Leeds. He was over the moon.

When Mum and Harold got home I wouldn't stop talking about the holiday. It annoyed them. Perhaps it was because I had found a family I liked that hadn't come from their stable as the Aprahamians, Flowers and Kaufmans had done. Perhaps it was just their own preoccupations – Mum was going into teacher training, and had got a job as a lecturer at Goldsmiths. In an ideal world she had wanted that head teacher's job, but perhaps training teachers was a good idea, she thought. There was the problem of the journey, though, Rickmansworth to New Cross Gate every morning and night.

A long journey to medical school would have been a problem for me, too, other than that we all reckoned that it would be a good idea for me to leave home and find some-where. Chick, the doctor friend who had helped me decide

I wanted to be a doctor, and whose daughter was at the medical school too, had a sister and brother-in-law (a doctor of course) who lived in the Sudan. Their son, Geoff, was also at the medical school, and they had rented a flat for him.

The flat was in Harrow, not far from where I was born and not far from Chick's house – the idea being that we could be checked up on. But Harrow? Why would I want to move out of home into a flat-share in Harrow, of all places? Everyone I knew who went to university was moving away from the suburbs, away from places like Pinner, Harrow, Northwood and Watford – to new places like Leeds, Manchester and Nottingham, or, on occasion, Oxford and Cambridge. If it was going to be in London, at least make it Muswell Hill, Crouch End or Camden. Not Harrow.

I kept my misgivings to myself. I knew I wouldn't get a hearing. In fact, I was compounding the misgivings: leaving home, leaving English, History and French, leaving school, about to start to do Medicine, which now seemed a decision made on a whim, and, bloody hell, now moving to a suburban flat back in suburban Harrow. Not much internationalism there.

The only thing going for it was that it was near to where my new girlfriend lived. It hadn't worked out with Janey. Perhaps the Hampstead Heath fiasco had put a damper on things. Perhaps I suspected that Janey agreed with her parents that it had ruined her life. Perhaps I didn't fancy her dad killing me. I had started going out with A., who was the daughter of Jimmy, the one who called Harold 'Johnny', and was now Harold's boss at the Institute of Education. I had known A. since she was about seven. She was in the sixth form and lived a bus ride away in Hatch End, round the corner, right where I had 'blacked up' as the Prince of Morocco's servant-boy in *The Merchant of Venice*. Definitely, I seemed to be going backwards not forwards.

# 12

---

# Not Doing Medicine

The first thing I did at Medical School was pretend I wasn't there. Then I pretended that I wasn't pretending. Instead of joining in the social life of the school, I headed off to the London Students' Union, which wasn't a students' union. It was a leisure centre: gym, swimming pool and canteen, and quite a few students like me, wandering around looking for somewhere that wasn't their own college. I joined a drama society that was for people who had chosen not to join their own college's drama society.

Early on that term there was the 1964 General Election, and I watched the results come in in the University College common room. I knew no one there and no one knew me, and I heard myself cheering the Wilson victory. In my mind, it felt as if a lifetime of Toryism was being swept aside. In reality it was only thirteen years of Churchill, Macmillan and Douglas-Home. Nevertheless, this regime had taken up so much of my childhood that it appeared as the natural order. A thread of continuity weaved from Tories in power all the way down to people in power in small local ways – headmasters, local businessmen who stood as Tory councillors, shopkeepers – even the owner of the Red Lion Pub, who Brian called 'The King of Pinner' because of the pompous way he stood outside his pub. It could be found in the uniformity of dress or accent of the long lines of suited men who walked past our flat in the mornings heading off to the city, or you could hear it in the way people phrased things, like when they said, 'It is often thought that …', meaning, 'I think …'; or 'It would be reasonable to say ...', meaning 'I think ...' There was an implied sense that 'the way things are' was the best and the only way things should be run. Throughout the fifties, the message we got was that there was no need for change.

By 1964, however, the ruling order looked ridiculous and hypocritical. Forever lecturing the population on how to run family life, how to have sex and how to be law-abiding citizens, a bunch of mandarins were caught, in their terms (not mine), having 'extramarital' sex, 'consorting with call girls' and getting 'dangerously' close to Russian spies. Such activities proved tricky for politicians claiming to be our natural leaders. They now looked like laughing stocks.

This was clear to all of us, but Harold Wilson also gave the impression that he would act to make a fairer society. He was no working-class hero, but at least he wasn't born posh, and he never seemed the kind of person who had been told by those around him that he was born to rule. Surely he would remember this when he came in to power.

Anyone with time to read the small print of the manifestoes could see that in actual fact, most of what Wilson was offering was little more than some vacuous guff about technology. But it made Labour sound modern. Mr Ordinary, Harold Wilson, would harness technology and we would all be better off. In contrast, the Tory machine did all they could to scare us into thinking that Labour in power would be like a cross between Guy Fawkes and Stalin.

None of this had much to do with the biology, physics, chemistry or medicine that I was pretending to learn at medical school. I quickly found out that the other medical students were mostly the sons and daughters of doctors. This explained the nature of students in the years above me: they had known they wanted to be doctors from the age of three, had done A-level science and were now proceeding with their Second MB (Anatomy, Physiology, Biochemistry) or even further, doing their 'firms' on the wards. (That MB bit stands for *Medicinae Baccalaureus*, Bachelor of Medicine.)

Less obvious was why such doctors' children were doing what I was doing in First MB. It emerged that some of them had flunked their A-levels, so Mum and Dad were giving them another chance. One or two others had taken the 'liberal' option and done arts A-levels, like me, while a group of mature students who had done degrees in other subjects or even led lives as solicitors had decided that they'd prefer to be doctors.

As for the course, some of it I found interesting, some of it I found too difficult. My problem was that it felt like I was wearing someone else's skin. I couldn't tell myself that it really was me doing this stuff, being this doctor-to-be person. I tried listening in on these students further ahead in the course, and as they chatted in the canteen about metabolism in the liver and sickle cell anaemia, it sounded even less like me. I couldn't see myself as someone sitting in the canteen in two years' time riffing about liver metabolism.

There was one immediate distraction: Silman. He looked unnervingly like Janey's dad, but without the aggression and back story. He had done a Philosophy degree at the Sorbonne, written a novel about people trying to assassinate de Gaulle some years before Frederick Forsyth, was running a cafe in Walthamstow Market to pay for his course, and was in the middle of an international legal case brought by Jacques Soustelle, the former Gaullist minister, more recently associated with the generals' plot to oust de Gaulle for having 'given away' Algeria.

In the novel, Silman and his co-author had claimed that Soustelle wanted to assassinate de Gaulle. As a result Soustelle was suing both of them for libel. Within days of us knowing each other, he nicknamed me 'The Stalinist' and had matched several of our fellow-students with leading Nazis: the Führer, Hess, Goering and so on. He never referred to them by their own names from that point on. The cafe in Walthamstow Market was mostly being run by his co-writer on the book about de Gaulle, who also had done a Philosophy degree at the Sorbonne and who – according to the plan – would start on a medical course the following year. Eventually they planned to win the Nobel Prize for discovering something – so long as the court case didn't drag on too long.

I was 'The Stalinist' because of my unwillingness to

condemn Mum and Harold outright as collaborators with the Purges, the Ukrainian genocide, the Nazi–Soviet pact, the Gulag and the invention of the 'Doctors' Plot'. I wasn't given quite as clear a picture of his background as I had given him of mine, but it appeared to start out in South Africa and pass through St Paul's School before a life-changing induction into Marxist philosophy and post-structuralism at the Sorbonne, where he attended lectures by Sartre and Jean-François Lyotard. Lyotard had even become a friend.

Within days of us knowing each other he had demanded that I read Sartre's *La Nausée* and *L'être et le néant*, Camus' *Le Mythe de Sisyphe* and de Beauvoir's *Les Mandarins*. He even drew up a list of further reading including Canetti's *Auto-da-Fé*, Upton Sinclair, Sinclair Lewis, Margarete Buber-Neumann's *Under Two Dictators, Hitler and Stalin* and *Milena*, and the complete works of Jean Genet.

I said that if I did get round to reading any of it, I couldn't read the French ones in French. 'Ridiculous!' he said. 'Of course you can.' I asked him if he had known much French before going to the Sorbonne. No, he hadn't. Once he was there, he went to classes and picked it up, he said. What? At the same time as trying to understand the philosophy? Yes.

He described the way French universities worked: if you passed your Baccalauréat (like A-levels, but with the added obstacle that you have to pass the whole raft), you were entitled to go to your local university for free. None of the rigmarole of interviews, entry requirements and clearing houses. But then the first year at university wasn't anything like English universities either. It seemed you looked ahead to the end of the first year, chose an exam you would do, then signed up for lectures in the great amphitheatres of the Sorbonne to help you tackle that exam.

He had gone to the lectures and loved the course. Now that he was in medical school, it mystified me as to why he didn't feel as much out of his skin studying the properties of matter, valences, rat dissection and Young's Modulus as I did. Instead, he tackled it philosophically.

Early on, we were doing Electricity. Just before the first seminar, he took me to one side and said in a conspiratorial way, 'They know what electricity *isn't*, but they don't know what electricity *is*.'

I said, 'Of course they know what electricity is. They teach it.'

'Typical Stalinist,' he said, 'accepting at face value what the authorities tell you.'

The first seminar was going fine, the tutor had talked about positive and negative charges and transfer of energy, electrons moving along wires, and good and bad conductors. He was drawing atoms on the blackboard with little arrows and plus and minus signs, when Silman whispered to me, 'Watch this.' He asked the tutor, 'What is electricity?'

The tutor – who like all the others that year was kind, helpful, interested and interesting – started up again, drawing atoms and trying, with his chalk, to make electrons move across the blackboard. It became clear that in the end the only way he could really describe electricity was with 'charge', 'positive and negative', and 'transfer of energy'. I think everyone was content with that explanation, but Silman said that with something as basic as electricity, which we can see in operation all day long, shouldn't we actually know what it is? You could believe in that moment that he thought he was unmasking the truth behind Stalin's Show Trials.

Maybe he would get a Nobel Prize by discovering what electricity really is. Or maybe what he was saying didn't matter. It was hard to know which. 'Just imagine if people could live forever,' he said, 'the exploitation of capitalism and the incessant wars and man-made famines would become so intolerable there would be world revolution.'

I dived in: 'But people don't live forever.'

To him, that seemed like a minor point.

Silman was Sartrean about the Vietnam War: if you weren't against the war, you were for it, he argued. In the middle of us dissecting a rat, he would argue with some of the sons and daughters of doctors. It was like a confrontation between people talking different languages. The students would use a word like 'democracy' as if it was similar to 'air' or 'house' – a term we all agreed on. I don't suppose they – or I – had ever wondered whether this use of the word 'democracy' was itself part of the way we were being recruited to support the war, or at the very least to not oppose it.

'It's called "democracy" because it isn't,' Silman said.

What?

'The people the Americans are supporting are a vicious, corrupt clique. If the South Vietnamese really were democrats, the Americans wouldn't support them. The American problem isn't with Communism, it's with democracy.'

'Have you found the carotid artery?' the tutor called out from the front.

I was spending plenty of time with A. – often going to folk clubs or talking about our parents. The deeper meaning of relationships could be explored by trying to figure out how or why our parents had got together and stayed there. She very much liked my mother, but I think she was of the view that Harold was a clever ogre. Some people treated him as if he was a cross between Lenny Bruce and Isaiah Berlin. On her side, she regarded her father Jimmy (Harold's boss at the Institute of Education, the 'Inst') as a kind genius and her mother (nickname 'Robert') as a nightmare.

Jimmy was an ex-RAF war hero who had nearly died in Crete. (He showed me a pebble in the drawer of his desk that he said he used to suck when they ran out of water in the siege of Crete.) He developed theories of language and learning that came out of the liberalism of Dewey. His partner in this was Nancy. And here was the intriguing bit for A. and me, getting close: Jimmy and Nancy were not a couple but inseparable professionals. They appeared to be together the whole time, in their whole working lives, at the Inst, at the London Association for the Teaching of English, doing research. But also in their private lives, with Nancy coming over to the flat and being part of how Jimmy and 'Robert' brought up their daughters, sharing holidays in Cornwall and the rest.

The way it seemed to work was by division of labour: Nancy was the partner in all things to do with the head, Robert was the partner in all things to do with the body, and there was a three-way co-operation over child-rearing. The trouble was that Robert made up for what she must have perceived as her lack of presence in Jimmy's intellectual life by paying obsessive attention to toast, trousers, hair, nails, armpits, feet, shoes, windows, jam jars, carpets, shelves, shirts and taps. The problem for her, though, was that as it involved every minute detail of the material world, there was too much of it to keep up with. Rather than being a spotless, modern, American-style apartment, the flat and its inhabitants stayed pleasingly bohemian no matter how fiercely she waged verbal war against bohemianism. People possibly thought that the way we Rosens lived was more arts-and-craftsy-casual than the suburban norm, but even so, at least once a month, Mum (never Harold) waged war with the mess, Robert-style, but when she did, she scorched the earth. Surfaces had to be cleared, 'droppings' (Mum's word for anything that had been 'left' – cigarette ash, newspapers, books, pens, matches, glue) had to be got rid of. It was terrifying. Robert – same words, completely different outcome.

A. fretted and chafed against this (I wasn't so bothered) but Jimmy sucked on his pipe and counselled the Crete plan: caution and patience in all things. If A. was raging against Robert's attitude to hair-washing, he would drift into his study to reread the later poems of Edward Thomas.

A. and I got into folk music: she sang and played the guitar. I did neither, but we spent hours at clubs and concerts. This was the era of the folk revival – or as the real aficionados called it, the 'second folk revival', or, as the cynics would put it later, another chapter in the long history of 'fakesong'. At this time it was Bert Jansch, Ann Briggs, the Watersons, Ewan MacColl and Peggy Seeger, the Critics Group, Bert Lloyd, Young Tradition, John Renbourne and Alex Campbell. Meanwhile Americans like Tom Paxton, the Darlingtons, Ramblin' Jack Elliott, Tom Paley, Mike Seeger, Odetta and Jesse Fuller were coming through London or staying here. The big groups – the Spinners, the Corries, the Clancy Brothers, the Dubliners, Robin Hall and Jimmy MacGregor – put on concerts in the big venues. There were also appearances from people we understood to be 'real' folk musicians, performers who were presented as coming from families where music had been part of their background forever. These were people like the Coppers, the Stewarts of Blairgowrie, or the McPeakes.

However they did it, they all sang 'traditional' songs or sang in what they said was a 'traditional' way. It was all performed in the shadow of 'authenticity'. The origins of the words and music were often obscure and contested. The same can be said for the transmission: did people pass these songs and instrumentals to each other on bits of paper, face to face, or both? And then there was the contentious matter of ownership: did some or all of this vast amount of material belong to individuals or to the cultural, national or ethnic group who supposedly or actually created it? Or was it always a product of human mixing, always coming out of the melting pot, so anyone anytime could and should feel entitled to give it a go?

This included a class question: did this traditional material originate with 'working people', rather than hired elites trained in conservatoires and ecclesiastical schools, or acts hired by big entertainment companies? There were people around who maintained that it did, and these origins were what made it authentic. The music spoke of the tensions, desires, hopes and tragedies in the lives of small farmers, miners, seamen, prisoners, soldiers, weavers, tinkers, carriers and many more different trades. Taken as a whole, it represented something of the outlooks of millions of people from between around 1500 to the first decades of the twentieth century. Its survival often rested on the persistence of 'collectors' and anthologisers, going back as far as people like Samuel Pepys, through various eccentrics and academics like Bishop Percy, the Reverend Baring-Gould, Professor Francis Child and Cecil Sharp, right up to people who were still active, like Alan Lomax.

Every so often, either 'Literature' or 'Music' had taken notice of all this, without necessarily seeing it as a significant social or cultural phenomenon. It's easier to select a tiny group of special, fine examples and say that they are, as individual pieces, a 'good ballad' or a 'marvellous tune'. Of course, you can't bash people over the head and tell them that they should like, love or admire some, any or all of this body of work. Ultimately, it's all supposed to be entertainment and if you ain't entertained, you ain't entertained. There's nothing more lethal for entertainment than being told you ought to like it.

The clubs and halls were full of crowds enjoying this music, but also full of debates, obsessions, rivalries and battles. There were moments watching and listening to some of the singers and musicians that were as powerful for me at this time as any movie, play or poem that I had ever enjoyed. When two little-known Americans, Sandy and Jeannie Darlington, sang a song from the Midwest about not wanting to be buried out in the open, on the 'lone prairie', it felt like it could cut through glass. There are something like 100 or so pieces, either live or on disc, that made me feel that way.

One group of pieces are called 'night visiting songs', where a 'rover' of some kind tells of how he makes his way to his lover's bed at night with the suggestion that it has to be secret, out of sight of his lover's parents. A.'s bedroom was on the ground floor, so I said that we could see if the night-visiting song worked. I arrived outside her house at about midnight, crept across the front garden and tapped on her bedroom window. She opened it up and let me in, I got into bed (just as it says in the songs) but she said that I ought to go again very soon. Just then, we heard Jimmy saying something to A.'s mum and coming towards A.'s door. I jumped out of bed, grabbed my trousers and slipped into the cupboard. Jimmy came in. 'Are you awake, dear?' he said.

'Mm,' she said.

'It's late. You worried about your A-levels?'

'No, not really.'

'Anything else?'

'No, everything's fine.'

'Night-night then, love.'

'Night, Dad.'

And he went out. I crept out of the cupboard.

A. said I ought to go. I agreed, put on my trousers, climbed out of the window, crept across the garden and walked back through suburban streets to the flat in Harrow.

A t Medical School, we started having lectures on embryol- ogy from Harold's old friend, David – the one who sent him off to find the Professor in the Berlin Natural History Museum. Though he had known me as a small boy and the families had sometimes met up and gone for walks in the park, now he kept his professional distance, and hardly acknowledged the fact that Harold and him had been insepa- rable friends in the Communist Party for a few years in their early twenties.

In spite of all my fears about studying medicine and being a doctor, I really did like zoology, and so I was genuinely fascinated. This positivity was knocked when I arrived one morning late to David's lecture. Water was streaming out of the ceiling of the lecture hall. David looked up as I pushed open the door wearing Harold's father's American plaid jacket (think *On the Waterfront*) and he said, 'Oh, I thought you were the plumber.' As my fellow students had spent the last few weeks revelling in the fact that I looked like a tramp, this was a gift.

I had to give myself the option of getting out of this medi- cine lark, so I started plotting. I'd heard that it was virtually impossible to switch courses at London University, and totally impossible to walk out of a medical school and transfer across to, say, University College, where I now really wanted to go. It seemed exactly like the image of a university I had in my mind: big, crowded, bustling, diverse and full of public argument.

But that, according to the rumours, wasn't open to me. Could I get myself somewhere else? Somewhere where I could start off doing medicine and if I really didn't want to carry on (which seemed more than likely), I could just switch. I'd heard that one or two of Brian's friends at Oxford had done exactly that. What if I could get myself into Oxford ... was that possible? Brian had finished there by now, and was on his way to the Seychelles to find coral and a PhD. I went to Mum and Harold and put on a show of how maybe it would be a good idea for me to try to get into Oxford, do medicine there. After all, wasn't I at just the same stage as others of my year applying to get into Oxbridge, as this was nearly always done in the post-A-levels year?

I don't know how I swung it, but we all agreed I should give it a go. And why not try at the same college as Brian had been to: Wadham? It had the reputation of being a bit radical – Michael Foot had been there – and, according to Brian, was more 'grammar-schooly' than the other colleges.

I applied and they called me to interview. It was fairly amicable. They were intrigued by the circuitous route I seemed to be taking, getting into medicine via arts A-levels, and we got into a pedantic conversation about whether you could ever prove anything. On the way back to London on the coach, I felt colder than I had ever felt before. I had an uncontrollable shiver and by the time I got home, it took me hours to get the chill out of my legs and bum. I thought it was strange – nothing more than strange – and it would take another twelve years to unravel that this was the first time I noticed a symptom of being attacked by my own immune system, probably triggered by the trauma of the car accident.

I thought that the inconsequential nature of the chat, and the fact that it piddled away into pedantry, had blocked off my chances of switching courses. Now what? I thought of Silman heading off to the Sorbonne with nothing more than school French. Maybe that was a way to go. Hey, why not study English at the Sorbonne?! Before that particular plan got any further, I heard that Wadham had accepted me. I didn't congratulate myself for getting in. I felt totally in debt to Brian, who had got there by his own efforts. I was in no doubt that the college had pressed its siblings button, looked at what they thought of as their success with Brian, and said, 'Let's give the brother a go too.' I thought I was a lucky bastard, but the cold reality was that whatever else I did, I had to pass my First MB. Not that it made me drop everything and get on with it.

I carried on with acting in a John Arden play at London University and spent a good deal of time writing poems about feelings I couldn't describe. Meanwhile the events in Silman's life got more and more fantastic by the day: in Paris he was meeting former colleagues of Soustelle, chiefs of police, generals – anyone who could vouch for the fact that Soustelle had indeed been part of the plot to kill de Gaulle.

On one occasion I went to Paris with him and met his old tutor Lyotard – before his fame as a postmodern philosopher – and Pierre Vidal-Naquet, who was close to Socialisme ou Barbarie, an organisation which had uncovered old and continuing links between the French ruling elite and fascism. He talked of the demonstration for the liberation of Algeria in 1961 when scores, possibly hundreds of demonstrators 'disappeared' and bodies were found in the Seine. I remembered having been in Paris not long after that demonstration and noticing – how could you not? – the way the police followed passers-by with automatic weapons.

On the course, we moved on to spectroscopy, which I didn't get; valences, which I got but thought I would never remember; and breeding fruit-flies in order to prove that Mendel got it right. This I loved; the tiny fruit flies with their white, red and tartan eyes, breeding away in the same distribution of features as Mendel's sweet peas.

I went to see my old friend Terry who was at Leeds University. I had never seen anywhere like Leeds. He said he ate every night at a 'Chinese chippy'. What was a Chinese chippy? We stood in a queue that went round the block and when we got inside, a tall, hot Chinese bloke was swathed in steam as he threw food into a wok, tossed it and threw it into cardboard boxes. I had never seen such a thing before. Outside, Sikhs worked on allotments and coming home from the take-away, three blokes were dancing in the street shouting 'Hunsle' for t'cup!' (Hunslett for the Cup). When Terry asked me to squeeze some more stuff into his dustbin, a woman walking past me as I jumped up and down in the bin to flatten the rubbish, said out of the corner of her mouth: 'Don't come very often, don't dustman.' This was, as people had suddenly started saying, 'something else'.

Terry shared a house with scores of people. There was no heating, no carpets, no curtains, and it was on a terrace of back-to-backs all blackened by soot, with back alleys and privies. One of the people in the house was a building worker who went to bed in his working clothes and boots. At five o'clock his alarm rang and he stepped out of bed, out of his room, down the stairs and out of the house. When I told

Harold, he said, 'That's how they get you: work invades the rest of your life.' Terry introduced me to Mike G., who was a Marxist and in the same outfit as the guys from Watford, Chris and Mike H., the International Socialists, now known (of course) by its acronym, IS; to Jack, who was needing help to be elected leader of the Students Union (on his way to becoming the Home Secretary); then to Yentob, who was wearing a black velvet suit (the first I had ever seen close up) and directing French surrealist plays on his way to being head of everything artsy at the BBC.

I wished I had gone to Leeds. How bloody ironic that Terry, who was the first in his family to go to university, had arrived at doing something he really wanted to do, while I, with all the 'help' from someone who had been at university and was now teaching at one, had ended up doing what I didn't want to do, in a place I didn't want to be.

In the flat in Harrow, Steve set up a camera and said that women would turn up, take their clothes off and have their picture taken. I said, I thought that I ought to live somewhere else.

I moved into a place in Lissenden Mansions, a high red Edwardian block next to Parliament Hill Fields. Also there was the owner Peter, who was a painter, and Rachel, a woman with dark hair who wore shawls and worked in the theatre. Peter painted in the flat; his works were, he told me, 'hard-edge abstract': they were made up of a few geometric shapes – three or four squares, triangles and circles, usually painted in primary colours. He took me to see his paintings and asked me what I thought. I really didn't know what to say about them.

I discovered that living and working just down the road, under the railway bridge, was John Foreman, the broadsheet king, who printed off old songs on to broadsheets that he sold and also sang from, accompanied by his concertina. He was a champion of old print and old printed songs, very suspicious of all the folky purism going on. A bit further down the road at the Tally-Ho they had Sunday morning live jazz, that always ended with a wonderful all-in rendering of

'Watermelon Man'. Across the road was an Edwardian men's shirt shop that sold collarless, buttonless striped flannel and cotton shirts, chef's trousers and workingmen's blue jackets. I dressed myself in these. I looked ahead to Oxford and how I might be able to wangle dropping medicine. I felt I was getting back into my skin.

Once it got to the summer term, Silman declared that he was coming over every day and all day for the next three weeks, to revise. I said I preferred to do revision on my own. He said, 'No, the way to do revision is to do it together; they don't want us to socialise our learning, Rosen, but we don't have to give in to that.'

He turned up next day, first thing in the morning, and we did exactly as he said: we spent all day and every day for three weeks going through the biology, chemistry and physics, learning and testing each other. In between sessions he told me I was mad to think of giving up medicine. It was just a means to an end. The work we were doing now was a short interval – four years. We do it, pass, get over it, and then get down to the fundamentals. With a medical degree, you could go anywhere in the world and people needed you. Or, if you got the hang of it, you could go into research at any one of hundreds of projects that would affect the lives of millions of people.

After these pep talks, we went back to chanting the order of the cranial nerves. There were times when we were in helpless laughter over the Latinate compound names for the neck and shoulder muscles, and succeeded in muddling each other up with whether it was acromio-deltoid or delto-acromius.

This made the exams bearable, but it also led me to think I had done better than I had. I was called back for a face-to-face with an external examiner who wanted to know if I understood anything about physics. I stumbled through the amplitude of waves and he asked me what I liked about physics. As I didn't like physics, this was a hard question. It wasn't that I had any argument with physics, or thought there was anything wrong with the subject itself. But I was afraid of it. I had picked up that physics was an explanation for how the universe worked, so I said that physics interested me because it answered questions. He seized on that and said, 'So it satisfies your intellectual curiosity?'

'Yes,' I said. I passed and walked away from the medical school.

# 13

## Rehearsing the Uprising

I bought a skull and put it on the mantelpiece. My roommate was a maths genius from Sunderland called Dave, and he said that he was fine about it. The skull's top had been sawn off and reattached with two hooks-and-eyes. We pulled back the hooks, lifted it off and looked in. No one told me whether it was a man or a woman. I wondered if I was going to look in skulls for the rest of my life.

'College life' at Wadham combined the extraordinary, the archaic and the banal. One night I was standing outside the building I lived in, talking to someone who said that I should listen to Coleman Hawkins, when one of the men who called us 'sir' (they were known as 'scouts') appeared and sent me to bed. The next day, I got a note telling me that I had to see the Dean. The Dean was a world-famous expert on the civil service in Imperial Rome. Or the last of the Peloponnesian Wars. He said I was making a noise after hours and I had to pay a fine. I paid the fine.

A few weeks later, some people who did rowing were very pleased that they had won. They celebrated long past bedtime and one of them pulled the toilet pan off the wall and walked around the college with it. I made enquiries. They weren't fined. I bumped into the Dean in the 'quad'. I asked him if I could have a word. Of course. I pointed out the anomaly of me being fined and the rowers not. He said I was learning something about justice. My immediate reaction was to think that he was an odious creep and that I had landed up in an antiquated and corrupt system, but everyone else said that he was a fantastic bloke.

The head of the college, known as the Warden, was a much-loved, much-admired scholar called Maurice Bowra, who had gathered around himself hundreds of stories that Brian had regaled us with when he was home for the holidays. He would imitate Bowra's voice, which was like no other. It was very deep and loud, he hit words like he was hitting a drum, and the last syllable of every sentence went even deeper and louder until the very last moment, when it suddenly rose up.

In those days, colleges were single-sex and we were locked in at eleven o'clock. Some people figured out a way of climbing in and out of the college, over the wall of Bowra's garden, through his back door, through his sitting room, and out of the door into the quad. Bowra was known to leave his doors open. One night a student was doing this and had got as far as Bowra's sitting room when he realised that Bowra was still there, just getting up off the sofa. The student dived down behind the sofa. Bowra now sat down again and sat there reading, the student crouching behind the sofa, breathing as quietly as possible. After about two hours, Bowra got up, walked to the door and said, 'Turn the light out when you go to bed.'

He was famous for taking the mick out of John Betjeman; for writing a book called *Primitive Song*, which he called 'Primitive Sin'; and for being passionately anti-war. This came from his experiences many years earlier in China and the First World War. He was said to do all he possibly could to save students from being thrown out, whether they had failed exams, or for sex, drugs or rock'n'roll, or for the whole package.

Another Bowra story took place while he was nude bathing with others along a stretch of river called 'Parson's Pleasure'. A woman came by on a punt. The men grabbed hats and clothes and covered their crotches. Bowra covered his face: 'I don't know how you're known in Oxford, gentlemen, but I'm known by my face.'

As always, Brian had experienced something before me, so when I met Bowra for the first time, I felt that I knew him. He invited groups of first-year students to come to his house in the corner of the quad for a meal. This way, he said, he would get to know each one of us. We were to knock on his door at seven o'clock, which we did, and he ushered us through to a room.

He was small and portly, always dressed in a three-piece suit. He had a large balding head that looked like a big pear sitting on a stuffed jacket. The unique voice came out of a mouth that turned down on one side, and he arranged the conversation with us at this meal so as to engage with each of us in turn, one by one round the table. But it wasn't a conversation. He just looked at the person and started talking. The guy next to me lived in Leeds. He didn't say he lived in Leeds but nonetheless Bowra just looked at him and said, 'Leeds. Mmm. Remarkable town hall. And lions.'

When he got to me, he looked at me and said, 'Lenin. Mmm. Frightful man, Lenin. Bertie went to see Lenin. Bertie Russell. Bertie said to Lenin, "What do you do with the bourgeoisie now that the revolution's happened?" And Lenin said to Bertie, "We string them up from the nearest tree." Frightful man, Lenin.'

Then he moved on to the next guy, who had come from Sri Lanka, then still called Ceylon. He looked at him, and said, 'Mmm, Ceylon. I was in Colombo. Walls. Very fine walls.' And so it went on.

At exactly eight o'clock he got up very suddenly and said, 'Time to go,' and saw us out of the door.

I spent a long time thinking about why he'd told me the story about Lenin. He hadn't asked me anything about myself or my background. Brian said that his technique was always to find out everything he could about people, then, in 'conversation', you would realise through his bass, staccato words that he knew much more about you than he let on. I hadn't ever mentioned Lenin, or the Soviet Union. Maybe Brian had? Or maybe there was a paper trail back to Mum and Harold in the NUT? Or was there something on a reference or testimonial from my schools?

I was embarrassed by the hierarchy I found in the college. The divisions between 'us' and 'them', the scouts and the students, felt worse when we ate 'in Hall'. It was just as it looked in films, long lines of us streaming into a great seventeenth-century hall, with high beams above, paintings down the sides, us all wearing gowns, a 'high table' up one end where Bowra and the 'dons' sat, while we were served by teams of waiters. I was more used to lining up in self-service canteens at medical school, or at various university student unions or at 'centres' like India House and the Africa Centre. Why was there all this rigmarole? I learned very quickly that the answer to that question is: because it was Oxford. We were being trained to see the world this way, layered into different levels of entitlement, duty and service. There were even different kinds of gown, depending on whether you were a 'commoner', a 'scholar', an 'exhibitioner', or a 'don'. Mentioning such things was considered petty. Better to say nothing.

So, I decided to disappear. This began with the mealtimes. The meals were compulsory and pre-paid by Mum and Harold, but I still had my £400 from my accident, so I used it up over the year eating in caffs and pubs. At the same time – and it felt part of the same move – I skipped getting involved in college groups. Instead I dived into university-wide drama and journalism and going to the folk club. The places where these happened – the city's theatre The Playhouse, a backstreet room lent to students by Robert Maxwell and the upstairs of a pub seemed free of Deans, fines, 'Hall', and scouts.

I started writing sketches and monologues and acting in them, wishing I was as good as Jonathan Miller. On my first outing, I got onto the stage and stood in front of an audience; all that I could say was 'Sorry, I've forgotten my words.' Not a great start. I spent hours writing and performing things like daft parodies of Chekov where 'The Doctor' spends all his time trying to get off with 'The Sisters'.

I turned up in the office of the students' magazine, *Isis*, and offered to write for them, and I was soon working with Robin on 'features'. Robin played the guitar and sang. While we were making up a 'folk song' about speed traps, we decided to dedicate one edition to the folk revival. We interviewed Bert Lloyd, the Watersons and Shirley Collins. Another issue was on the 'left' and we interviewed Ralph Miliband, the editor of *Tribune*, and Paul Johnson who was editing the

*New Statesman.* Miliband was moving leftwards; the editor of *Tribune* was very hopeful, and Johnson was moving rightwards. I liked Miliband and went away and read his book *Parliamentary Socialism*, which I thought should have been called 'Why Parliamentary Socialism isn't going to happen.'

I liked the feel of this interviewing business. We went to the Oxford dog track and wrote about that. We also went to see Lord Boothby in his flat. He was just as I remembered him from his time on TV with Michael Foot: bumbling about in his bow tie, talking about Winston and how they had saved the country. He had hurt his hand and kept making suggestive jokes about it with a man who was serving us drinks.

'Why did he do that?' Robin said on the way back.

'I've no idea,' I said.

Sometimes A. came to visit me. She stayed with the Australian friends of some Australian friends who knew her father, Jimmy, who was Harold's boss. The man, Ian, happened to be an English tutor at Wadham, and lived with his wife and two children in a house away from the centre of Oxford. It was a corner of domestic Australia. At bedtime, I told the children stories and they said I was a 'pommie drongo'. For a moment, this homeliness seemed something I wanted to have – the sooner the better. Afterwards I floated the possibility to Ian that I could switch to doing English. He thought it was just that – a possibility.

A. decided that she was going to go to Leeds Art School and become a potter.

Sometimes A. and I went to see Ian's Australian friends in London. They had two children as well. I played with them and wrote a poem about them called 'billy and sarah'. I was thinking of e. e. cummings poems. For the first time in my life, I was feeling a tug towards thinking about poetry-and-children, children-and-poetry. It was part of this yearning for homeliness.

After a few weeks of Anatomy (cutting up the body we called 'Gladys'), Physiology (finding out how fast our blood took up oxygen) and Biochemistry (learning the benzene ring), I made a decision. I would tell Mum and Harold that I didn't want to go on doing Medicine. I wanted to do English. That would pull together the things I was interested in: journalism, acting, writing sketches and monologues, poetry, literary criticism and the politics of culture that I'd enjoyed at school.

I broached it in the first Christmas holidays. It was a road crash. Harold went up in steam: the moment I found something difficult I ducked it, he said; sometimes there are things we aren't good at, but it might still be better to do them. (That made no sense to me at all.) Mum said that seeing as I had come this far, then surely the best thing would be to carry on. (That didn't make sense, either.) I felt desperate. I said I had no argument with medicine, it's just that I couldn't see myself being a doctor. I'd be a doctor who wanted to write. What was the point in setting myself up for life with a conflict I wouldn't be able to resolve? They said this was nonsense, look at Chick. Oh no, I thought, back with the saintly Chick and his bloody photography.

I failed. I didn't convince them that I should switch course. My strategy for getting out of Medical School – getting into Oxford – had come off the rails. All I had done was give myself an extra year of doing medical studies than what I would have done if I had stayed at the Middlesex Hospital Medical School: that's because the Oxford route to becoming a doctor entailed doing a whole three-year degree in Physiology before going on the wards, while the London medical school route was a twenty-month course called '2nd MB'. I was stuck. And stuck for a long time with skulls, Gladys, oxygen and the benzene ring. Beyond that, beckoned the ward where I had been strung up in my sling, dealing with blokes pissing broken glass or young men who had lost their legs.

I moaned about it to A. who told her father, Jimmy. He called me into his study, looked out the window, and asked me about the sixth form. He tried to find out why and how I had come to think that it was medicine that I wanted to do, and how I was – or was not – enjoying Oxford. He said very little, just nodded and sucked on his pipe and went on looking out the window to where Hatch End station glowed in the dark. At one point in the conversation, I mentioned that when my friends were applying for university, I had tried to put the brakes on medicine and apply to Sussex to do sociology, but Mum and Harold had said no. He seemed very struck by that. He said that he had no idea that had happened; no idea that I had tried to change direction, no idea that they had said no. He stared even harder at Hatch End station.

A few days later I had another conversation with Mum and Harold and this time it was completely different. Harold was emotional and apologetic and put his hand on my shoulder. He said that he'd had a long chat with Jimmy, and if I really did want to stop doing medicine then I should. I was stunned. I don't know what A. said to Jimmy or what Jimmy said to Harold, but it changed everything. At least now I had the chance of seeing if the college would let me switch courses.

I've often thought about why Mum and Harold were so desperate for me to be a doctor, and why this moment was so hard and so sad for them. Some of it was to do with the saintly role they had assigned to doctors – especially Jewish Communist ones, like Chick. It seemed to them, I think, that it was the most worthwhile of all professions, devoted solely and selflessly to the benefit of others. The Communist part was important because it was this set of ideas that had brought in the National Health Service, which to them was socialism in action. They had known from the 1920s and '30s how back-street medicine worked and didn't work, and they had seen how right-wing doctors resisted the setting up of the National Health – yet it was won all the same. And they felt part of that victory. It was something that they and the people they knew had won. All this was poured into their hopes for me. And I was, in this moment of decision, rejecting it – and them.

I think there may have been something else. They had both made the journey from a working-class Jewish community which, as they grew up, became embroiled in big fights over its right to exist. As they absorbed British culture and made careers at the heart of it, part of Europe went into one of its greatest ever convulsions in an attempt to rid itself of Jews – of them. Each one of their group knew that if they had been living where some of their relatives were living, it would have been their end too. With a wave of the arm or a shrug, my father would mention his French uncles and aunts who had just 'disappeared': 'there at the beginning of the war, not there at the end.'

By the time I was in my late teens, however, my parents were, by any measure, English. Outside of the house, both of them looked and sounded like English middle-class people – 'of Jewish origin', perhaps, but no more. Mum felt that school and Englishness had emancipated her. For Harold it was more complicated, in that he felt his emancipation came from his mother and Zeyde but he had learned how to 'make the right noises', as he used to put it. He talked of how, no matter how oppositional he was, he felt at times that he had ingratiated himself. But if Judaism and the social life around a synagogue was not for them, what was the alternative? You became as English as you could and hoped that people would accept you; and yet, even in the midst of that hope, there was a part of him that disliked the way he'd had to ingratiate himself.

In his case, much more than Mum's, Harold hoped that he could hold on to some things about being Jewish, being a bit different. It was a contradiction, but I think that's what he wanted to do. Before the days of multiculturalism, interculturalism, theories about the melting pot, diversity, the 'mosaic of identities' and the rest, the pair of them lived out a mesh of feelings to do with wanting to be accepted while knowing there was always the danger that they wouldn't be. They wanted to be oppositional, but not for reasons of difference or of having a separate identity. The oppositional element arose because they held views that they thought should be universal, not national. And yet, ironically, the reason why and how they had come to hold these universal views came from the nature of their particular Jewish backgrounds: poverty and persecution in Eastern Europe, migration to Western Europe and the States.

The way this interacted with me being a doctor was, I think, that they perceived it as the best way to be accepted. Perhaps, sometimes, they thought that their adoption of English Literature and 'Education' was inauthentic – or at least not as totally authentic as, say, when Jimmy spoke and wrote. It was 'his culture', which they had had to learn.

Medicine, though, was seemingly without culture. Medicine had no passport. Like their political views, it was universal. And yet here was crazy bloody Michael, ready to jack it in and do that English Literature thing instead. 'It's just books about books,' Harold said again, as if there was something inauthentic about that. Books-about-books had no real value beyond itself, even though books-about-books was what he had spent his own life doing.

No matter: he agreed that I should give it a go. We would try to arrange it for me to change course.

The routine, we gathered, was to talk to Bowra. 'What? No forms?' Harold said, whose notion of academia was shaped by London University, an institution that had struggled to validate itself against the domination of Oxbridge. One way it had done this was to be ruthlessly meritocratic, thus making everyone fill in forms.

I rang Bowra. He picked up. 'Bowra!'

'Er ... it's Michael Rosen here, can I come and see you to ...'

'Tuesday four o'clock.' And he put the phone down.

Harold cancelled the day's work and we went to see him. We knocked at the door, and Bowra opened it and took us into his room. He looked at me and belted out, 'Mm?'

I had prepared a speech. 'I would like to change course and ...'

'From what to what?'

'From Medicine to English.'

'Can you write a sentence?'

'Well, I think so, and ...'

He turned to Harold, who had prepared a London University pleading speech. 'I think it would be the best thing to do in the circ ...'

'Good. Convince your father, convince anyone.' He turned back to me. 'You'll have to start all over again. That's three more years.'

He turned once more to Harold: 'That's more money for you to pay to keep him. I haven't got any. Fifty pounds, that's all.' Back to me: 'Pass your Prelims. Bye.' And he ushered us out.

Harold was shocked. He kept brushing his hair back off his forehead and saying, 'Extraordinary.'

When I told Brian, he laughed and laughed and explained to us that the whole thing was staged. 'When he said "From what to what?" he knew exactly what course you were doing and what course you wanted to do. He would have heard from the tutors. And that "Convince your father, convince anyone" – he must have heard that Harold had been against you changing course, probably via Ian, who'd got it from the friends who were friends of Jimmy. And the fifty pounds he's given you is what they call an "exhibition", it's like a little scholarship.'

'Extraordinary,' Harold kept saying.

Mum was still sad; but also hopeful that I would now do what I wanted to do. She had plenty of reasons to not worry about it: she was now deep into her commitment to teacher training at Goldsmiths, presenting poetry programmes for BBC Schools Radio, doing talks for the London Association for the Teaching of English (LATE) and writing chapters in books on primary education. People listened to what she said, read what she wrote. She was taking off.

Feeling euphoric that I had at last come out of a corridor of misgiving and fear, I decided to write a play. It was about me living in the flat with Geoff and Steve. I called it *Stewed Figs*. I showed it to the university theatre club to see if they would put it on. They agreed that I could put it on for one night at the Oxford Playhouse, I just had to find a cast.

I had made friends with Chris P. who was from Lancaster, and was the singer in a students' soul band, The Blue Monks. Soul music was one of my cultural gaps: I had kept up with Chicago blues, Tamla Motown and the new British rhythm and blues, but not soul. I hadn't heard of Otis Redding, Solomon Burke or Sam Cook. Otis sang like he was crying. It seemed at that moment like one of the most beautiful and painful sounds I had ever heard. Chris tried to imitate him. I didn't know whether he was good or crap, but when someone wrote up the Blue Monks in a music mag, they called him 'the singing goat'. He agreed to play the character of Benji, which is what I called myself in the play.

I threw everything into it: rewriting, casting, designing posters and leaflets and then directing. At night I lay in bed thinking, how the hell am I going to pass my Prelims? There's a green book called 'Organic Chemistry' to learn and I don't know any of it. I discovered that the Taj Mahal made chicken liver curry. I lived off it.

The play went down well; I sat in the audience loving the way people laughed. I hadn't known how to end the play, so I had finished it with a party, Geoff having a crisis and throwing everyone out. I met Ian afterwards, and he said he thought it was great but it felt as if I hadn't known how to end the play, and so I had written in a party scene and Geoff having a crisis. I had the feeling that if Ian was that good at figuring out what was wrong with the play, he'd be pretty good as my tutor. Many years later, I heard that Geoff had come to see it. He had snuck in and out without letting on that he was there.

I passed my Prelims. Chris failed his and was 'sent down' (expelled). He had been so good at acting me, his going made me feel I'd lost a bit of me.

I was going to start university all over again. It felt like I was at the beginning of a long road: since the end of A-levels, I had done two years at universities and I hadn't even started yet. In contrast, Terry up at Leeds with Mike G. and Yentob only had a year to go, and was talking about what he would do when he left: work in film. Sounded good. I was envious.

Home was now, ironically and infuriatingly, Muswell Hill! After the years of hating being stuck out on the road between Northwood and Rickmansworth, complaining to my parents that we weren't living in Muswell Hill, they had waited till I had gone to Oxford and moved there! When I came back for the ludicrously long Oxford University holidays, I would go upstairs to the top-floor attic rooms, look out over London and start to write some poems about me and Brian when we shared a bedroom, or about the things Harold and Mum said at home when I was seven or eight years old. I wanted to find out what it had been like and why I liked that time so much. I wrote some of them as I imagined Carl Sandburg or e. e. cummings might have written them. Why was it that Americans did 'informal' so well? The group of poems written at that time would end up in my first book of poetry for children, *Mind Your Own Business*, in 1974: 'I share a bedroom with my brother ...'

When the new academic year started, I had to find somewhere else to live in Oxford. One or two of Brian's friends were still around. There was a bloke who played a one-string fiddle who put me onto a bloke doing chemistry who told me about some rooms in a Victorian terrace house in Walton Street. It needed three of us, so I collected up Dave the maths genius and John who liked doing sketches. He lived in Durham Castle, as his father was the boss of Durham University.

John was going to be a lawyer, but wasn't enjoying the course. Some evenings he would sit in my room till late. I wanted him to go to bed because I had a tutorial in the morning. He wouldn't go. He would recite Lewis Carroll's 'Jabberwocky' as if he was a sergeant-major on the parade ground, or do imitations of the classics prof reciting obscene lines about fellatio from Catullus, his Burmese grandmother telling him off, and Geordie women in the sausage factory where he had worked between school and Oxford. On his first day there, the women had grabbed him, whipped off his trousers and pants and smothered his balls (his 'stotts') in sausage-skin syrup, which then hardened so that he had to spend the next few weeks picking off the bits. He conjured up a picture that couldn't have been further from the life we were leading.

The landlord (who drove a taxi and arranged the rides in a loud voice from the communal phone downstairs in the dank hallway) and his Polish wife lived on the ground floor. I bought four blue Denby plates, a towel and two dark brown mugs. Mrs Porter, the Polish landlady, said that we had to wash our dishes in the communal bathroom. I started with the best of intentions, but a few weeks in and the four Denby plates and two brown mugs weren't getting washed up.

Instead, I got interested in different kinds of mould. Brian had said that the definition of a bohemian was that they wash up before a meal instead of after it. I became a bohemian, though sometimes it was easier to eat off the unwashed plate. John invented the saying, 'A bit of old egg never did anyone any harm.' You could say it when faced with a bit of old egg, and it also worked for a bit of old sausage, a bit of old ketchup, or a bit of old mould. I knew that I would have to do all I could to stop Mum and Harold seeing this place.

The first weeks of doing English were not as I expected: the Oxford idea of the study of English was that it should be historical. It followed from this theory that at the beginning of the course you're at the beginning of English: the Anglo-Saxon epic poem, *Beowulf*. That was the first kind of beginning. There was another beginning: the beginning of the 'modern period', and that was the poetry of John Skelton (1463–1529). We were taught in tutorials, where the tutors set us a translation or an essay. The following week you came in and read your work to the tutor, who then criticised it, before setting you the next week's work. There were also lectures at the English faculty, one of the few modern buildings in Oxford. These were optional but open to all. I went to the first one of the first term which was, of course, on *Beowulf*. Not content with *Beowulf* being the beginning of English, a woman in a gown gave a one-hour lecture on the first word in *Beowulf*. The word is 'Hwaet'. It gives us our word 'what', but in this moment of the epic it means 'Lo!' or 'Listen!' It's how the storyteller grabbed people's attention.

I should have been excited by *Beowulf*. Wasn't this the folk tradition in action, face-to-face storytelling and singing, recorded and preserved more by luck than design, in the sole epic to have survived in England? The manuscript had once been flung out of a library window, its edges singed by a fire that destroyed hundreds of unique medieval books. The lecturer talked about 'Hwaet' – the sound, the letters, the meaning, the calligraphy, the vellum. People around me were making notes. I kept saying to myself, I should be interested, I should be interested, this is what I have chosen to do. The whole lecture was about 'Hwaet'. She never got past 'Hwaet'. She pored over 'Hwaet'. She loved 'Hwaet'. I didn't go to another English department lecture for the rest of my time in Oxford.

My Anglo-Saxon tutor was Alan, who played jazz piano, and started several sentences at the same time, none of which he finished.

'You might like to take a look at ... some of the students are ... Sherry? – Oh it's South African, sorry ... Anti-apartheid aren't you? ... Theory of oral formulae ... have you had a chance to go over the ... did you go to the lecture on ...?'

He could carry on like this for the whole hour unless you dived in and picked up one of the threads. I took my chances on the theory of 'oral formulae' and Alan sent me off to read Francis Magoun, Jr, on the oral formulae of *Beowulf*, which showed that the composition of *Beowulf* involved a form of folk composition whereby stories and songs are made up of phrases that reappear many times. These oral formulae could be found in any epic poem or saga. They had been found in the *Odyssey*. Alan also sent me off to the library to read a paper that showed how the poetic style of *Beowulf* involved patterns of alliteration and assonance linked to varying rhythms. I tried inventing ways of writing it down: it came out as 'a-BOOM, te-BAM; FAH-choo-wow, FAH-sham-te'. Harold was amused that I borrowed his copy of *Beowulf* from University College, London, 1938. Every line had his translation scribbled next to it.

'Use the libraries,' I was told, and there were three: the 'Bod' (the Bodleian), the English Faculty library and the college library. I discovered something I loved doing: browsing, sniffing round shelves to see what books were there. In this way I 'found' E. K. Chambers' *The English Folk-Play*, and sat one afternoon reading about the history and spread of mummers' plays. I 'found' the Child Ballads, the classified collection of what Francis J. Child reckoned to be the core folk ballads of the English-speaking world. But then, I wondered, where did Ewan MacColl and Bert Lloyd find the 'industrial' songs and ballads about, say, lead miners, that they had put on the album *Shuttle and Cage*, or the song about the sailor on a

slave ship that was on the Critics Group album ? I always felt
that whenever it came to any of this alternative and oral material, I was only ever scratching the surface. How did Geoffrey
Summerfield 'find' all that oral poetry he put in *Voices* and
spread out on our front-room floor?

At the university folk club, Hedy West, an American from
the Appalachians, sang songs and ballads she had learned
from her father and friends. She said these songs had come
to America with the arrival in the mountains of people
from Northern Ireland and Scotland. The drama of 'Matty
Groves', the detached, melancholy way she sang it over the
top of a five-string banjo, blew me away. When the 'high-
born' husband in the song comes back and finds his wife in
bed with the lowly Matty Groves, he says to him:

> 'How do you like my fine feather bed?
> And how do you like my sheets?
> How do you like the fair lady
> who lies in your arms and sleeps, sleeps,
> lies in your arms and sleeps?'

I loved that irony with detachment. Wouldn't it be great to be
able to write irony with detachment? The English Literature
course, I could see more clearly now, was a historical charge
through 'English' novels, plays and poems. 'English' included
Scots, Irish and Welsh authors, but not anyone else who
wrote in English in, say, America, Australia, Canada, the
Caribbean, Africa or the Indian subcontinent. Why not? I
thought. Though English Literature started in a time when to
us it was unreadable without a translation, it came to a rapid
full stop in 1900 because, for our teachers in Oxford in 1965,
it was 'too early' to come to a critical judgement on 'more
recent' material. Down at the English faculty, though, you
could go to lectures on T. S. Eliot and W. H. Auden. I didn't
go. It felt like flirtation to me: a flash of stuff we couldn't
have. I did once go to a big public lecture by the Professor
of Poetry, Edmund Blunden, on Edward Thomas. I thought
Jimmy would have liked that.

I played a servant in a dramatisation of *Tristram Shandy*

and got an inkling that this was a revolutionary book, but we wouldn't get to eighteenth-century fiction until next year. Meanwhile, I started to become preoccupied with not understanding what was happening between me and A. When she had been in Leeds she had discovered a new life, and loved it. Now she had moved to college in London, and I resented all that independence but couldn't admit that I did. It takes a lot of time and energy to avoid admitting things to oneself and so I kept busy, getting more and more involved in writing and performing sketches. Mum and Harold came to see one of the shows and thought it was awful. One sketch involved me acting stupid while being beaten by someone with a stick who also held a fishing rod over the top of my head, with a beer bottle dangling from it. I wore a flat hat. The idea was that I was a stupid worker, who could only be driven onwards by being beaten or bribed with beer.

Harold gave me a pasting over it. 'Why are you mocking the working class?' he said.

I said that it was meant to mock the person doing the beating and the bribing.

'What do you think the audience were laughing at?' he said. 'It was you pulling stupid faces, trying to grab the bottle while you squealed every time you got a beating.'

The conversation reminded me of the times I had come home and, wanting to sound stupid, had put on a Cockney accent. 'Why do you do that?' Harold had always said. 'Are you saying that people who talk like that are stupid?'

I heard via A.'s mother that Mum and Harold were worried I was pissing away my time, hanging out with silly people, doing silly sketches. It was going to end badly. Meanwhile, far away in the Seychelles, Brian had discovered a coral. It was going to be named after him: *Coralis Rosenensis*, or something. That's what clever, sensible people do.

I was still writing articles for *Isis* and the student newspaper, *Cherwell*, when the paper got banned. It was something to do with dope. I didn't touch dope, wouldn't touch it, have never touched it, but I wasn't against others smoking it and I defended their right to do so. I sat in rooms while the joint came along the line to me, but I always passed it on without

taking a puff. The editors asked me if I would support a campaign against the banning. The paper itself was not able to
run the campaign.

A guy called Trevor P. said it was a simple matter of freedom
of speech. I said, if Oxford had a real student union instead
of the debating chamber where public school boys and girls
strutted about saying 'True, O king, true', we could organise something. Together we wrote a leaflet calling people to
march to where the Proctors (the university police) hung out.
We spent several days distributing them, some at the gates
of the Union where various 'members' (fellow students)
explained to us that the Proctors were just doing their job
... Our freedom of speech wasn't an absolute ... We had to
be controlled ... The Proctors had the right to do that, and if
we didn't like it, we should have gone to another university.
Trevor P. pointed out that we had no say in how the Proctors
were appointed. Of course not, they said, nor should we.

Trevor also had the idea that we should wear our gowns
and carry our mortarboards. He said that would show that
we were all students of the university, and we were taking
them on on their own terms. In the end about 150 of us turned
up, and photos appeared in several of the national papers.
Probably because the *Cherwell* editors had a hotline through
to London newspaper scandal pages, and sent them regular
reports on what the brother of the bloke who was having
an affair with Princess Margaret was up to. As the *Cherwell*
editors and writers that I got to know ended up being MPs
and editors of national newspapers, leaking stories about
the brother of Princess Margaret's lover must have been a
good move.

But something had stirred. A tiny group of people had
questioned why Oxford University was structured the way it
was. I got a whiff that there were some smart folks in Balliol,
Somerville (a women's college) and Nuffield (a post-graduate
college), who had a knack of talking about such things in ways
that related to the Philosophy, Politics and Economics courses
they were doing. This included people like Christopher H.
and his brother Peter H., Tony and Paul, who all talked very
fast and enthusiastically about Marx and Trotsky. I connected

up with Leebs from Harrow Weald (the one with German parents who was friends with Mart), who was doing a post-graduate degree on Development Economics and referred to 'aid' as the 'new imperialism'; and Mike H., from Watford, one of the founder members of IS, now doing post-graduate study on town planning and friendly with someone called Paul Foot, the nephew of Michael Foot. Mike talked about America's 'permanent arms economy' and 'state capitalism' in the Soviet Union. I came across Martin R., an old friend of Malc's and family friend of the Aprahamians. He was still going on about 'peace-loving peoples' and 'socialist coun-tries' (meaning the Soviet Union and Eastern Europe). He was close with Martin K., son of one of Harold's Communist Party heroes who had written a Marxist account of the rise of the novel in Britain.

Reports were coming in of student occupations in America when it was announced that Enoch Powell would speak in Oxford. There was a demo with some pushing and shoving, followed by headlines in the local and national press about the right of Enoch Powell to go wherever he wanted, as well as make up stories about black people putting turds through white people's doors. To the press, the demo was evidence of two things: left-wing people are against freedom of speech, and Oxford had become infected with lefties.

The next year, I moved into a flat in a road called Upper Fisher Row along with Leebs and Mike H. We looked at each other. I was living with one guy from Harrow Weald and the other from Watford. The suburbs had caught up with me again. The flat overlooked the river in central Oxford, just off the road between the station and the town. This time we had a kitchen, and my Marxist flatmates organised a cooking, cleaning and washing-up rota.

In the old part of the course we had now left Anglo-Saxon and were heading towards the doldrums of early Middle English: chronicles and devout Christian poems. I started bunking off tutorials as I was getting involved in so much other stuff. For the 'modern' part of English, I adopted a new routine: start on the essay the night before the tutorial, work all through the night, go into the tutorial, read the essay, come home and sleep. This was tricky if the essay was on a whopping great novel like *Tom Jones*. I came a cropper one week, with my essay on some letters by Swift. I had assembled an argument about Swift's problems with bodily functions, saying that this led him to despise anyone or anything who departed from what were at that time the new bourgeois norms. Talking to Mike H., I had just 'discovered' norms and how norms are used to police us. I was finding norms all over the place. I read the essay to Ian. Very good, he said in his cool Australian way. 'Have you ever wondered,' he said, 'whether Swift was being ironic?'

I felt my hypothesis collapse. The word knakke (clever dick) came to mind. I had been a knakke and thought I could rumble Swift. I hadn't realised: you can never rumble Swift.

Ian said, 'Why would Swift have been ironic solely with *A Modest Proposal*?' (where he advocated the cooking and eating of babies to solve the 'Irish problem'). I had no answer and sat there blushing.

Ian's way of thinking turned *Gulliver's Travels* itself upside down. What if even the last chapter, where Swift appears to be extolling the virtues of the horses' culture, was ironic? Ian told me to read George Orwell on Swift. I did. It started me off on piecing together a chain of books that engaged with literature as if it was about ideas, not just about structure and metaphor – ideas linked to the society that the literature arose in: Danby on *King Lear*, Watt on the rise of the novel (even if, as Harold claimed, he had nicked some of it from Martin K.'s Communist dad). Even Tolkien talking about dragons and myths in *Beowulf* treated these as ideas belonging to a society. I tried applying Orwell to *Beowulf* and came up with an account of it being in support of a warrior-based society and promoting the value of loyalty to the warrior-hero, as at that great moment – after all the others have given up on Beowulf, thinking him dead from battling with Grendel's mother – one warrior alone waits for Beowulf to rise from the deep.

I started using the word 'ideology' a lot. Christopher H. and Mike said, 'Read *The German Ideology* by Marx and Engels.' I bought a copy: it was the same size and colour as

Joyce's *Ulysses* that Brian bought me for my birthday, and it sat alongside it on my shelf, neither of them completely read. Also recommended were Marx's *Economic and Philosophical Manuscripts* and *Wage Labour and Capital*. I gobbled them up. I held in my head the way in which capitalism's ultimate, final interest is in the worker's labour-time, as exemplified by how British workers in the 1830s were called 'hands'. All the owners cared about were the hands. Even when factory owners provided accommodation, it was only so that the hands would get to work on time every day, and not go off anywhere else: language and class.

The Vietnam War was becoming a major tragedy. A horror. Students in America were occupying campuses and getting killed for it. Civil rights marches were happening in Alabama and Northern Ireland. Students all over the world were asking questions about how universities were run and in whose interests. In London, an occupation began at the LSE. One of the leaders was Chris H., from Watford, friend of flatmate Mike. Some of us went down to see and hear for ourselves what it was all about, and I got to know some of them. It was a time of hope.

The big demonstration against the Vietnam War in London was coming up in March, and we started holding meetings to organise for it. One question was whether Harold Wilson would or would not ask British troops to go to Vietnam. His foreign minister, Michael Stewart, seemed to be itching to do it; BBC journalist Ian Trethowan lovingly described Stewart giving us anti-war campaigners a 'drubbing'.

Neither the University Labour Club nor the two Martins in the Communist Party could contain or channel the ferment. Meetings and discussions were everywhere. I was getting to know a new vein of people: I headed over to Nuffield, listening to activists from Jamaica, Africa and Pakistan talk about 'neo-colonialism', 'Maoism' and 'Third Worldism'. The whole world was changing. Trevor M. from Jamaica said I had to read Eric Williams's *Capitalism and Slavery* (which I did) and Sydney Lens's *The Military-Industrial Complex* (which I did). Christopher and Peter H., Stephen and Dave discussed whether all countries in the world calling themselves socialist were 'state capitalist', while Adam (son of one of Mum and Harold's old CP friends) was in a group with the 'Weasels', the Workers' Socialist League, some of whose members had jobs in the Cowley motor factory. Revolution begins at home, they said. A very angry bloke called Ben talked of people he disagreed with as 'elements'. 'We all know what kind of element you are,' he said. No matter: we were a movement.

At the same time I was trying to get a new play about Brian and his new girlfriend, B., off the ground. I had called it *Backbone*. B.'s parents had objected to her choice of boy-friend, what with him being Jewish, and in the end B. had left home to live with Harold and Mum. On one occasion my parents had to deal with the police after they were accused of abducting B. The drama society put it on for one night, and it won the *Sunday Times*–NUS drama competition, which eventually led to it being put on for a week in Oxford. It was then 'bought' by Peggy Ramsay, the legendary literary agent. I met her in her London offices just behind the Wyndham's Theatre. She said that she was the agent for all the revolu-tionaries, like David Mercer and John McGrath, and I should read Marcuse; she threw a copy of *Eros and Civilisation* at me. She claimed that she was the first to discover Joe Orton's body in his flat: 'The place was covered in spunk and shit,' she said. It sounded like a story she liked telling. She said she'd find me work to do, writing screenplays and TV scripts of published novels.

One of the people who often spoke at our revolutionary meetings was Andy from Zimbabwe, who told me that my play wasn't revolutionary. He put on an evening of revolu-tionary theatre in a converted fire station: several short plays by Ionesco, and his adaptation of Eisenstein's *Battleship Potemkin*. He was right, my play wasn't revolutionary. The Royal Court Theatre in London scheduled it for a one-night reading, and then for a two-week run in the main theatre. I stood outside and, exactly as the cliché has it, I looked at my name in lights. Adam (the Weasel) said that he liked my play because he liked bourgeois knockabout. Arnold Wesker told me that he didn't like it, because it was rude. 'There's no need to be impolite,' he said. Back at the flat in Oxford, Leebs and Mike pressed on with the chores rota. 'Just because you're famous, Rosen,' Leebs said, 'doesn't mean that you get out of doing the washing up.'

Peggy said that *Backbone* was going to 'transfer' to the West End. Then it wasn't going to transfer, because the Royal Court production was too cumbersome. I said that you could dispense with all the scene changes in the dark; the actors could bring on their own chairs, and it would make it more Brechtian. Peggy said, 'Don't be fucking daft, darling.'

Yorkshire TV loved the play. Then they got a letter from B.'s mother saying that if they put it on she would go to the papers saying that it was all about her, and she would sue them. Peggy said, no she fucking can't. The big cheese at Yorkshire TV was very religious, and Peggy said that he had no fucking balls and that's why Yorkshire wouldn't do it.

The March demo was one of the biggest of that time. We marched to the American embassy in Grosvenor Square. I had the image in my head of a Vietnamese woman harvesting rice and bombs landing around her. The richest country in the world bombing one of the poorest. We had to show the Vietnamese we were on their side. There was an unstated intention to get at or into the embassy, but a row of police stood between us and the building. Several hundred of us – perhaps a thousand – pushed against the police. They arrested many of us, me included. I landed up in a coach with Don, who had played Harold in my play. We sat in the coach for a time, until several of the police came round to identify us and the crime we had committed.

One policeman – who hadn't arrested me – asked me for my name. I refused to give it, so he wrote 'Big' on his sheet and we were taken off to Savile Row station. We sat in a large room, singing and telling stories. We speculated about an Indian guy called Manchanda, who we'd spotted leading several hundred people in the opposite direction. We agreed that he was an agent provocateur. One by one, we were taken out and photographed.

Every so often a policeman came in and identified someone and they were taken off and charged. But no one came for me.

I reckoned that 'Big' wasn't good enough to identify me. At around four o'clock we were let out into the street. I thought, I've got a bloody long walk home to Muswell Hill from here, but then I saw Harold and Brian waiting outside for me.

'We heard where they were holding most of the demonstrators,' Harold said, 'so we came here. They wouldn't say if you were in there or not.'

I said, 'They didn't know. They didn't have our names.'

I loved it that they had come and waited for me. We put our arms round each other and walked to the car.

Back at Oxford, the Proctors banned students from leafletting Cowley, so Jamaican Trevor M. suggested that we occupy the Proctors' office until they lifted the ban. The office was in the Sheldonian, the round eighteenth-century university theatre with venerable busts mounted above the railings outside, though by now they had got eaten by acid rain, so Harold called them the 'syphilitic heads'. There were a few hundred of us calling for a lifting of the ban and the end of the Proctor police system. Bob Reich (later Bill Clinton's Minister of Labour) said to me that he agreed with our objective but disagreed with our methods. The gates were bolted, so Trevor suggested we give them a bit of a shove. We did, they pushed open and we streamed in and sat down.

After a while, the Proctors came out and started to negotiate with us. Trevor spoke for us and said that there was no compromise, the ban had to be lifted. We were adults and had the right to leaflet if we wanted to. We elected a committee to take negotiations forward. Later, Clive, a sombre and serious guy I hardly knew, came up to me and said that this was dangerous because the moment a committee is elected it comes to stand not for the masses but instead of the masses, and simultaneously becomes part of the spectacle, not part of change. Clive was introducing me to 'Situationism'.

Around then, I received what felt at the time more like a summons than an invite. I was asked to a dinner-party discussion about the student revolt, and went, more out of curiosity than anything else. There was the host, Lenny, who taught Law, Lenny's wife, the cartoonist from the *Daily Telegraph* and his wife, and one or two others. I was the only student.

They treated me as if I was an expert on world student revolt and the one in Oxford in particular – not only an expert, but also personally responsible for it. Lenny was angry that the free arena of argument and debate had been violated. I said that there was a connection between how the war in Vietnam was being run by the 'military-industrial complex' (hah!) and the way institutions, in a chain, through governments, through to universities, maintained the status quo.

Lenny choked on that and said that he and I were free to dissent. But then his wife spoke up and said in a strong South African voice, 'Oh come off it, Lenny. Nothing would change if that's how we behaved. You don't seriously think apartheid is going to end if it isn't through all-out resistance. That's why you and me left, because we couldn't commit ourselves to it, but we both know that's what's going to bring about the change.'

Lenny withdrew into his shell after her outburst, but the others went on and on at me as if I had disrupted their lives. I came away thinking it was a strange way for people to behave: interrogation by dinner-party. Still, perhaps that's what Oxford academic life was like, and Lenny and his friends would probably be there for the rest of their lives. I was wrong: Lenny became Lord Chief Justice.

In the summer I auditioned for an Oxford and Cambridge production of *A Midsummer Night's Dream* and a revue written by Clive James (yes, that Clive James), working with Rob Buckman, Pete Atkin and Julie Covington – who would all go on to do TV and theatre work. I got the part of Robin Starveling the Tailor and a few monologues and songs in Clive James's revue. In rehearsals the professional director, Richard Cotterill, said the performance had to involve movement. And so we attended dance classes with S., who began every session with Miriam Makeba's 'Pata Pata'. There were moments when the sound of Makeba and her band seemed like the most hopeful sound I had ever heard, a hope that connected Vietnam with South Africa with Luther King and now us doing our dance classes. For the revue, the Cambridge part of the cast included people who would one day become very well known, like Mark Wing-Davey (*Hitchhiker's Guide*), Dai

'Russell' Davies (radio presenter) and Jonathan James-Moore (radio producer). I had a strong feeling that the material from the Cambridge folks was much better than ours: cleverer, wittier, more talented, more experienced in all departments. Our side included Nige, who would go on to write, amongst many other things, *The Wimbledon Poisoner*. Between rehearsals, Nige said that he thought the flaw in Marx's theory of surplus value was that it was a moral judgement.

I was OK in *Midsummer Night's Dream*, but when it came to the revue, Clive's long monologues had me beat. I couldn't remember all the words. As for the dancing, I couldn't keep time. After one session where I was still buggering it up, Clive blew his top. He came for me, shouting, 'I'll fucking have you. You're ruining everything I've ever worked for.' He was pulled off by Jonathan and Dai. Later, Clive explained that for him revue was the art form of the future: via sketches and songs it could tackle every theme, every emotion, every kind of politics, in a popular way. He was putting together a team that would take it to the next level, and I was an obstacle to success. I was demoted to a few walk-ons and pulling funny faces. The whole thing – the Shakespeare and the revue – migrated to Oxford and then, without me, on tour to the US.

In the next term, I was chair of the university Experimental Theatre Company and we put on the UK premiere of a play by Günther Grass, *The Plebeians Rehearse the Uprising*. It takes place during the 1953 revolt of East German workers, which happened while Brecht was rehearsing his *Coriolanus* adaptation with the Berliner Ensemble. I took the part of the first Mason, the leading revolutionary in the Shakespeare and the Grass play.

Reviewers from London came to see it, but once again Harold was unhappy. This time it was about the portrayal of the Communist actions against the workers. He said 1953 was only seven years after the war, and no one knew who held Nazi sympathies and who didn't. I said that the moment any Communist regime acted against workers, we should be alarmed, shouldn't we? Remember Kronstadt, I said. Christopher H. (brother of Peter, and later to become the world's most famous 'contrarian') had got me to read about Trotsky's suppression of that sailors' and workers' uprising. Harold was still of the opinion that to attack the Eastern bloc countries in public was to give succour to the enemy – even when he himself held very few hopes, if any, that things would work out well in the Communist world. My view was that we had to examine, explain and where necessary condemn the Eastern bloc countries, if we wanted any chance of building organisations and campaigns that weren't damaged by totalitarianism.

In the third year, Ian said that I could study the Romantics with F. W. 'Freddie' Bateson, renowned critic of Wordsworth and one-time *enfant terrible* of the English faculty for having opposed the exam system. He reasoned that it was little more than a training in journalism – writing quickly to deadlines. Not everyone wants to be a journalist, he said. He was a very kind, witty, clever tutor, and when he laughed he wheezed like an old machine, as he did over my essay on Keats's 'La Belle Dame Sans Merci' in relation to popular ballads. A lot of things I was doing were connecting up and making sense to me.

The strong whiff of rebellion hung in the air; we were all raising questions about who controls the syllabuses and why. Why weren't students part of the course design process? Why couldn't you pick and mix, rather than accept the course boundaries set by universities? We looked at the anomalies of the English course, with its arbitrary definition of 'English', its end at 1900 and its notion of literature as something which travelled in a corridor passing 'influence' along the corridor from one writer or one 'school' to the next for no other reason than that it was what one literary gent after the next fancied. 'Society' hardly existed in this scheme of things, let alone exerted any influence on writing. What the university referred to as 'Language' was purely and only 'philology', a description of changes in words and grammar over 1,500 years. Linguistics, whether of the new Chomskyan school, the Bloomfield school of descriptive linguistics, the sociolinguistics of Dell Hymes or any other form, was kept outside of the university walls: stuff those redbrick oiks do.

We called a faculty meeting and invited anyone from the English faculty to come. Professor Dame Helen Gardner attended, as did one of the Proctors, who in his academic life was a chemistry don. We made our submission, and Professor Dame Helen Gardner replied. She said that she and the other tutors strove with might and main to provide the most excellent course in English in the world, and that she herself experienced disappointment, if not anger, when she and other dons spent many hours preparing lectures which hardly anyone attended. I interjected and said that people voted with their feet. She exploded and said that that was rude and unacceptable.

We went on to discuss the 'Language' course and paper, and we pointed out how it was equivalent to a science course from the nineteenth century. The meeting broke up with nothing resolved. The Proctor took me to one side and asked if, seriously, the language course was really as antiquated as I'd suggested? I said it was, and that none of the developments in linguistics occurring in the twentieth century were included. He shook his head: 'I had no idea, I had no idea.'

Another upheaval was happening: Raphael Samuel, a history teacher at Ruskin Trade Union College in Walton Street, was building up what he called History Workshop Conferences. Each conference was a mix of university professors – usually Marxist, often ex- or still-Communist, like Christopher Hill, Eric Hobsbawm, E. P. Thompson, Tim Mason, Dorothy Thompson – and his trade union students.

One historian said that Hill, Hobsbawm and Thompson were infected by Stalinism and this prevented them from seeing the full potential in the self-activity of the working class but Raphael Samuel's students had all got their places at Ruskin through their trade unions, and were doing special studies on aspects of history and practice in their industries or places of work. They gave papers on, say, how Irish labour came into Britain and made it possible for the harvesting to be done in the nineteenth century, or how the labourers in nearby Otmoor rioted over enclosures. This was a new history that drew on some of the work that sat on our shelves at home, in the fading red covers of the Left Book Club.

These conferences were packed with hundreds of people, crowded into the halls and corridors, listening, talking, arguing, and writing. Dave (later to run the FA as Lord Dave,) played football in one of the hallways. I felt that it was all very well for me to argue with Helen Gardner about the English syllabus, but here was Raphael Samuel and hundreds of others redefining history, how it was taught, how it was studied, who was entitled to research it, and how it was disseminated. This, I thought, was one of the most exciting things happening, and I wanted to be part of it.

Others thought that the LSE was where it was really happening – or, I should say, still happening. Their occupation was like a permanent History Workshop, putting all their prescribed courses in politics, economics and history under the microscope and running their own versions, inviting in speakers from all over the world, and questioning the economics and politics of universities themselves.

Then, in May that year, trouble broke out in Paris.

This felt even more serious. It began when students on one of the new campuses in Nanterre started to question how they were taught, and built up to when the streets were a permanent battleground, there was a general strike, and President de Gaulle disappeared.

I went to a meeting in the LSE theatre addressed by Danny Cohn-Bendit, the head of the French student movement, who warned of a 'pre-fascist situation'. I hadn't ever heard of a pre-fascist situation before. I went to another meeting at the Mermaid Theatre addressed by a shop steward from Renault's Boulogne-Billancourt factory, now occupied by the workers. He described the endless grind of the production line (he used the word 'boulot' just as Gaudemarre had done in the Colonie!), and how the upheaval had triggered many of them into noticing that they made the cars but didn't own or control the fruits of their labour. A large Argentinian bloke with very long hair stood up and made a speech that mixed long volleys of revolutionary cliché with accusations that the shop steward and all of us listening to him were counter-revolutionaries. He was told to sit down, and he said that telling him to sit down was part of the problem, not part

of the solution. He went on. And on. Someone said that
he did this at all the meetings, and he was either insane or
a plant.

In September I went over to see my friends the Miquels in
Paris, by which time the tide had receded. But I still caught
some meetings in the Sorbonne amphitheatres. These had
now turned into debates about tactics. Every now and then
when one person took the floor, others leapt to their feet and
denounced them for belonging to a Stalinist, or Trotskyist, or
Maoist, or anarchist group. I soon learned the words *gauch-
iste* and *groupuscule*, and my favourite poster, designed in
response to the new buzzword '*participation*' and using the
old-school style of chanting conjugations, was: '*Je participe,
tu participes, ils participent, nous participons, vous partici-
pez, ils profitent*' (they profit).

But my time as a student was coming to an end. After five
years, I was finally going to get a degree. So what next?
I could do teacher training, but would probably end up on
the course that Harold, Jimmy and Nancy taught. And did
I really want to be an English teacher? There were theatre
scholarships, some of them run by TV companies. Having
acted in or directed a host of plays – like Dürrenmatt's *The
Visit*, Wedekind's *Spring Awakening*, Osborne's *Inadmissible
Evidence*, *Romeo and Juliet* – that would make sense. And
there were TV traineeships at Granada and the BBC.

Maybe that was the way to go. I talked it over with Ian and
Mum and Harold. They reckoned that though it was a long
shot and the competition was crazy, why not give the BBC
a try? At the time, the BBC was producing radical things:
Garnett and Loach were there; history and arts documenta-
ries were coming out that were exactly the sort of thing that
would interest me; the Open University, and many further
education, schools and children's programmes, all looked
inviting.

They offered what they called a 'General' traineeship to
six graduates a year, and when you came off the end of that,
after two years or so, you applied for jobs within the BBC.
Though it wasn't written in black and white you'd get one, all

being well, you would. That way I'd keep my options open. So I applied for the theatre and Granada traineeships, but the BBC was my preference.

I was offered an interview. Beforehand, however, Ian called me into his room in college and said that a man had turned up asking questions about me. What sort of man? I asked. Well, he was from the BBC but not actually at the BBC. He asked whether I was alright. Ian said that I was. He then went off to ask some other people if I was alright. Was he a spook? Ian shrugged. I told Harold. 'He was a spook,' he said.

Then the interview. There were about six or seven people there. One of them was the head of drama, Shaun Sutton. Another was Karl Miller, editor of the *Listener*. Another was a genial and friendly bloke called Laird. They asked me about *Backbone* and the Royal Court, about writing for *Isis*, about acting and directing, till we got on to politics.

'How would you describe your politics?' Laird asked.

'An unlearned Marxist,' I said, coining a phrase on the spot.

'Unlearned or unearned?' Karl Miller said.

'Unlearned,' I said.

A few weeks later, I was asked back to Broadcasting House to meet someone called Lance Thirkell. He was a grey-haired, abrupt, snappy talker, who wore shirt-sleeve garters. He stood the whole of the time he was talking to me, opening and closing a drawer in a large grey filing cabinet and reading my file. He looked at me and said, 'I think we'll go nap.'

When I got home I asked Harold what that meant.

'It means they're backing the outsider.'

'Is that me?' I said.

'Yes,' he said.

I then made a bad error. The editors of *Cherwell* had given me a weekly column to write, and when connections were discovered between the post-graduate college of All Souls and various property holdings, I wrote what we would now call an appallingly homophobic piece, making fun of the 'Master' of the college and others on the basis of their supposed homosexuality. It was a classic case of using one oppression in an attempt to defeat another.

There was a kerfuffle at the level of masters of colleges.

Bowra was approached by the leading figures at All Souls, and called me in.

'You're in trouble. They want you out. I've told them you're not going. You're going to write a letter. Now. And I'm going to go round myself and take it to them.'

I sat down and wrote a letter apologising for my intemperate and inexcusable article and for personalising the abuse. Bowra looked at it and said, 'Mmm, very clever, you haven't apologised at all. It'll do though. What you're going to do is work and get a good degree. Bye.'

He saved my skin. The boss of All Souls was one of his oldest friends. Only one person could get rid of me, and that was Bowra – and one thing he would never do was take orders from anyone, not even from an old friend, over the matter of what he regarded as a student's indiscretion. The price was for me to prove the hanging judges wrong. News was coming in from all over the country of students threatening to walk out of Finals to undermine the system. He didn't want me to be one of them.

I figured that if I stayed around, I would get into even more of a mess, so I packed up all my books and old essays and translations and went home for the twelve weeks leading up to Finals. I lived in the attic rooms in the house in Muswell Hill. Every morning I got up, did a few hours' work, watched BBC Playschool, did a few more hours' work, and wrote poems. I started to think that I would like to work on Playschool, writing poems and scenes for them. I looked through past exam papers and discovered that the finals were just about as liberal as a public exam can be. Each paper had a set of entirely predictable questions. Only Anglo-Saxon offered one or two tricky problems, because you were expected to translate chunks of Anglo-Saxon poetry. On nearly all the papers, there was one question that to all intents and purposes went: 'Is there anything else you would like to write about? If so, write about it.'

So, I devised a course for myself in poetry, plays and novels that I was interested in. I started to make discoveries and connections between literature, history and ideas. Books that had meant one thing started to mean something else. I thought I knew *The Tempest* and 'discovered', when leafing through one of Harold's old books – an anthology put together by the Marxists Jack Lindsay and Edgell Rickword – that Caliban could be regarded as a rebel rather than as I had always seen him played, a balls-scratching savage. At least some of the play was about or to do with colonisation, wasn't it? And then the native Caliban unites with European working people in an attempt to overthrow the coloniser. Yes, it's all masked by jokes and drunkenness but the essence of it is a revolt. Meanwhile, old Gonzalo chats on about a kind of utopia in the context of a never-ending nastiness of usurpation and revenge amongst the aristocracy. How had I missed this before?

Then, in the midst of my swotting, *Twelfth Night* suddenly seemed to be about class in Elizabethan society. The play showed various effete, idle members of the aristocracy, in contrast to various dissolute members of the next class down – the gentry – and a couple of people from the new aspiring middle class, one informed by Puritanism, the other, Viola, by striving, sexual desire and social mobility. I went back to Danby to see what he said about the upset to the social order caused by the Machiavellian Edmund in *King Lear*, and jotted down all the Machiavels across Shakespeare's plays. I 'discovered' that Shakespeare was writing about changing times: 'Love cools, friendship falls off, brothers divide, in cities mutinies, in countries discord, in palaces treason, and the bond cracked 'twixt son and father.'

I came across a chapter by the Cambridge academic, Muriel Bradbrook, which posited something else I'd never thought about: in *A Midsummer Night's Dream*, when the 'rude mechanicals' put on their play, *Pyramus and Thisbe*, Shakespeare appears to be at the very least giving audiences a laugh at their efforts. Bradbrook pointed towards the precise kind of popular entertainment Shakespeare was poking fun at, which contemporary audiences would have recognised.

I was excited by this. Bradbrook was saying that alongside the Mystery Plays – the seasonal town pageants put on by tradesmen's guilds, which represented actual or apocryphal scenes from the Bible – touring companies staged

'Romances', tales of kings, monsters and fairies culled from classical dramas and legends: thus the rude mechanicals' production of a play, which is a kind of *Romeo and Juliet* story from Antiquity. This was popular theatre from four hundred years ago. Bradbrook then went on to name some of these other plays and gave references to them, like *Sir Clyomon and Sir Clamydes*.

I thought: I know, for my dead cert question on Elizabethan Comedy, why don't I – instead of doing the usual round of Dekker and Fletcher and the rest – go to the Bod, (the university library) dig out these popular romances, read them, make notes and prepare a question on them? Original research, eh?

For Chaucer, to speed things up, I bought two translations. Three of the tales I had read properly and closely in their original late Middle English, but the rest I thought I would read as if they were folk tales and did all I could to get hold of the stories that embodied similar motifs and themes from Boccaccio and others. I was amazed to find that the bawdy Miller's Tale was part of a French tradition of tales (known as *fabliaux*) that revelled in farcical sexual encounters, disruptive of law and order. There was even one called *Le con qui parle*.

I retranslated *Beowulf*, quite mechanically at first, but then starting to fancy the way I was doing it, trying to keep as much of the original alliteration as I could, amazed how some of it survived intact from the original: Grendel was 'grim and greedy' in the year 1000, and still was.

One of the questions that always cropped up was on The Ballad, and the set text for this was the *Oxford Book of Ballads*. I looked closely at it and saw that there were no living sources for the texts. I thought I could make an argument for saying that these ballads existed in a living, oral tradition, and the only way to be absolutely sure of treating this in a scholarly way was to use examples from actual singing. That united form and function. I selected versions of the ballads from my records: Shirley Collins, Hedy West and others. I learned these.

In the week before Finals, I went back. I was walking into Wadham, Bowra was walking out. He looked at me: 'Working?' he said.

I shrugged.

'Thinking?' he said.

I shrugged again.

'I've completely lost the capacity to do either,' he said and walked on.

The night before my Anglo-Saxon paper, I realised that the way the exam worked was that one year they asked us to translate part of the Anglo-Saxon poem 'The Wanderer', the next, 'The Seafarer'. They just alternated. I checked my book of past papers. Last year, they did 'The Seafarer', so all I need do was look up my crib or translation for 'The Wanderer'. I couldn't find it. I must have left it at home. I asked K. if I could borrow hers. That night, I pretended it was a part for a play that I had to learn and learnt the translation off by heart.

For Oxford Finals exams, you wore a black suit, black shoes, white bow tie and black gown, and carried your mortarboard. This was called 'sub-fusc'. It was encouraged, but not official, for people to wear a white carnation. I didn't have a black suit, black shoes or a white bow tie. I matched up a pair of black jeans with a Levis cord black jeans jacket, tied a bandage round my neck and blacked up a pair of white gym shoes. I bought a small round cardboard disc-badge, wrote on it, 'A carnation', and pinned it to my jeans jacket.

We filed in and the moment we were asked to turn over the first paper, I looked ahead to the question on the poems: was it 'The Wanderer' or 'The Seafarer'? I was right, it was 'The Wanderer'. I looked to see what I reckoned was the section of the poem we had to translate; I recited the poem in my head till it got to the right part; I wrote it down as fast as I could. Then it was back to the beginning of the paper. Neither then nor at any time since have I worked out what this had to do with 'doing English'. Acting, yes. Academic study? Surely not.

The exams lasted a week or more. When it came to the morning we had to do the Language paper, the front of the hall filled up with what looked like every English tutor in the university. Later, I heard that they thought we were going to stage an uprising. We weren't. Rebels never know till afterwards how close the powers-that-be get to full-on panic.

I enjoyed the papers. I wrote plenty and said what I wanted to say. I thought, given that exams are exams, it was fair. It wasn't a test of what I didn't know, it was a test of what I did know. Halfway through one of the papers, Professor Dame Helen Gardner walked up the aisle and stopped next to me. She handed me a card. On the card she had written: 'Gentlemen must wear sub-fusc: black shoes, black suit, white shirt, white bow tie, if not, they will be excluded from the exam.'

The night before the last exam, I got some white paint and wrote in large letters on the back of my gown, 'Hells Angels. Jeff Chaucer'. I wore the gown with this message inside so that it couldn't be seen. In the last minute of the last exam, I turned my gown so that the message was showing, walked up the hall, collected some paper, turned round and came back. Moments later, it was the end of Finals.

I went back to the house. They told us that we all had to be available in case we had a 'viva' – an oral exam – which would be held if there were problems with any of our papers, or if our marks were marginal between the grades.

Howard Marks ('Mr Nice') wanted to rent my room with his girlfriend Ilse, but I was suspicious. When there was the trouble over my article in *Cherwell* he had stopped me in the street and said how he had been talking with the people from All Souls, and they were going to get me thrown out. It seemed so incongruous: Howard, proud-to-be-drunk and proud-to-smoke-dope, perpetually seen in pubs and music venues, and here he was claiming to be chatting to these upper-class college masters about me.

Anyway, I did rent him and Ilse the room and even as I was getting ready to go, he was filling up the shelves with hundreds of singles. 'Rock'n'roll,' he said. 'Everything important that anyone has ever wanted to say is in rock'n'roll.'

'Everything?' I said.

'Listen to this. Where's your record player?'

He put on the Duke of Earl singing 'Duke of Earl'. It was good. I liked it.

He put on Chris Kenner's 'I like it like that'. He put on Fats Domino. I said it was great, I had Chuck Berry and Bo Diddley myself. That gave me a thought: I'd better take my collection with me, or he'll nick it. I gathered up my singles: Tommy Tucker's 'High-Heeled Sneakers', Aretha Franklin's 'Natural Woman' and 'Spanish Harlem', the worn-out Canned Heat and Dionne Warwick, and a hundred others. Then my LPs and EPs: Delta Blues albums like Robert Johnson's and *Blues Fell This Morning*, field recordings of English, Irish and Scots songs, MacColl, Guthrie, Leadbelly, Mozart's clarinet concerto, Beethoven's *Pastoral*, Dylan's second album, the Stones's first album, Gus Cannon's Jug Band, Léo Ferré, Georges Brassens. Then I headed home.

A week later, I heard that I would be needed for a viva in six weeks' time. It was because I was marginal between a Second and a First. I didn't know how to prepare for a viva, and no one told me. Six weeks later I was back in my room. Howard had blown the amp in my music equipment. I walked over to the exam halls, went in and for the first time felt nervous. I was cross with myself that I did. Surely it didn't matter. I had a job. I didn't need a First in order to do any post-graduate work.

Sitting in a row were the examiners, one for each one of the papers – which added up to something like twelve people, all in their gowns, with their red hats and hoods filling in the spaces around them. In front of me, in a velvet waistcoat, was the chair of the examiners, Professor Dame Helen Gardner.

'Sit down, Mr Rosen,' she said. 'You have alphas or alpha betas or alpha gammas on all your papers apart from mine, which is a delta – no alpha. For you to get a First Class Honours Degree in English Literature and Language, you have to raise your mark on my paper to at least an alpha gamma. You have to have alphas on all your papers for a First.'

For a moment, I thought, well I'm really not bothered. I've done fine, I don't need to raise anything; I could just walk. I shuffled in my seat, but I've never been all that good at split-second judgements and I stayed put.

'Your question on Elizabethan comedy was absurd,' she said. 'You chose obscure plays of no literary merit, rather than follow the usual course of writing about Dekker and Fletcher. Why's that?'

I said that it was because I thought that there was an interesting and serious question about what was the popular dramatic entertainment of the day, and I was interested in the history of popular theatre. 'Pyramus and Thisbe' was a pointer to that, and Muriel Bradbrook had provided the pointer. I said I thought I'd referred to that in the question. She muttered that it was absurd nevertheless, and that she had drawn a line through that essay and given it zero.

'Next, you wrote on the ballad but refused to use the reputable source, *The Oxford Book of Ballads*. Your reason for this was the spurious one of needing to use living sources. In fact, the Shirley Collins example was from the Vaughan Williams collection. I have drawn a line through this question and given it zero.'

She seemed to be getting angrier and angrier. I thought again to myself, I really don't need to be here. Why am I getting told off? I haven't failed, I'm being viva'ed for a First.

'Now to the Metaphysicals.'

This was the subject she was world famous for, having produced celebrated editions of John Donne and been the editor of the Penguin *Metaphysical Poets*, one of my favourite books.

'You wrote on Henry Vaughan and produced some mediocre stuff on "light" in Vaughan's poetry, as if that was all there is to it. You didn't write on Donne. Why's that?'

'The question didn't ask specifically for me to write on Donne.'

'Donne is the most important poet of the period. Let's talk about him. Do you know what a "paradox" is?'

'It would be a paradox if I got a First after this kind of questioning,' I said.

'No,' she said, 'that would be an irony, not a paradox.'

I thought, yes, that's true.

She was finished with me, and handed the rest of the discussion over to the row of men – and they were all men. One of them, Wordsworth's great, great, great something or other, said that he wanted to take me up on why I had claimed that John Clare was 'nearer' to the natural world than Hopkins. I said that Clare wrote about agricultural work because that was his background, his father was a farm labourer – and as a boy Clare had been a bird-scarer – whereas Hopkins was a spectator. Wordsworth said, 'Case unproven.'

There were a few more questions and then they asked me to leave. On the way out, the Chaucer examiner, a small man with glasses, leant away from the table and whispered, like he was apologising for burping, 'I really liked your Chaucer paper.'

Later that day, I met up with Ian. He said that there had been a kerfuffle. After I went, the examiners demanded that Helen Gardner apologise to me. She refused, and said that she would pass on a note to Ian to thank me for my 'demeanour'.

'There's something else,' he said. 'She thought you'd made up the Elizabethan comedies you wrote about. She had never heard of them. She went to the Bod and dug them out to see if they were genuine or not.'

Bowra asked to see me. 'Well done,' he said. 'Helen Gardner. Frightful woman.'

And I left.

Harold's aunts, Bella and Stella Rosen (married name, Rechnitz) with her son Michael. Bielsko-Biala, southern Poland.

Oscar 'Jeschie' Rosen, Harold's uncle, in WWI French army uniform.

Oscar with, we guess, his wife, Rachel.

# Postscript

## To Harold, Who Died in 2008

There's something I didn't ever tell you, Harold. When Connie died in 1976, you told me that some time after that, Ronnie came to see you and was cross with you that you didn't tell him his sister had died. You told me that you said to Ronnie, 'Connie didn't ever ask to see you when she was dying.' And that was that. You didn't ever see Ronnie again and neither did Brian nor I. What I did do, though, was write to him. I didn't ever tell you this. I was curious. I remembered Ronnie. I liked him.

He wrote back irritated. He said that when Brian and I were children, Bubbe and Zeyde used to come and see us very often in Pinner, but you never thanked them for coming so far. I thought, well, they didn't come all the time, it was fairly even stevens as I remember. Sometimes we went to see them, sometimes they came to see us. Then he went off on a whole thing about how awful you were: he claimed that you said to him, 'Connie said she didn't want to see you.' Ronnie responded in his letter to me: 'I don't believe that Connie would have said that.'

So we've got two versions here: you say that you said to him, 'Connie didn't ever say she wanted to see you.'

He says you said, 'Connie said she didn't want to see you.'

No way of knowing, now.

He then wrote that I mustn't tell anybody that he had written this letter. What was that about? Who knows.

So I wrote to him again and I pointed out that I'm not you, Harold. I said that whatever you said or didn't say, should have said or shouldn't have said, was nothing to do with me. Couldn't we start again and perhaps meet up? I suggested meeting in a restaurant somewhere. I said that I didn't keep kosher so perhaps he wouldn't be happy coming to the house, but if we went to a kosher restaurant, it was sorted. And I put a couple of my latest books in with it, including a copy of *The Golem of Old Prague* – my adaptation of the Jewish Golem stories.

He wrote back to say that he didn't like my Golem stories: whatever happened hundreds of years ago, it gave a very bad impression of Jews now. It wasn't going to help with anything nowadays. He said that he liked the idea of meeting up though, where? When?

Then, just as I got going finding a kosher eatery near him, he wrote again to say that this correspondence was finished. I wasn't to write ever again.

And I didn't.

A couple of years after you died, we went to see your cousin Ted again in America. He was 103. On the occasions I went before, you know he always wanted to talk to me about your father, but when I came back with stories, you didn't want to know. When Ted was growing up he lived with your father, so he knew some things:

Morris and your mother, Rose, met in London in the early 1900s. Morris had come to London in around 1892 from Poland as a teenager with his parents, Jonas and Martha. They were in the fuel business, but they couldn't make it work in London so they went back to Poland, leaving Morris there. He was always very bitter about that. He was just left in London. He met Rose, Ted said, in something called the Yipsels. Work it out, it's something like Young People's Socialist League. They got married and went to the States around 1912 with the two kids they had already, Sidney and Laurence, both born in London. Just like Ted, who was born in Buxton Street, right by the Whitechapel Road, in 1908.

Ted said it wasn't exactly that Morris lived with them. More that Morris sometimes came to live with them. In the house was Max (Morris's brother), Max's wife Sarah and their children, Ted and Ted's younger sister, Olga. When Max went off to work in the boot and shoe factories, just as Morris did, Max's wife ran a little store, selling candy, kerosene, cans of beans. Ted said it was no great shakes. People came by and bought one or two things.

Morris didn't always have a job. It seems he got blacklisted for union organising. He went off to Rochester. One time, when Ted was a teenager, Morris came back and said to Ted, 'Let me show you this.' He took out a billfold and showed Ted a picture of a boy.

'What do you think, Ted?' Morris said.

Ted shrugged.

'It's my landlady's son,' Morris said. 'Do you think he's a smart-looking kid?'

Ted said he didn't know.

I asked Ted why he told me this story. Ted said he was just telling me. I didn't say any more. Neither did Ted.

Now, this time some ten years later, with Ted aged 103, he said, 'Did I ever tell you Morris had an illegitimate son?'

I said, 'No you didn't, Ted. You did tell me how one time Morris showed you a picture of his landlady's son.'

'That's the one,' Ted said. 'When Morris showed up here, he was always dressed beautifully: suits, spats, new shoes. He came with a trunk and I shared the room with him. It was one of those trunks that's like a closet. It stood in the corner of the room, he opened it up and there were five suits hanging in there. Five suits, he had. He always came with five suits.'

Ted went on: 'My father said that when Morris spoke, people listened. He spoke at meetings and people listened. At the Workmen's Circle, Arbeter Ring we call it in Yiddish. But we didn't know where he went or what he did. He just showed up, stayed a while and then went off again.

'He stood in an election somewhere, Pennsylvania. The story always was that he got more votes than the big guy ... you'll know his name, Michael ... leader ...'

'Eugene Debs?'

'No ...'

'Norman Thomas?'

'That's the one. In whatever election it was, Morris says he got more votes than Norman Thomas ... on the same ticket ...'

'What election?'

'I don't know. Pennsylvania, somewhere ... He turned up one time in a convertible. He took us out in the convertible, my father and me, but not my mother. She wouldn't go. She took against Morris after he had the illegitimate child ... Did I ever tell you that Morris died in the Mattapan?'

'Mattapan?'

'Boston's biggest mental institution.'

'No, you didn't say.'

'My father said his condition had so deteriorated I shouldn't go see him. So I didn't go. That's where he died.'

So, Harold, that's what Ted told me and I tried to find out more. I know it didn't interest you, but it interested me. Google has changed everything. I kept googling Morris Rosen. There was a Morris Rosen who was in the mob, another one who was a Communist carpenter. Their names kept coming up. Then I put in 'Boot and shoe worker' and up came a report of a 'Convention' of the Shoe Workers Union in St Louis, Missouri from 1921, a year before your mother and Morris split up.

It said that Morris Rosen, the delegate from Brockton, Mass., 'moved the following motion':

WHEREAS, the world war is over – has been over for two and one-half years – and we see no good reason why there should still be men and women behind prison bars for no other reason than that they had certain convictions and exercised what they thought to be their constitutional rights in publicly expressing them; and

WHEREAS, our country stands alone today as the only one of the leading nations of the world that has not granted amnesty to its political and industrial prisoners; and

WHEREAS, Eugene V. Debs, who has given a lifetime of loyal service to the working class, is now occupying a felon's cell; likewise, there are some two hundred and fifty other political and industrial prisoners in the federal Jails of our country; Now, therefore, be it that we demand of the United States Government the immediate release and the granting of amnesty to all persons whose political belief formed the basis of their persecution, trial and imprisonment.

The same delegate Morris Rosen moved another motion:

WHEREAS, the workers of Russia after suffering untold per-secution, misery, and hardships for many years under the rule of tyrants, have thrown off that yoke, and

WHEREAS, the Workers' Government of Russia has now been established for more than three and one-half years, and from all information available it is the kind of government the people in that country want;

therefore, be it RESOLVED: that we demand of our government that there be established an immediate resumption of trade and diplomatic relations with the Russian Workers' Republic.

I thought you might be interested in that.

Anyway, I went on googling and up popped another thing: a pageant in Brockton.

The Book of the Pageant of Brockton
Written by
Suzanne Cary Gruver
Produced in Connection With the Centennial Celebration of
the Incorporation of the Town of North Bridgewater,
Now Brockton, at the Fair Grounds,
June 15–16, 1921

Morris Rosen took part in the following scene of the pageant:

Episode IV. Arbitration and Industrial Peace. Scene IV.

ARBITRATION AND INDUSTRIAL PEACE
The City views from her dais the coming of her Arts and Industries. They arrive to stately music and take place either

side her throne. The Industries are a united group. Peace and Justice stand near the City's dais, prominent among the Civic Virtues.

There is a clash in the harmonious music. The figure of Discord, in yellow-green, appears. At her approach there is a movement of unrest among the group of Industries. Peace trembles as she advances menacingly toward her; she raises a protesting hand. Discord continues her threats and Peace sadly steps down from her place and leaves the City. Discord whispers words of dissension into the ears of the Industries. The group separates into two factions – representing now Labor and Capital. The leaders appeal to the City. She bids Justice decide between them. Justice, balancing in her golden scales the arguments presented, announces that Arbitration alone can settle the grievances. Arbitration is summoned. She listens impartially to both leaders. Discord is driven away. Then, uniting the two factions into a solid group again, she summons Peace, who returns gladly to her place near the City's throne.

What do you think, Harold?

I asked Ted if he knew where Morris was buried. He didn't remember. Online there's an organisation that keeps lists of who's buried in the American Jewish cemeteries. I found out that there are cemeteries for the Arbeter Ring, and in one of them there was a Morris Rosen. It was in Melrose, Boston. I found out that Max and Sarah were buried there, too. I had a trip lined up to the States, I got myself to Boston, having written to the cemetery supervisor who said he would mark the grave for me.

One grey, rainy morning in November, I got on a bus from Somerville out towards Melrose. The bus didn't go all the way, so when it stopped, I started walking. First it was small single houses, nearly all white and 'shingled' with clapper-boards, a bit like houses in East Anglia. Then there were some 'row houses' or terraces, and then that petered out so all there was were tattoo parlours, car sales places, occasional night clubs. And of course there was no pavement, so I was walking on gravel and mud. Cars swooshed past me spraying up the rain.

I started to wonder why I was doing this. It wasn't like I was going to meet anyone. I was just going to look at the grave of someone who you didn't know after the age of three.

I got to the Jewish cemeteries and found the one fenced off as being for the Workmen's Circle. I looked around and saw that one grave was marked with crime incident tape that the cemetery supervisor had put for me. It was over to one side, under some trees, on its own: it said, 'Morris Rosen'. Who put the stone there? It couldn't have been your brothers Laurie or Wallace, as both had died before Morris died. It could have been your brother Sidney, who had left Morris in the 1930s. It wasn't you, Harold, or Sylvia, because you were in England. It might have been the 'illegitimate' one, I suppose.

I looked some more. Like all the other graves, it had a carving to represent the Arbeter Ring, a circular chain with the letters A R and a number. I took photos. I wandered about some more and there were messages to do with brotherhood and hope. I also found the graves of Ted's parents Max and Sarah, side by side.

Later I checked with Ted's son. On Jewish graves, there's a tradition of writing the name of the deceased's father in Hebrew. The name in Hebrew on Morris's grave was right – Jonas, Max and Morris's father. The date of Morris's death was earlier than I thought, 1950, (birth 1878). The number? It was the number of the branch of the Jewish Workmen's Circle that must have clubbed together to bury him, and the branch name, I found online, was 'Mattapan'. Did that mean they had a branch in the Mattapan, or was that just a coincidence? Mattapan is a district in Boston, perhaps where Morris lived before going into hospital.

That's about it.

No, there was another thing.

Do you know where he was born? Krośniewice. I found that out from his First World War registration card. A small village west of Warsaw.

So, there's your father Morris, his brother Max in the States, and two more brothers in France – Oscar and Martin.

In Poland: Morris's sisters Bella, Stella (mother of Michael Rechnik), her husband Bernard and some others ... These are your uncles and aunts.

You know how much I've been interested in France. Well, I started to get interested in your uncles, the French brothers, Oscar and Martin. Do you remember how some years ago, I picked up a book that listed every one of the Jews deported from France? It was put together by Serge Klarsfeld, who almost single-handedly set out to tell the story of what happened to Jews in France under Vichy and the occupation. I didn't find an Oscar Rosen, but I found a couple of Martin Rozens ... No way of telling anything from any of that.

All you knew, all Ted and Olga knew, all Michael Rechnik knew, was that they were in France before the war and they weren't there after the war. That's how you always put it. Your cousin Olga said that she remembered writing to them when she was a girl. Olga and Michael remembered that Oscar and Martin lived in a road called 'rue de Thionville', but they weren't sure which town this was ... Metz? Nancy? They were pretty sure that one of the brothers was a clock-mender and the other a dentist. That was it. And that's all you knew, too.

I tried finding a rue de Thionville. There are a few of them, because Thionville is a place so there's bound to be roads going to and from it. That was no good. Dead end.

I thought about how two people mending clocks and teeth can live in France, a country so close to where we lived, a country we had visited dozens of times, could just disappear. Or be disappeared. But then, that was the project. To disappear them. And in their case, it had worked. Their lives and their deaths had been wiped. It annoyed me and it saddened me.

Then, quite out of the blue, Ted's son Teddy wrote to me. He said something had turned up: some letters and cards. These were in German, and they came from France and Poland. He sent me the scans (translations by his partner, Nadia):

1. **Sender:** Rosen, 11 rue Mellaise Niort (Deux Sévres) France
Addressee: Monsieur Max Rosen
96, West Cedar St. Boston Mass U.S.A.

Niort, March 18, 1940

My Dears, I have received your dear letter dated January 17, 1940. I am glad that you are healthy and I can tell you the same about us. I also hope that you received my letter dated February 6, 1940. But I am very surprised that you write so little. I can inform that I have still not received a sign of life from Poland. Now I am asking you whether you have already received a letter from Poland. If yes, please send me a copy (not the original). I am asking you again and let me know immediately.

As for my business, I can tell you that since August 20, 1939, I have not worked and that we live from our savings. Our money is getting less every day.

I forwarded your dear letter to Martin.

I am glad that you are sending money to our dear brother.

I am pleased to hear that your dear brother send money to Poland.

Unfortunately I cannot do the same.

Otherwise no news. I am sending you heartfelt greetings and kisses.

Your Oscar who is thinking of you.
My dear wife sends many regards.

This first letter told us straightaway that Oscar was living in Niort, Deux-Sèvres, which is nowhere near Metz or Nancy and that he was is touch with his brother, Martin. The letter is dated just a few weeks before the invasion of France in May 1940. At that point virtually the whole population of the areas where the German army invaded fled to south-west France. Maybe Oscar and his wife got wind of it early, and fled ahead of the invasion.

Here's the second letter:

2. Sender: Rosen, 11 rue Mellaise, Niort (Deux-Sèvres), France

Addressee: Monsieur Max Rosen, 96, West Cedar St. Boston (Mass)

Niort, 23 March, 1940

My dears,

Only today did I receive your dear letter dated 29 February. I hope that you already received my card dated 18 March. We are glad to hear that you are in good health and I can tell you the same from us. We were very pleased to receive your letter and we thank you very much. I just learned from you that dear Bella is no more in Biala. I tried to make inquiries but unfortunately I can't get any information. I am very surprised that you have not yet received any news from Poland. You live in a neutral country, therefore it is much easier for you to find out something about our sisters in Poland. Who knows whether they are still alive. I am giving you the following addresses. Write immediately. Also let me know right away whether you received this card. You may also write to me in Yiddish. Tea Weinstock in Opoczno, Ziemia Radomska.

Stella Rechnitz, ulica Żeromskiego No. 17 in Dombrowa-Górnicza, bei Sosnowiec, Poland.

I learned that it is best to write in Polish to Poland, and up to 25 words, not more.

If you receive a letter from Poland, only send me a copy. Nothing else new, as I am awaiting good news. Best regards, your brother, brother-in-law

Oscar

My dear wife also sends you many regards and wishes you the best. Awaiting immediate answers, as it takes very long.

The 'dear Bella' is Oscar's sister but we don't know who Tea Weinstock is. And I'm not sure why he says 'brother-in-law', as he's Max's brother. Stella Rechnitz, also a sister, is Michael's mother.

3. Hand-written registered postcard with German stamps, airmail stamp, and a German military censorship stamp:
Sender: Bernard Rechnitz Dombrowa 6/S Schlesischestr. 14
Addressee: Mr. Max Rosen, Boston-Mass West Cedar 96 U.S.A.

Dombrowa, 22 January, 1941

Dear Brother, I have written to you several times and urged you fervently to take in my only child. Michal/ Mordka / Rechnitz in Joszkar – 6 Ta, Maryjskoja U.S.S.R. pocstowy Jasscryk No. 8 barack / 7. Sowjet Union.

He was sent way from Lemberg and only America can rescue him. Therefore I am fervently asking you to take the necessary steps immediately. Many thousands have already gone to America. I am asking you again and fulfil my request. I have sent you my son's birth certificate. Born 16 November 1923 in Dombrowa 6/S.

What are you doing my dears? Kisses to you and your dear wife. Maybe for now you can send him a few dollars? I beg you very much.

This is from Michael Rechnik's father, Bernard Rechnitz (Michael changed the spelling), who though he says his 'brother', in fact he's Max's brother-in-law! Perhaps it was his wife, Stella, who actually wrote it.

4. Hand-written postcard with German stamps and airmail stamp:
Sender: Bernard Rechnitz Dombrowa 6/S Schlesischestr. 14
Addressee: Mr. Max Rosen Boston-Mass West Cedar 96 U.S.A.

Dombrowa, 11 February 1941

Dear Brother, I hope you have already taken the steps to take in my son. Maybe you could adopt him to make this work? Dear brother, I urge you. For now send him a few dollars and packages with food because he has nothing. I fervently urge you to send something as soon as possible. Don't be upset with me but only you ... [remainder of the sentence obscured by airmail stamp]

Kisses to you and to your dear wife and children. Your sister Stella

I googled 11, rue Mellaise, Niort, Deux-Sèvres, France and it's an ordinary French street, the kind I've walked down thousands of times, shop downstairs, flat above, shutters. It looks like it's been there, unchanged in appearance, since the 1880s. I went on searching and came across a reference to a book, *Les chemins de la honte. Itinéraire d'une persécution, Deux-Sèvres, 1940-1944,* by Jean-Marie Pouplain: the paths of shame, the itinerary of a persecution.

I ordered it. It arrived just as we were moving out of a house I had lived in for about twenty-five years, boxes were piled up but I couldn't resist pulling open the package. I went straight to the index to look for 'Rosen', and it said there was a Rosen mentioned on pages 34, 65, 96, 108, 197, 202, 203 205, 210, 212, 213, 236, 240 and 244. On page 34 there was a list of Jews drawn up by the Vichy regime, and one of them was: '*Rosen, Jeschie, né le 23 juin, 1895, polonais, bon-neterie, marié à Kesler, Rachel, née en 1910, 11 rue Mellaise.*'

Some things were right, some not so right, some unknown. Address: right; 'Jeschie': not right; wife's name, ages, job ('*bonneterie*' – hosier): didn't know that before. If 'Jeschie' was an alternative name for Oscar, there could be a reason. Jews have Hebrew names as well as official names for the country they live in. Sometimes in Eastern Europe the Hebrew names are 'Yiddishified'. 'Jeschie' is a Yiddish familiar name for 'Yehoshua'. Just sometimes, Jews' official state names have echoes of their Hebrew names – the same first letter or a rough rhyme ... Yehoshua kind of rhyming with Oscar? Perhaps ...?

Then I went through the other pages. On one of these, Jeschie was listed as 'horloger de carillon' (literally: mender of chiming clocks). The 'Prefect' or 'Sub-prefect' had made these lists of Jews, and then they went on to document how Jeschie and Rachel were given yellow stars, and how they had to pin a sign saying '*Entreprise Juive*' and '*Jüdisches Geschäft*' (Jewish business) wherever they were working. And then they were 'Aryanised' – a special Vichy France term to mean that they had to hand over everything they owned to Vichy. It also said that Jeschie was arrested and got away, '*clandestinement*'.

The next time his name is listed is in a document featured in the Klarsfeld book I have. He is on a 'Convoy 62':

> On convoy 62, a convoy of 1,200 Jews leaving Paris-Bobigny at 11.50 am on 20 November 1943. Arrived Auschwitz, 25 November, as cabled by SS Colonel Liebenhenschel. 1181 arrived. There had been 19 escapees, they were young people, who escaped at 8.30 p.m. near Lerouville. In the convoy there were 83 children who were less than twelve years old. Out of the convoy 241 were selected for work and given numbers 164427-164667. Women numbered 69036-69080 were selected too. 914 were gassed straightaway. In 1945, there were 29 survivors, 27 men and 2 women.

There was a grim satisfaction for me here: I had started on this investigation because I didn't want the people in our family to be disappeared. So, pulling their names out of these internet sites and books was a way of resisting this.

Harold, I thought you would like one aspect of this: you often used to say, as an ironic aside, 'After all that expensive education we gave you ...!' I think you meant that the education hadn't cost anything, as we didn't pay any fees. But there was a lot of it, school, college, and then MA and PhD, and now I had used the stuff I'd learned by beavering away through papers, websites and books, and got to the point of retrieving all this. I thought of your admiration of Dimitrov, sitting in his cell, defending himself against the accusation that he had burnt down the Reichstag. OK, I'm no Dimitrov, but at least I had found this stuff. And hasn't it given me the chance to prevent our relatives from having no records, you know – just disappearing completely? I was explaining to myself why I was doing this research: I didn't want the Nazis to be successful in 'disappearing' them.

This led me to ask more questions: where were Jeschie and Rachel picked up? Most of the others on the Vichy list had been taken from Niort. But Jeschie and Rachel had escaped. I went on googling and suddenly up popped Oscar (not Jeschie) and Rachel Rosen, in papers and on a monument to victims of Nazi barbarism in Sedan, in north-east France. Sedan? No one ever mentioned Sedan.

I got in touch with Gérald Dardart, the author of the papers, and he told me that he had found that Oscar and Rachel had been picked up in Nice.

Nice? Why Nice? Back to the books. France wasn't only occupied by the Nazis. The south-eastern corner was occupied by Italy. As the round-ups of Jews in the rest of France progressed through 1943, the Italians resisted them. The Germans asked the Italians to hand over the Jews in the part of France they occupied, but they refused. An Italian banker, Donati, started to get Jews out of France because he had more than an inkling of what was going on in the camps. He arranged false passports and commandeered two boats which would take several thousand Jews to North Africa, recently recuperated by the Allies following the Battle of El Alamein.

Jews from all over France heard about these things and started to do everything they could to reach Nice and its environs. If possible, they checked into hotels to wait for Donati to spirit them away. This is why Oscar/Jeschie and Rachel would have made for Nice.

This rang a bell, though. Weren't Klarsfeld's parents sent to Auschwitz from Nice? Yes, I remembered right. They were taken from the Hotel Excelsior, and only recently he had arranged for a small monument to remember the Jews deported from there. But how come my relations were deported? Why hadn't Donati saved them?

Precisely as Donati was trying to complete the rescue, the Allies were busy defeating Italy. Donati got a message to Eisenhower, pleading with him not to announce the victory. Just hold off a few days. But Eisenhower announced it all the same. Within three days of that victory in September 1943, the Nazis marched into Nice. Amongst them was Alois Brunner, one of the most eager executors of the 'Final Solution'. He found the Jews in the hotels and rounded them up, apparently in the most violent way possible.

Could I be certain that Oscar/Jeschie and Rachel were there? I had an idea. The Wiener Library in London would likely have the records. I went and sure enough, they had

Klarsfeld's papers listing the Jews in the Hotel Excelsior along with his parents. There were the names, Jeschie and Rachel Rosen. They were in that hotel when the Nazis came looking for Jews.

But there was one more bittersweet truth. Sometimes when I run through this, I'm bewildered by the terror of it.

Here are two people who in their youth come out of Poland, where hostility and persecution make life difficult or dangerous. They settle in Sedan on the Franco-Belgian border – I found a document confirming that they lived in rue Saint Michel, more on that in a minute – where they run a clock-mending business. It so happens that the country they've adopted is invaded, so like everyone else they flee. They get to south-west France, and move into a flat above a shop.

Then, the country creates a new kind of government that decides that foreign-born Jews need to be put on lists, given yellow stars and signs to say that their business is Jewish. The 'business' at this point, I figure, has been reduced to working in a market (the words '*bonneterie*' and another, '*forain*' on one of the lists, suggest he had become a stallholder selling knitted socks and stockings). Then everything they've got left is taken away from them because it is 'Aryanised'. (I pause a moment and think this one through: Jewish money and property is made not-Jewish and transformed in some mystical way, 'better' or 'purer' or 'more proper', by being transferred to 'Aryans'. This is Vichy doing this, not the Nazis, I remind myself.)

And then they run. How? I don't know. They get themselves to safety in Nice. This Donati fellow is getting Jews out. He's chartered some boats. All they've got to do is wait a day or two. But then, in a blink of an eye, it seems, the streets are full of soldiers and a madman is rounding up Jews, shoving them on trains, and the trains travel to Paris, then across France, then into Germany, then to Poland, to Auschwitz.

And did they, did Oscar/Jeschie realise at that moment that he had, in a horrible inversion of the normal meaning, come home?

Oscar/Jeschie's birthplace is listed as: Oświęcim, the Polish word for Auschwitz. He had returned to the place of his birth.

And then, by whatever means, gassing, overwork, random violence, starvation, typhus, the pair of them were disappeared. Gone. Nothing left. The End.

No, Harold, not the end, I'm afraid.

There is yet another bitter twist to this. Still googling for information, I found an American site that lists applications for immigration. Your cousin Olga – Ted's sister, Morris's niece – applied for permission to bring Jeschie and Rachel to America. (It's the first definite time, by the way, that I find someone in the family calling Oscar, 'Jeschie'.) It lists their home address as 18, rue Saint Michel, Sedan. The application is dated 10 February 1939. Just think: you and Mum were hitchhiking round France only five months after that. In the commentary accompanying Olga's and other applications, we read:

> These files document the extreme difficulties and frustrations of sponsors and those seeking entry to the United States, particularly around quotas and other barriers to immigration. Generally there is very little resolution to case files and further research will be required to learn if the person successfully entered the United States or other country.

Maybe Olga was unsuccessful. From this statement, that seems likely. Strange that she never mentioned it. Perhaps those who knew Oscar, Martin, Stella, Bella and their friends and spouses, (that is, people like Max and Morris) and people like Olga and Ted who only knew them by name, felt so awful after the war that they hadn't been able to get their relatives out, that they couldn't even talk about the parts of the story they knew. To be blunt about it, they didn't tell me the truth. No one mentioned the letters from Niort and Poland or the application for immigration into the US. When I had asked Olga about Oscar and Martin, she just mentioned that she used to write to them when she was a girl to practise her French.

I've sent all this round to my relatives. Some comment

on it. Some don't. The one survivor, your cousin, Michael Rechnik got back to me. He remembered that while he was in the camp in Siberia, he received $50. He always wondered who it came from and why. He knows now that it came from his Uncle Max in America.

Lots more to tell you, Harold. I'm afraid that closing borders is becoming fashionable again. Did I tell you I was doing a book about Émile Zola? I finished it. In my researches on that, I found out that Dreyfus's granddaughter, Madeleine Dreyfus Levy, was on the same convoy as your uncle Oscar and his wife, Convoy 62: those anti-Dreyfusards got their revenge. Zola, though – what a mensh!

Love
Mick

PS On the very weekend that I've been proofreading this book, Teddy in America (son of your cousin Ted) has written to me to say that they've been sorting out the house now that Ted's wife Gladys has died. Teddy opened up Ted's 'storage closet', which was filled with all sorts including a 'recycled shoe box with peeling tape from many uses and sealed with tape, marked "family photos"'. He opened that box up too and inside was a set of seventeen black-and-white photos of your uncles and aunts – Oscar (Jeschie), Martin, Willi, Bella, Stella and Genia, and, I think, your Polish grandparents, Jonas and Marta, going right back to the early 1900s.

After years of thinking I would never get to know what Jeschie and the others looked like, they appeared in my email inbox. To tell the truth, it's been a bit overwhelming. Imagine: looking at these people, some of whom I've been tracking for years on their journeys from Poland to France to Auschwitz. I sent them round the family with questions about who was who. In one, I couldn't make out the writing saying who it was with Bella and Stella walking down the street. Back came a note from Grant, the son of your cousin Michael:

'Wow. Since 1939 my father, Michael, has only had one photograph of his mother Stella. Now he has a second one ... and the man in the photograph is him!'

'I saw my father last night. He was mesmerised by the photograph. You will readily appreciate that this is the first time in almost seventy-eight years that my father has seen another photograph of his mother. And as if that was not enough, they are together.'

The photos are all gifts with little messages saying 'from your brother' and the like. This generation of Rosens stayed in touch by sending each other photos from Poland and France to America. Then, after the war: nothing. All these people had just disappeared. At some point, maybe after his father Max died, Ted must have put the photos together, put them in a box, taped them up, hid them in the closet and never mentioned them to his cousins, that's you, Harold, and your sister Sylvia, and never mentioned them to his own son, Teddy, or to me or to Sylvia's daughter, Gillian.

I wrote to Teddy:

'As you and me have talked about before, the effect of losing all these people in the Holocaust must have left Olga, Ted and Gladys with some terrible feelings that they could or should have done more. You will all have seen Olga's letter to US immigration that I found online, so she definitely tried to get Oscar/Jeschie out of France in Feb. 1939 but I spoke to her for some time and she was seemingly quite clear that she had no address and no knowledge of anything to do with Oscar. We can only imagine the feelings that your US relatives had about all this. Harold used to just shrug about it, but he had lost touch with all of them – or rather was never in touch with any of them anyway. The problem for Max and Morris was that these were all their brothers and sisters.'

I wonder what else is going to come out Ted's storage closet.